KT-228-156

The Editors wish to thank all the individuals and organisations who made this publication possible. In particular: Susan Watts, Debra Royal and Chiara Binetti for their assistance and dedication; Roel Cosijn from The Ecovolunteer Network, who encouraged the Editor to put together this guide; Anita Prosser of BTCV for her encouragement and assistance; and the Expedition Advisory Centre of the Royal Geographical Society. The above organisations are listed in the guide.

To be updated for the following years on new and previously published projects and to join our non-expiring free e-mail newsletter, readers must send an e-mail to: network@greenvol.com. Proof of ownership of this guide will be asked to receive a UserID and password, which will allow to access the *Green Volunteers* Network pages at www.greenvol.com where the updates are listed. Free annual updates of this guide will be available unless the Editor and Publisher cease operating but no such interruption of activities is anticipated.

TABLE OF CONTENTS

Before joining any project or organisation prospective volunteers should carefully read the Warning on page 3 and the Important Note on pages 15–16.

The Editors highly recommend the following introductory pages are read. These pages explain what conservation volunteering involves and will increase the volunteer's chances of being accepted to a project.

Green Volunteers

The World Guide to Voluntary
Work in Nature Conservation

Green Volunteers
The World Guide to Voluntary Work in Nature Conservation

Editors:	Fabio Ausenda, Erin McCloskey
Cover design:	Studio Cappellato e Laurent srl, Milano
Cover photo:	Volunteer at the Gibbon Rehabilitation Center, Thailand
	Courtesy Rossella Rossi

This Guide is not an annual publication: the password that readers can obtain upon request (see page 3 for details) and the e-mail newsletter which they can join allow the readers to keep the information in this Guide always up to date and to be constantly informed on new opportunities.

Published by: Green Volunteers di Fabio Ausenda
Via Canonica 72
I-20154 Milano, Italy
www.greenvol.com
E-mail: network@greenvol.com

US & Canada distribution: Universe Publishing
A division of Rizzoli International Publications, Inc.
300 Park Avenue South,
New York, NY 10010

UK distribution: Vacation Work Publications
9 Park End Street,
Oxford OX1 1HJ, England

Australia and
New Zealand distribution: Woodslane Pty Ltd
Unit 7/5 Vuko Place
Warriewood NSW 2102

Printed in Jan. 2005 by: Consorzio Artigiano L.V.G. srl, Azzate (VA), Italy
ISBN: 88-89060-03-4
Library of Congress Control Number: 2004195402

PREFACE

In recent years there has been a growing demand for volunteers for nature conservation projects in general and for wildlife related projects in particular. Volunteering provides wildlife and nature enthusiasts with an opportunity to become involved in worldwide conservation efforts. Students can gain experience allowing them to pursue a career in nature conservation as well as ideas for a thesis. Until recently, large organisations were mostly responsible for offering this kind of opportunity, but usually the financial contributions required limited the number of people who could afford them and become volunteers. However, there are many smaller nature conservation and wildlife protection projects with a constant shortage of funding which greatly need volunteers for research assistance and financial resources. Often these contributions by volunteers can maintain projects for years. The Gibbon Rehabilitation Project in Thailand, for example, has been running successfully for over 10 years exclusively on the contributions and help of international volunteers. Until now many of these projects throughout the world did not have a worldwide forum. With this guide these valuable projects have the opportunity to connect with prospective volunteers and vice versa.

The objective of *Green Volunteers* is to provide information to fill the communication gap between people who are willing to join interesting and valuable projects worldwide, and the projects in need of volunteers. For this reason, the Geneva-based World Conservation Union's Species Survival Commission (the body which publishes the "Red Lists" of endangered species) considers the *Green Volunteers* guide a useful instrument for supporting conservation projects throughout the world.

HOW TO BE LISTED IN *Green Volunteers*

If you are an organisation or project based anywhere in the world and you would like to be listed in the next edition or on our website at www.greenvol.com, please contact *Green Volunteers* at the addresses on the previous page. Should you require any information on how to recruit and organise volunteers as a valuable instrument to support a nature conservation project *Green Volunteers* is willing to assist you.

INTRODUCTION

Green Volunteers is a directory. There are 2 sections: one dedicated to organisations and one to specific projects.

Organisations play an important role in providing opportunities for volunteer work; listed are those offering projects on a wide range of species, habitats and geographic locations, at various costs to volunteers (from zero to a few thousand dollars.) Organisations are listed in alphabetical order. Should an organisation have an acronym, as many do, the organisation is listed according to the alphabetical order of the acronym. For example, BTCV, CVA, WWF, are listed according to the acronym's alphabetical order. For some of the larger organisations, or for those offering interesting projects to prospective volunteers, a few projects have been described in greater detail in the second section. These projects are listed at the end of the organisations' descriptions under the heading: Selected Projects. For most of the organisations no projects have been described in the second section due to limited space in this guide. Prospective volunteers are therefore encouraged to contact the organisations directly (or visit their websites), and inquire for further information about available projects.

Projects are found in the second section of this guide. Greater detail about the projects offered by the organisations is provided, and many more independent projects, which are not part of major organisations, are listed.

MEANING OF ABBREVIATIONS

For each organisation and project the guide lists:

The **address** and the **telephone** and **fax** numbers with the international codes. Remember to change the local area code according to the country's telephone system. For example, to call The Monkey Sanctuary, (UK) phone number (listed as ++ 44 (1503) 262 532), people calling from the UK should not dial ++ 44 (the international code), but should add 0 (zero) before 1503 (the local area code). People calling from the Netherlands should add 00 before 44 to call the UK. Whereas people calling from the US should dial 011, then 44, the international access codes from the US to the UK. **E-mail** and World Wide Web (**www**) addresses are listed where available. If these references are not listed, a quick phone call to ask an organisation if they have recently activated an e-mail or www address will help you to communicate and get information much faster than through regular mail and will speed your selection of the right organisation for you.

Desc.: The main activity and objectives of the organisations or projects.

Spp.: The species or the group of species involved. The common name, and Latin name if necessary for clarification, is provided. For projects involving groups of species, families, classes or communities, these groupings are cited in more general terms such as marine mammals, tropical birds, African herbivores, etc. Abbreviations are occasionally used.

Hab.: Specific habitats or wider biogeographical areas an organisation is involved with, such as tropical seas and coasts, African savannah, Mediterranean islands, etc. Abbreviations are occasionally used.

Loc.: The countries, regions (such as Southeast Asia) or continents where an organisation conducts its projects.

Travel: A basic summary of travel directions. Organisations and projects will give full details to the volunteers once accepted.

Dur.: The duration of the volunteering time, either a set period or a minimum and maximum duration.

Per.: The period of the year when a volunteer can join a project such as year round, the summer, July to August, etc.

L. term: Long-term volunteering is a longer stay than the set volunteer duration. Some projects do not allow long-term volunteering, others do, but they typically continue charging the volunteers the same contribution (per week, for example) without recognizing any discount for the additional experience acquired by the volunteer. Other organisations or projects encourage long-term volunteering for this benefit. The Ecovolunteer Network is one organisation that encourages a longer permanence on some of the projects by considerably decreasing the cost to the volunteer the longer a volunteer stays. Some projects or organisations require professionally qualified labour and staff and accept graduate students for their thesis work.

Age: Minimum and maximum age for joining a project.

Qualif.: The qualifications and skills required of a volunteer who wants to join a project. Most of the time no special qualifications are needed, other than a strong motivation and enthusiasm. Adaptation to harsh climates, long walks, hot or cold temperatures, basic accommodation and very little comfort is almost always required. Where possible, the Editors have specified particularly extreme working or lodging conditions present at a given project. However, specific information is to be obtained from the organisation or project. Other typical requirements include a strong flexibility to work with other people, a willingness to accept very little privacy (very rarely volunteers will be able to lodge in a single or even double rooms) and the ability to adapt to different cultures. These requirements apply to almost all projects but are not always stated. A volunteer may offer special skills, such as photography, good computer literacy, mechanical skills, etc. Never expect, nor impose these skills onto a project—there may already be very qualified people performing these duties with the accuracy required by the project. For long-term volunteering, or for organisations or projects where little or no contribution is required, volunteers are often selected according to their qualifications or previous experience in related work. Contact the organisation directly for more information on the skills and qualifications required.

Work: The main activities performed by volunteers are listed for projects. Since most organisations manage several projects, the work performed by volunteers is not described in detail because it will vary with each project. Prospective volunteers can predict what kind of activities to expect from the description of an organisation and the projects it supports. Further details are given by the organisations directly.

Lang.: The languages that are required for a volunteer to work on a project. The importance of communicating with the project staff or with local or international researchers should not be overlooked. Prospective volunteers should never underestimate the importance of this aspect and never overestimate their ability to understand a foreign language in a working environment.

Accom.: (Not described within the organisation description.) The style of accommodation the volunteers will be lodged in. For most of the projects volunteers should be prepared for very basic accommodations such as bunk beds in research stations (rarely in houses) tents or hammocks. Bathroom facilities can also be very basic and hot showers, particularly in the tropics, can be quite rare. Chores such as housecleaning, cooking, washing dishes, etc., are often expected. Comfort and privacy is rare. The ability to do without these privileges must be considered for environmental volunteering.

Cost: Most of the projects require a contribution from the volunteers, which is often the major funding for a project. Projects are often conducted with the financial contribution and the work volunteers perform. The cost of projects may vary from a few hundred to a few thousands dollars US. The Editors have tried to list as many organisations as possible requiring little or no contributions. These organisations, however, are difficult to find; they are either small projects in developing countries that have no means for communication or until now did not perceive the importance of taking volunteers. It is fair, however, that even these small projects or organisations ask for a small contribution, especially in developing countries. Usually, the volunteer's contribution covers food and accommodation or there may be a common kitty for food costs. Very rarely will the cost include the international airfare to reach a project site.

9

Some projects have introduced a very useful 'progressively decreasing cost' policy, depending on the length of stay. The rationale is that the longer a volunteer stays with a project, the more useful he or she becomes because of the experience he or she gains. Long-term volunteers selected according to their skills are often reimbursed for their living expenses. This is typically the case for long-term volunteers with Government Agencies, such as the US National Park Service, the US Forest Service or The US Fish and Wildlife Service. Part of the volunteer contribution likely pays for the project costs: marketing, reservation staff, rent, telephone, mail, etc. Money going towards an agency or larger organisation or overhead should not be considered money diverted from the conservation objective. Larger organisations perform a basic role in a world-wide conservation effort by providing volunteers and funding to projects that alone would not have been able to reach these important resources. However, when overhead costs are in excess of a reasonable percentage (max. 20–25%) an organisation should try to become more efficient by reducing costs, in order to devote a higher percentage of a volunteer's contribution to actual projects. It is perfectly in the right of a volunteer to know how much of his or her contribution goes into a project, and what is the organisation's overhead.

Agents: The agents or organisations where a prospective volunteer can or should apply. Many organisations have branches in other countries that act as agents for projects. Other organisations use outside agents such as travel agencies to recruit volunteers. Many organisations do not have agents and require direct application.

Applic.: This section briefly describes application procedures that may be required such as filling out an application form, sending a deposit or initial contribution, or becoming a member of a specific organisation.

Selected Projects are listed for some organisations. If detailed description of projects are not provided, volunteers should contact the organisation directly in order to receive further information.

WILDLIFE REHABILITATION CENTRES

To volunteer with wildlife you don't necessarily need to cross an ocean or stay away for weeks or months. You may indeed be able to volunteer and get in close contact with various species, mostly endemic but also exotic, in your own town, county, district, province or state at Wildlife Rehabilitation Centres. These centres, usually managed by local or national Non-Profit Organisations or private individuals – rarely local governments, take care and try to rehabilitate wounded or mistreated animals. Animals may have been wounded by hunters or car accidents or have been victims of plain cruelty. Often exotic wildlife that is confiscated by local authorities is handed over to Wildlife Rehabilitation Centres. Rare species illegally imported or detained against the CITES convention (International Convention on Trade of Endangered Species) cannot be released into a foreign habitat and rarely are re-exported to the country of origin.

Wildlife Rehabilitation Centres are always in need of volunteers. They often don't charge any fees and, if they are located near where you live, they may allow you to work just a few hours a week. There are several hundred Wildlife Rehabilitation Centres throughout the world, and they are mostly concentrated in First World countries. We did list a few in this guide as examples because we have had direct communication with them, but it would not be difficult to find a Rehabilitation Centre nearby where you can volunteer for a short period, a weekend or even a few hours a week.

We recommend that you do a web search with the key words "Wildlife Rehabilitation" and the name of the geographical area of your choice, such as Bedfordshire, Oregon, Alberta or New South Wales, depending on where you live or where would you like to volunteer. To help with your search, we have selected a few websites with a comprehensive international list of Wildlife Rehabilitation Centres.

www.catchat.org/adoption/notcats.html
A very thorough list of animal rescue centres in the British Isles, divided by species.

www.ispca.ie/content/links.html
The website of the Irish Society for the Prevention of Cruelty to Animals, a good list of Irish Wildlife Sanctuaries.

www.tc.umn.edu/~devo0028/contact.htm
The Wildlife Rehabilitation Information Directory. A complete list of Centres throughout the US, Canada and the world.

www.greenpeople.org/sanctuary.htm
A list of over 200 sanctuaries in the US, Canada, Australia and throughout the world.

www.wildliferehabilitators.com/links.htm
The link page of the Association of Wildlife Rehabilitators, it has a good list of Wlidlife Rehabilitators and Rehabilitation Centres in the US, Australia, Canada and the UK.

Finally Yahoo has a good list of Wildlife Rehabilitation Centres under Wildlife > Rescue and Rehabilitation.

TIPS FOR CONTACTING
AN ORGANISATION OR PROJECT

1) **Have clear in mind what you want to do, the species or habitats you prefer, the geographical location, the duration of your volunteering period and the costs you can afford.** This will help you in selecting and reducing the number of organisations or projects you want to apply to. Select a list of both organisations and projects and divide them into your first and second priority. The first priority should include not only those organisations or projects that are of primary interest to you, but also those which are more remote and harder to contact.

2) **Use the fastest possible method to contact an organisation.** Remember that interesting projects or organisations also have many applicants, and they usually fill their available positions on a first come, first serve basis. Therefore, you want to be as fast as possible in letting them know that you are interested in taking a position with them. You may send via e-mail the *Green Volunteers* standard application form found at page 255. Should you not receive a reply within 3–5 days, be prepared to send reminders or telephone them to confirm their e-mail address. These addresses often change, particularly when an organisation finds a cheaper internet server.

3) **Inform as much as possible the organisation or project you would like to work for about yourself.** With your request for information, send a description of your skills and interests and possibly a CV. You can find at page 255 the *Green Volunteers* standard application form, modeled on the application forms of many organisations. This form may be sufficient for applying and it may help you to save time. The form (which is not an official application form but just a tool to help in the application process) is also available from the *Green Volunteers* **Network Pages** at www.greenvol.com (these webpages are accessible with your password, see page 3 for details). Always enclose a cover letter (preferably typed and not handwritten) and ask if the organisation accepts the *Green Volunteers* application form.

4) **Make an organisation's response easier.** Remember that organisations and projects often are short of funds. Therefore, help them by enclosing self-addressed stamped envelopes. If the organisation is located in a foreign country, enclose an international reply coupon. You

may also offer an organisation to fax you collect (give them an appointment, because in order to receive a fax collect you should first be able to answer vocally, accept the call, then switch on the fax mode). Better still, since a fax goes both ways regardless of who calls, you can offer the organisation to call them on their fax line, and have them fax back the information. Remember that you should arrange this over the phone. If you interact with a large organisation, well equipped for recruiting volunteers, they have all the means to contact you, particularly if they are in the more expensive range of projects. In general, the cheaper the project or organisation you want to volunteers for, the more you should try to help them by reducing their cost of contacting you. In the past few years, however, the diffusion of the Internet, also in developing countries, has considerably reduced communications costs.

5) **Do exactly what is required by an organisation for being accepted.** If they do not accept the *Green Volunteers* standard application form, fill in the proper application form, pay the required deposit or membership fee and comply with other requirements. Once accepted, don't miss an opportunity by not paying a deposit on time. Inquire about the fastest method to transfer funds: by international telegraph money order, credit card, money wire from bank to bank, etc.

6) **Contact many projects and organisations.** Select the projects well in advance. Properly plan your vacation or time off, find the best air fares and select the best research period. Get detailed information on what to expect: the type of work, accommodation, food, climate, clothing and equipment necessary, etc. Owing to a lack of space this information is not included in the *Green Volunteers* guide. This guide aims to give a general overview of a given project or organisation. Do not show up at a project location without having applied first and having been accepted and confirmed. Most projects have limited positions, lodging and personnel. Very rarely are they equipped to take on an unexpected volunteer. If you want to do so, because you were already travelling in a certain area, do not be disappointed if you are rejected.

IMPORTANT NOTE AND WARNING

The Editor and Publisher of *Green Volunteers* has decided, both in order to offer prospective volunteers the widest possible choice and most valid conservation instrument, to cite, whenever possible, small projects and organisations, particularly in developing countries, for the following reasons:

1)   **Without *Green Volunteers* many small projects and organisations would not be able to receive volunteers** from developed nations. We think that we should help as best as we can this conservation potential, particularly if it comes directly from local organisations, without an input from large organisations from our side of the world.

2)   **Prospective volunteers**, by purchasing this guide, **expect to find something different and unique** from what is normally offered by large organisations in developed countries.

3)   **Often small projects require non-paying and long-term volunteers**, which is what many of *Green Volunteers* readers expect. These opportunities are also usually offered at extremely affordable costs to the volunteers, which is not the case of projects offered from large organisations, which are often expensive and don't allow long-term volunteering.

BEFORE JOINING PROJECTS AND ORGANISATIONS, PROSPECTIVE VOLUNTEERS SHOULD CAREFULLY READ THE FOLLOWING CONSIDERATIONS AND WARNINGS:

1)   **Because of obvious cost reasons**, which would then reflect on the cover price, **the Editor and Publisher cannot personally visit every project** listed in this guide but have to trust what projects and organisations (or the websites or previous volunteers) declare.

2)   **Small projects and organisations**, particularly in developing countries, mainly because of shortage of funding or qualified personnel or because of conflicts with local populations and/ or local authorities, **often change their programmes or even interrupt their activities without informing the Editor and Publisher of** *Green Volunteers*.

3)   **Before joining a project volunteers should verify the validity of what is declared** on the project website (if one exists) or in this guide.

4)   **Prospective volunteers should exchange frequent e-mails**, or even fax or phone calls, **with project leaders** and ensure that communication is always prompt and clear. They should also confirm the project details, such as the living, working and safety conditions, prior to departure.

5)   **Prospective volunteers to any project should ask names** and addresses **of previous volunteers and correspond with them** to further verify the conditions of the projects.

6)   **Volunteers should never join a project by going directly to the location** without previous correspondence and verification of existing conditions.

7)   **Prospective volunteers should read carefully the WARNING on the third page of this book.**

ORGANISATION LIST

À PAS DE LOUP 'VOLUNTEERS FOR NATURE'

12, rue Malautières
26 220 Dieulefit   France
Tel.: ++33 (4) 75 46 80 18
Fax: ++33 (4) 75 46 80 18
E-mail: info@apasdeloup.org
www.apasdeloup.org

Desc.: À Pas de Loup is a conservation volunteering organisation founded in 1994. Its objectives are to support local organisations in both developing and executing their schemes of nature conservation and to improve their local natural environment. During an assignment, volunteers are monitored by local staff to ensure quality results. Projects are in France, Europe, South America and Africa. À Pas de Loup volunteers are required to pay only for transportation and living costs.

Spp.: Some projects are wildlife related (seals, elephants, wolves, turtles), others are related to vegetation or reforestation (in France, Guatemala and Togo).

Hab.: Coastal Mediterranean, African savannah and tropical forests.

Loc.: Europe, Africa and South America.

Dur.: From 1 to 6 weeks.

Per.: In Europe in the summer, year round elsewhere.

Age: Min. 18.

Qualif.: No qualifications required.

Work: Depends on the project, often is mostly manual, such as work planting trees in Togo, cutting trees for recovering the Grouse habitats in the Alps or building pigeon houses for the Bonelli eagle Project, in Portugal. Scientific observation is also involved, such as of birds migration or elephants behaviour. Cultural activities and excursions are also planned.

Lang.: English, French, Spanish, Portuguese.

Accom.: Always very simple; in a campsite or in local houses.

Cost : Volunteers must pay for travel and food and must join the organisation (EUR 16).

Applic.: Send CV and letter of presentation and intentions.

AFRICAN CONSERVATION EXPERIENCE

P.O. Box 9706
Solihull, West Mids. B91 3FF UK
Tel.: ++44 (1626) 879 700 – (870) 241 5816 (from the UK only)
Fax: ++44 (1626) 879 700
E-mail: info@conservationafrica.net
www.conservationafrica.net

Desc.: The organisation organises Educational Work Experiences with conservationists, game rangers and biologists. Applicants may attend an optional Open Day to gain first hand information on the Game Reserves and Conservation Projects.

Spp.: Large and small game, including mammals, reptiles, birds, marine and freshwater life, plants.

Hab.: Sub-tropical coasts, seas, mountains; southern African savannah, plains, bushveld; semi-desert, fresh water marshes, wetlands; coastal lowlands, mountain ranges.

Loc.: South Africa, Zimbabwe, Botswana, Mozambique.

Travel: All travel arrangements included in the package.

Dur.: 4 – 12 weeks.

Per.: Year round.

L. term: Only in exceptional circumstances and by special arrangement.

Age: Min. 18, no maximum. Reasonably fit and healthy.

Work: Varies with Reserves. May include relocation or collaring of rhinos and elephants; capturing, tagging, releasing and game counts; animal monitoring and habituation. Whale and dolphin, seal and seabird research projects. Use of horses on conservation programmes. Volunteers usually work as part of a team under the supervision of experienced co-ordinators.

Lang.: English.

Accom.: Shared house in staff accommodation.

Cost: Approx. GB£2,700–4,000 (US$5,000–7,300); inquire for details.

Applic.: Request Application Pack. An optional donation is requested.

Notes: Essential qualification required is enthusiasm for conservation and must be reasonably physically fit.

AFRICAN EXPERIENCE

18 Emerald Hill, 87 Ridge Road
New Germany, 3620, Kwa-Zulu Natal South Africa
Tel.: ++27 (82) 433 2319
Fax: ++27 (31) 705 36 35
E-mail: louise@african-experience.co.za
www.african-experience.co.za

Desc.: An opportunity to experience a real African adventure in the beautiful setting of Southern Africa on "big five" game farms. The opportunities suit the individual needs of each volunteer.

Spp.: Various species of African Mammals.

Hab.: Bushveld and savannah.

Loc.: Various areas around South Africa, from the coastline to Kruger National Park.

Travel: Volunteers fly to the nearest local airport to the project.

Dur.: Varies from project to project; the main duration is 4 weeks.

Per.: Year round.

Age: Min.18.

Qualif.: No qualifications necessary, just a willingness to help and the desire to make a difference.

Work: The Wildlife volunteer work covers many broad spectrums that includes preparing the food and feeding the wild animals, hand rearing and bottle feeding the young animals (the lions and baboons in particular), cleaning the enclosures, general game farm management (alien plant eradication and bush clearing, etc.), working with the veterinarians to aid the sick, ill and injured animals. Some of the volunteers have the opportunity to spend time learning about various conservation related topics.

Lang.: A minimum knowledge of basic English is required.

Accom.: Varies from project to project, always clean and comfortable!

Cost: Prices start from US$200 per week, which includes food accommodation, transfers to and from the local airport.

Agents: Volunteers must contact African Experience directly.

Applic.: On-line application form.

AMERICAN BEAR ASSOCIATION

Vince Shute Wildlife Sanctuary
P.O. BOX 77, Orr, Minnesota 55771 USA
Vince Shute Wildlife Sanctuary
Tel.: ++1 (218) 757 0172
E-mail: bears@rangenet.com
www.americanbear.or

Desc.:	This non-profit organisation is dedicated to protecting the welll-being of the black bear, other wildlife and all natural resources through a better understanding. The Vince Shute Wildlife Sanctuary offers the opportunity for the public to view black bears in the hope to instill an appreciation and respect for the bears as well as the habitat that supports all wildlife.
Spp.:	American black bear (*Ursus americanus*).
Hab.:	Forest.
Loc.:	Northwoods of Minnesota.
Travel:	Airplane to Duluth, Minnesota.
Dur.:	Volunteers min. 1 week max. 4 months; interns (U.S. citizens or residents only) min.8 weeks max. 14 weeks.
Per.:	Summer.
L. term:	Volunteers can stay up to 4 months with project leader's approval.
Qualif.:	All volunteers must read the Volunteer Handbook and complete a liability waiver. Where possible jobs will be matched to the specific interests and skills of the volunteer. Students are encouraged.
Work:	Greeting and escorting visitors to and from the viewing platform, interpreting bear behaviour to visitors, assisting in construction projects, conducting daily clean-up chores, cooking, completing routine maintenance projects, grounds-keeping, maintaining records on bear activity, etc.
Lang.:	English.
Accom.:	All services available in the town of Orr. Campgrounds and numerous resorts are at nearby Pelican Lake. On-site lodging may be possible.
Cost:	Volunteers are responsible for off-site lodging and extras.
Applic.:	Contact the Association for more information.

APPALACHIAN TRAIL CONFERENCE

1280North Main St., Blacksburg, Virginia 24060 USA
Tel.: ++1 (540) 961 5551
Fax: ++1 (540) 961 5554
E-mail: crews@appalachiantrail.org
www.appalachiantrail.org

Desc.: The Appalachian Trail is America's best-known long-distance trail. Each year over 400 volunteers help with trail construction and rehabilitation. Volunteers can enjoy great scenery, and are provided with food, lodging, tools, equipment, training, and the opportunity for lots of fun.

Hab.: Appalachian Mountain Range.

Loc.: Great Smoky Mountains National Park, Southwest Virginia, Pennsylvania, Maine, and Vermont, USA.

Travel: Detailed access directions to base camp are provided.

Dur.: From 1 to 6 weeks.

Per.: May through October.

L. term: Volunteers can work up to 6 weeks.

Age: Min. 18.

Qualif.: Enthusiasm, good health, physical vigour, and adaptability. Willingness to follow instructions and safety rules and to share equally in camp chores. Experience is not necessary.

Work: Trail work is hard, physical labour, with hand tools. The crews work 8-hour days, rain or shine, hot or cold, regardless of black flies, mosquitoes, and other insects.

Lang.: English.

Accom.: Rustic cabins at base camp and tents out in the field.

Cost: Only transportation to base camp. Most expenses are covered including shelter, food, transportation to and from work projects, tools, safety equipment, and group camping gear. Crew members need to bring work clothing, sturdy boots, and their own basic camping gear.

Applic.: Request an application from the Appalachian Trail Conference.

Notes: International applicants are responsible for necessary visas. Weather conditions can vary from very hot to below freezing.

ARCAS – Asociaciòn de Rescate y Conservaciòn de Vida Silvestre.

4 Ave. 2-47, Sector B5, Zona 11, San Cristobal Guatemala
Tel./Fax: ++(502)2478 4096 – 2480 7270
E-mail: arcas@intelnet.net.gt – arcaspeten@intelnet.net.gt
www.arcasguatemala.com

Desc.: ARCAS has 2 projects: a Wildlife Rescue and Rehabilitation Centre, established in 1990, in order to rescue, rehabilitate and release wild animals confiscated from traffickers. It has released 300–600 animals per year into the Mayan Biosphere Reserve (MBR). The project is also a focal point for environmental education and awareness-raising in the MBR through its Environmental Education and Interpretation Centre. The second project is a Sea Turtle Conservation Centre. Its goal is the conservation of the endangered sea turtles that come to beaches on the Pacific Coast to nest. The primary way to conserve the turtles is to collect and incubate as many eggs as possible. ARCAS has also a caiman and iguana breeding programme, mangrove reforestation and environmental education.

Spp.: The centre receives many different species from the MBR, which include: birds (parrots, scarlet macaws, toucans, aracaries), mammals (spider and howler monkeys, raccoons, coatimundis, pacas, margays, kinkajous, peccaries, bairds tapirs, jaguars) and reptiles (iguanas, turtles, crocodiles, caimans). The seaturtles are: Olive Ridley Sea Turtle, Leatherback Sea Turtle.

Hab.: Tropical forest, tropical beach, mangrove coastal wetland.

Loc.: The Wildlife Rescue Centre is near the city of Flores; the Seaturtle Conservation Project is on the Pacific Coast.

Travel: Airplane to Guatemala City, then bus to Flores or Monterrico, then by boat to the projects.

Dur.: For generic volunteers min. 1 week. For internships or research projects, min. 1 month.

Per.: Year round for the Rescue Centre. From September to May, for the Seaturtle Nesting Project.

Age: Min. 18.

L. term.: Volunteers can stay for as long as they want. Volunteers can also spend some time in each project.

Qualif.: No specific skills required for generic volunteers. Candidates for internships or research projects must be students or researchers in a conservation related field.

Work: Volunteers help cleaning cages and feeding and caring for the animals. Special projects may include: observing the animals in the rehabilitation area, building cages, animal releases, etc. Research and internship opportunities are in the area of wildlife veterinary medicine, rehabilitation, nutrition and environmental education. In the Seaturtle Project volunteers assist in patrolling beaches at night in search of nesting sea turtles, collection and burial of eggs in the hatcheries and collection of data. Volunteers can also take part in caiman breeding, mangrove reforestation, construction and upkeep of park facilities and environmental educational activities in area schools. Everyone is expected to help in house cleaning and dish washing.

Lang.: English, basic Spanish is highly desirable.

Accom.: Volunteers live in a confortable house with toilet and kitchen facilities and electricity (110V, 12 V in Peten). Sheets are provided, own sleeping bag useful in cooler months (Dec. – Feb.), msquito net is otional.

Cost: US$100/week for room and board at the Rescue Center. US$50/week for room at the Seaturtle Project. Volunteers must pay all travel expenses.

Agents: Contact ARCAS directly.

Applic.: A simple application for the regular volunteer programme. For the research and internship opportunities candidates shouold send a letter of reference from their university or employer, a short essay explaining their personal motivation, a CV and a photograph.

Notes: ARCAS, as an under-funded non-profit volunteer organisation, may not be able to meet all expectations in terms of personal attention and work experience. Mail may also be sent to: Section 717, P.O. Box 52–7270 Miami, FL 33152–7270 USA.

ARCTUROS

Victor Hugo 3
546 25 Thessaloniki Greece
Tel.: ++30 (2310) 555 920
Fax: ++30 (2310) 553 932
E-mail: aec@arcturos.gr
www.arcturos.gr

Desc.: The management and conservaticn of wildlife and the natural environment focusing on the brown bear, a priority species, that encourages global management of the mountain forest ecosystems in northern Greece. Since 1993 ARCTUROS has operated the Environmental Centre at Nymphaion and Aetos in northern Greece, in an effort to solve the problem of captive and, especially, the 'dancing bears'. A project for the conservation of the wolf is also being carried out.

Spp.: Brown bear (*Ursus arctos*), wolf (*Canis lupus*).

Hab.: European temperate, deciduous and alpine forests.

Loc.: Mountains of Pindos and Rodopi (bear); central Greece (wolf).

Travel: Airplane to Thessaloniki, Greece.

Dur.: 2 weeks.

Per.: June to September.

L. term: With project leader's approval.

Age: Min. 18; most participants are between the ages of 18–30.

Qualif.: Biology or relevant background is strongly desired.

Work: Ranges from manual tasks to assistance in scientific research, participation in awareness-raising campaigns, preparing food for the animals, maintenance and construction of facilities.

Lang.: English.

Accom.: Fully equipped house (kitchen, fridge, washing machine) in Nymphaion. Field work in rented facilities or tents.

Cost: A food budget might be provided. Transportation not included.

Applic.: By April. Green Volunteers standard application form accepted.

ASVO – Asociacion de Voluntarios para el Servicio en las Areas Protegidas

Programa de Voluntariado
P.O. Box 11384–1000 San José   Costa Rica
Tel.: ++(506) 258 4430 Tel./Fax: ++(506) 233 4989
E-mail: info@asvocr.com lmatarrita@asvocr.com alopez@asvocr.com
www.asvocr.com

Desc.: ASVO is the organisation providing volunteers to Costa Rican National Parks and Reserves. Volunteers are needed for research, construction and maintenance work, english teaching, tourist assistance and interpretation. They can also participate in seaturtle conservation programmes on the coasts. Biology or Ecology students can participate into special projects, such as "reintroduction of monkeys" in a given area.

Spp.: Primates, tropical birds and mammals, sea turtles.

Hab.: Tropical coast, rainforest, cloud forest, beaches.

Loc.: Parks and Reserves throughout Costa Rica.

Dur.: Min. 30 days, 2 months for special projects. Volunteers who stay at least 30 days can work in two different projects.

Per.: Year round.

L. term: Inquire with organisation.

Age: Min. 18.

Qualif.: Flexibility, motivation, a good physical condition and ability to tolerate the tropical climate. Two reference letters by Costa Rica residents or by organisations in the home country are required along with a copy of passport and two photos. Special qualifications are necessary for some research projects.

Work: Various tasks: construction and maintainance of park structures and trails, providing information to tourists, assisting in research on biodiversity or in wildlife surveys, etc.

Lang.: Spanish. Inquire for English.

Acc.: In general in rangers' lodges.

Cost: Approx. US$14/day for room and board. Travel costs are extra.

Applic.: Contact ASVO (Alexandra Lòpez, Volunteer Coordinator, or Ing. Luis Matarrita Cortés, General Manager).

Notes: Health and repatriation insurance is strongly recommended.

BIOSPHERE EXPEDITIONS

Sprat's Water, near Carlton Colville,
The Broads National Park, Suffolk NR33 8BP UK
Tel.: ++44 (1502) 583 085
Fax: ++44 (1502) 587 414
E-mail: info@biosphere-expeditions.org
www.biosphere-expeditions.org

Desc.: Worldwide wildlife conservation expeditions. The projects are not tours, or photographic excursions, but genuine expeditions with real conservation content. Adventure, remote locations, different cultures and people are part and parcel of these expeditions, but also the knowledge for paticipants to play an active role in conserving part of the planet's biosphere.

Spp.: Snow leopards, wolves, bears, primates, rainforest birds, etc.

Hab.: Rainforest, desert, savannah, tropical coasts, seas, etc.

Loc.: Worldwide.

Travel: Volunteers are met upon arrival and taken to the project area.

Dur.: Min. 2 weeks up to 3 months.

Per.: Year round.

L. term: Volunteers can join an expedition for several months.

Age: No age restrictions. Minors with parents' consent.

Qualif.: No specific skills or fitness required. Disabled/minority expeditioners are encouraged.

Work: Expect to work (e.g., surveying, tracking, identification) for several hours a day, often independently but never alone. All necessary training is given and a Biosphere Expedition leader is always present.

Lang.: English.

Accom.: Varies from B&B to research stations to tent camps.

Cost: Variable and depending on project. Expedition contributions start from GB£ 990 (approx. EUR1,400/US$1700) for 2 weeks, for longer periods discounts are available.

Agents: In Germany tel. ++ 49 (7127) 980 242, fax. (7127) 8878 776.

Applic.: Contact organisation for more details and application forms.

LES BLONGIOS

La Nature en Chantiers
Maison de la Nature et de l'Environnement
23 rue Gosselet   59000 Lille   France
Tel.: ++33 (3) 2053 98 85 - Fax: ++33 (3) 2086 15 56
E-mail: lesblongios@free.fr
http://lesblongios.free.fr

Desc.: Les "Blongios" (*Ixobrychus minutus)* is anNGO which organizes more than 30 workcamps in natural reserves in France and Northern Europe.

Loc.: Natural reserves with a managment plan in France and in Northern Europe (The Netherlands, Great Britain, Ireland, Belgium).

Travel: Depends on the location, details on the website.

Dur.: From one week-end to one month.

Per.: Year round.

Age: Min. 18.

Qualif.: No qualifications required.

Work: Maintenance work in natural reserves: habitat restoration (cutting bushes to restore natural sites, digging ponds for amphibians), trail blazing and building board walks, bulding visitor centers.

Lang.: French, English, Spanish is also spoken.

Accom.: In huts, lodges or hostels near naturals reserves. Cooking and dish-washing is in the group's responsibility.

Cost: Just travel to the site. Room, accommodation and meals are provided. Membership EUR16 (EUR11 for students or unemployed).

Applic.: Via e-mail or with the online application form available in various languages.

Notes: All the available workcamp locations are on the website.

BLUE VENTURES

52 Avenue road
London N6 5DR UK
Tel.: ++44 (208) 341 9819 - Fax: ++44 (208) 341 4821
E-mail:enquiries@blueventures.org
www.blueventures.org

Desc.: Blue Ventures co-ordinates expeditions of marine scientists and volunteers, working hand-in-hand with local biologists, marine institutes, NGOs, and communities whose livelihoods depend on coral reefs, to carry out research, environmental awareness and conservation programmes at threatened reef habitats around the world. Blue Ventures continues to offer opportunities and field experiences to people wanting to become actively involved in marine conservation, whether a beginner or an expert. The teams are made up of dynamic, enthusiastic and committed volunteers, coming from a wide range of backgrounds and cultures.

Spp.: Tropical marine (coral reef) species.

Hab.: Tropical coastal seas.

Loc.: Madagascar.

Dur.: Min. 4 weeks.

Per.: Year round.

L. term: Enquire with organisation.

Age: Min. 18.

Qualif.: Blue Ventures offers: Scuba training up to PADI Advanced Open Water (or up to Divemaster on site if required).

Work: Comprehensive marine science training course, learning from international team of marine biologists. Relaxed learning environment, maximum number of 12 volunteers per expedition. Staff to volunteer ratio of 1:2.

Lang.: English.

Accom.: Comfortable eco-cabins plus excellent food provided.

Cost: GB£1,280 - 1,780 (approx. US$2000—3,200), including food, accommodation, equipment and training. Flights not included.

Applic.: Call or write to Blue Ventures for an application form.

BRATHAY EXPLORATION GROUP

Brathay Hall
Ambleside, Cumbria LA22 OHP   UK
Tel./Fax: ++44 (15394) 33 942
E-mail: admin@brathayexploration.org.uk
          brathay.exploration@virgin.net
www.brathayexploration.org.uk

Desc.: The Brathay Exploration Group, a non-profit organisation founded in 1947, runs 10–15 expeditions each year in remote areas all over the world. Projects concern field sciences from glaciology to ornithology. They are lead by former experienced volunteers.

Hab.: Mountain, tropical rainforest, desert.

Loc.: Europe, Africa, China.

Dur.: 2–4 weeks.

Per.: July to August.

L. term: Inquire with organisation.

Age: Min.15, max. 25.

Qualif.: No special qualification or prior field experience is required, but self-motivation and a sense of humour are needed.

Lang.: English.

Cost: GB£200–700 (approx.EUR300–1,000) for European expeditions, GB£1,400–2,750 (approx. EUR2,000–4,000) for worldwide expeditions; grants are available (ask for bursary grant application form).

Applic.: Ask for application form and medical questionnaire, to be sent in with a deposit.

Notes: Each expedition can be joined by 20 or less volunteers. Members of the Brathay Exploration Group join a club with benefits such as the use of a mountain hut, an information magazine, discounts. The Brathay Exploration Group also offers courses in Mountain First Aid and Leader Training. Further information is available from the above address.

BTCV

Conservation Centre
Balby Road,   Doncaster, DN4 0RH   UK
Tel.: ++44 (1302) 572 244
Fax: ++44 (1302) 310 167
E-mail: information@btcv.org.uk
www.btcv.org.uk

Desc.: BTCV was founded in 1959 under the name Conservation Corps and is now the largest practical conservation organisation in the UK. BTCV provides information and advice on urban and rural projects, organises conservation holidays, weekend and weekday projects and supports around 2,500 community groups.

Spp.: Wolves, sea turtles, vultures, otters.

Hab.: Wetlands, woodlands, grasslands, rainforests, desert, mountains, islands, coastline.

Loc.: UK, several countries in Europe, North America, Africa, Australia, Iceland, Japan.

Dur.: 1 day to 3 weeks.

Per.: Year round.

L. term: Volunteer Officer positions available (min. 3 months).

Age: Under 18 with parental consent for UK projects; min. 18 for international projects.

Qualif.: Some international expeditions require reasonable fitness.

Work: Diverse, e.g. UK: restoring paths & dry stone walls or hedgelaying. International: revegetation, construction, sustainable development, habitat management or animal research.

Lang.: English. Other languages encountered with various projects.

Cost: From GB£45 (approx. US$80) for UK projects; GB£200–1,000 (approx. US$350–1,800) for overseas expeditions.

Applic.: GB£50-100 deposit required (approx. US$90-180).

Notes: Conservation Holidays Brochure available on request.

Selected projects:

Wild Bird Rehabilitation, Bulgaria
Skaftafell National Park, Iceland
Wolf & Bear Conservation, Slovakia

CARAPAX – European Center for Conservation of Chelonians

International RANA Foundation
C.P. 34 – Località Le Venelle
58024 Massa Marittima (GR) Italy
Tel.: ++39 (0566) 940 083 – Fax: ++39 (0566) 902 387
E-mail: volunteers@carapax.org – carapax@cometanet.it
www.carapax.org

Desc.: The Carapax Center was established in 1989 by the International RANA Foundation (Reptiles, Amphibians in Nature) the European Union and the Tuscany Region. The Carapax Center conducts research and works towards the recovery and reintroduction of tortoises. Carapax reintroduces animals saved from captivity (private donations to the centre) and from illegal sale (confiscated by the authorities) back to nature. Once set free in natural reserves, the tortoises are marked and followed using radio-tracking techniques or by local environmental organisations or responsible authorities. For 8 years volunteers have worked at the Carapax Center to provide general care of the animals. Volunteers also help experts in their scientific research in the field.

Spp.: Priorities are the Mediterranean tortoises and fresh water turtles or terrapins. *Testudo hermanni hermanni, T. hermanni boetgheri, T. marginata, T. graeca.*

Loc.: Central Italy, in the Tuscany region, 18 km from the west coast.

Travel: Airplane to Rome, train to Grosseto and Follonica, then bus to Massa Marittima where Carapax staff will pick up volunteers.

Dur.: Min. 2 weeks.

Per.: Mid-April to mid-October.

Age: Min. 18.

Qualif.: Experience is not required; motivation and interest is important.

Work: Management of infrastructure (upkeep, build or repair); care of animals (feed, sometimes help with veterinary care, scrupulously respecting hygiene standards); provide information to the public (receive and guide visitors); scientific research inside and outside the centre (depending on individual knowledge of the programmes linked to universities).

The activities take place mainly in the spring and September, the most active period for tortoises. Participation in the repatriation of tortoises (Italy, Greece, Tunisia, Morocco, France) is generally reserved for volunteers who have already taken part in field projects, are able to recognise species and are familiar with the marking system. Basic training is given to volunteers on their first day.

Lang.: English, Italian, German, French, Dutch.

Accom.: The centre can accommodate about 20 people. Accommodation is in wooden chalets (1 room; 6 beds) with electricity. There are 4 outdoor showers and 2 toilets (1 for women and 1 for men). There is an open-air kitchen protected by a large roof.

Cost: Travel expenses are not reimbursed by the centre and volunteers pay a daily participation fee of EUR13 (approx. GB£8.50 or US$16) for accommodation and food. This must be paid at least 2 weeks prior to arrival at the centre.

Applic.: Contact Carapax directly for an application form.

Notes: Volunteers must carry health and accident insurance.

CENTRE FOR ALTERNATIVE TECHNOLOGY

Machynlleth, Powys
SY20 9AZ Wales   UK
Tel.: ++44 (1654) 705 950
Fax: ++44 (1654) 702 782
E-mail: info@cat.org.uk
www.cat.org.uk

Desc.: The Centre for Alternative Technology, open to the public since 1975, has working displays of wind, water and solar power, low energy buildings, organic farming and alternative sewage systems. It offers residential courses on topics such as water power, bird watching, organic gardening and rustic furniture making. The Centre also hosts an information service and a bookshop (with mail-order service). The Centre receives 80,000 visitors per year.

Loc.: Wales, Great Britain.

Dur.: Short-term volunteer programme of 1–2 weeks.

Per.: Specified weeks between March and September inclusive.

L. term: A limited number of long-term volunteers work in specific departments such as engineering, building, gardening and information for 6 months. Prospective long-term volunteers must stay for a 'trial' week before any offer of a placement can be made.

Age.: Min. 18.

Qualif.: Particular skills are not needed for short-term volunteers. Certain skills and previous experience may be criteria for the selection of long-term volunteers, as places are limited.

Lang.: English.

Cost: Volunteers contribute GB£5,50 (EUR7,50) per day for the cost of room and board. Accommodation and food are provided.

Agents: Contact the Centre directly.

Applic.: Application forms for the short-term volunteer programme are published in January. Early booking is necessary. Contact the Centre for details on the long-term volunteer programme.

CHANTIERS DE JEUNES PROVENCE CôTE D'AZUR

La Maison des Chantiers La Ferme Giaume
7 Avenue Pierre de Coubertin
06150 Cannes la Bocca France
Tel.: ++33 (4) 93 478969 – Fax: ++33 (4) 93 481201
E-mail: cjpca@club-internet.fr
www.cjpca.fr.st

Desc.:   This organisation offers programmes for teenagers who want to experience community life, work for heritage protection, and spend an unusual summer holiday.

Loc.:   St. Marguerite Island, Cannes, in the Region of Provence, France, and in the region of Piedmont, Italy.

Dur.:   2 weeks.

Per.:   Summer, but also year round during school holidays.

Age: Min. 13, max. 17.

Qualif.: No qualifications necessary.

Lang.:   French.

Cost: Approx. EUR 350 (approx. GB£ 220).

Agents: Contact the organisation directly.

Work: Different for each project, from simple construction to trail maintenance.

Applic.: Call or e-mail the organisation to receive an application form.

CONSERVATIONS VOLUNTEERS NEW ZEALAND

New Zealand Department of Conservation
PO Box 10420
Wellington New Zealand
Tel.: ++64 (4) 471 0726   Fax: ++64 (4) 471 1082
www.doc.govt.nz/Community/006~Volunteers/
(to obtain the ~ sign press Alt+126 on the numeric keyboard)

Desc.: The goals of the New Zealand Department of Conservation include environmental conservation, supporting and strengthening links between local communities, the public and other conservation groups. Volunteers help with many different conservation tasks such as bird counts, historic building restoration, hut maintenance, weed control, whale strandings, tree planting and giving public presentations.

Spp.: Birds, plants and animals of New Zealand. Projects are mainly habitat focused.

Hab.: Various throughout New Zealand..

Loc.: Most projects are on specific islands of New Zealand.

Dur.: From a few days to a year, depending upon project. Local long-term volunteers can participate on agreed upon days per week.

Per.: Year round.

Age: Min. 18.

Qualif.: Fitness levels, from low to high, are considered for various projects; minimum level of endurance is the ability to trek 3 hours with a pack.

Lang.: English.

Cost: Varies with project; board is often provided; volunteers are often responsible for their own food; costs are usually minimal.

Applic.: Local applicants are given first priority, followed by nationals and then foreigners. Contact the Conservation Volunteer Co-ordinator at the relevant office for details. See the Online Calendar for Conservation Volunteers link in the Volunteers Webpage (see address above) to find current openings and contacts throughout New Zealand. Application form is online.

Notes: See list of what supplies and equipment to bring.

COORDINATING COMMITTEE
FOR INTERNATIONAL VOLUNTEERS

1 rue Miollis
75015 Paris France
Tel.: ++33 (1) 4568 4936 – Fax: ++33 (1) 4273 0521
E-mail: ccivs@unesco.org
www.unesco.org/ccivs/

Desc.: The Coordinating Committee for International Voluntary Service (CCIVS) is an international non-governmental organisation that plays a coordinating role in the sphere of voluntary service. CCIVS has 250 members and branches in over 100 countries. The aims of the CCIVS are to fight against the dangers of war, social and racial discrimination, underdevelopment, illiteracy and the consequences of neo-colonialism; to promote international understanding, friendship and solidarity as pre-conditions to firm and lasting peace on earth; to enable social and national development and to establish a just international economic and social order. Volunteers from different countries live and work together on a common project to benefit the local population working in the fields of agriculture, archeology, construction and re-construction, disaster relief work, protection of the natural environment and health and welfare.

Dur.: Usually 3–4 weeks.

L. term: CCIVS member organisations also organise long-term projects for medium (1–6 months) or long-term (1–3 years) volunteers.

Agents: Contact CCIVS for further information.

Notes: CCIVS produces several publications on volunteer service. Contact CCIVS for the list of publications and ordering.

CORAL CAY CONSERVATION (CCC)

The Tower, 13th Floor
125 High Street, Colliers Wood
London SW19 2JG   UK
Tel.: ++44 (870) 750 0668 – Fax: ++44 (870) 750 0667
E-mail: info@coralcay.org
www.coralcay.org

Desc.: Working in partnership with governments, NGO's, local communities and education groups, CCC sends teams of volunteers to survey some of the world's most endangered coral reefs and tropical forests. Since 1986, CCC volunteers have been responsible for the establishment of World Heritage Sites, marine reserves and wildlife sanctuaries. CCC offers the opportunity to combine marine and terrestrial scientific research with international travel and cultural exploration.

Spp.: Terrestrial and marine organisms.

Hab.: Tropical coasts and forests.

Loc.: Philippines, Honduras, Fiji and Malaysia.

Dur.: Min. 2 weeks.

Per.: Year round.

L. term: Inquire with organisation.

Age: Min. 16.

Qualif.: CCC offers: 1 Scuba Training wk, 2 Skills Development wks and numerous Conservation wks. PADI Open Water divers are trained up to Advanced Open Water (AOW). PADI AOW divers (BSAC Sports/Club/Sports, CMAS, SAA- equivalents) are accepted directly onto the Skills development Programme.

Work: Training in marine and/or terrestrial ecology and survey techniques. Reef and forest data collection.

Lang.: English.

Accom.: Basic on-site accommodation provided.

Cost: Start at GB£550 (US$900). Prices include food, accommodation, equipment and training. Flights not included.

Applic.: Visit www.coralcay.org or call for an application form.

Notes: Monthly presentations are organised throughout the UK. Contact Volunteer Recruitment (recruitment@coralcay.org) to reserve.

COTRAVAUX

11 Rue de Clichy
75009 Paris
France
Tel.: ++33 (1) 4874 7920
Fax: ++33 (1) 4874 1401

Desc.: Cotravaux coordinates 12 French workcamps. Its role is to promote voluntary work and community projects concerning environmental protection, monument restoration and social projects. The organisation offers many workcamps in different regions of France. Many of the organisations members of Cotravaux work with foreign partners.

Loc.: France.

Dur.: 2–3 weeks.

Per.: Year round; most projects run between June and October.

L. term: Certain projects offer 4–12 month volunteering.

Age.: Min. 18.

Qualif.: No specific skills needed.

Lang.: A few projects require French.

Cost: Volunteers must pay for their own transportation to the camps. Room and board provided (some camps require a daily contribution).

Agents: Some partner organisations (inquire with Cotravaux).

Applic.: Contact Cotravaux by fax or mail to obtain the list of partner workcamps in France or other specific countries.

Notes: A list of Cotravaux member organisations can be obtained by the website of Jeunesse et Réconstruction, one of the largest French volunteering organisations. Their website is www.volontariat.org, while the list of Cotravaux members is at the bottom of the page www.volontariat.org/cotravaux.htm; no links are provided but any search engine can help.

CTS – Centro Turistico Studentesco e Giovanile

Sezione Ambiente
Via Albalonga 3
00183 Roma Italy
Tel.: ++39 (06) 6496 0306 – Fax: ++39 (06) 6496 0335
E-mail: ambiente@cts.it
www.ctsambiente.it

Desc.:	Founded in1974, CTS is now the largest youth association in Italy. Its Environmental Department organises research activities, ecotourism and environmental education programmes, training courses and workshops. It also publishes books and produces videos on environmental subjects. Projects concern endangered species, animal behaviour, habitat protection, and wildlife management.
Spp.:	Bears, dolphins, whales, sea turtles, wolves, chamois.
Hab.:	Alpine, Mediterranean Sea and coast, temperate forest, lagoons.
Loc.:	Italian Alps, Appennines, Mediterranean coasts and islands, often inside protected areas.
Dur.:	Depends on the project; average period is 6–15 days.
Per.:	Year round.
L. term:	Inquire with organisation.
Age:	Min.18. Younger members with parental and CTS consent.
Qualif.:	Physically fit, flexible, cooperative. Able to swim for marine projects.
Cost:	EUR250–700 (approx. GB£170–450), excluding food and transportation.
Lang.:	Italian, English.
Agents:	CTS offices are throughout Italy and in London, Paris, Madrid, Barcelona and New York.
Applic.:	Membership is required to join the expeditions (EUR 28).
Notes:	CTS cooperates with organisations such as the Ecovolunteer Network (see organisation list).

Selected Projects:
Bottlenose Dolphin Project, Italy
Loggerhead Sea Turtles in Linosa, Italy

CVA – Conservation Volunteers Australia

National Head Office
P.O. Box 423, Ballarat 3353
Victoria Australia
Tel.: ++61 (3) 5330 2600 – Fax: ++61 (3) 5330 2655
E-mail: info@conservationvolunteers.com.au
www.conservationvolunteers.com.au

Desc.: Founded in 1982, CVA is a non-profit organisation dedicated to practical conservation. CVA's activities concern environmental topics such as salinity, soil erosion, biodiversity and endangered species. Volunteers are primarily between the ages of 18–30. Each team working in a project is provided with a vehicle (usually a minibus or 4WD with trailer), first-aid equipment, hand tools and cooking equipment. CVA projects offer a unique opportunity to see parts of Australia, off the regular track, as well as to make international friendships through team activities.

Spp.: Turtles, penguins, birds, koalas, wallabies, vegetation.

Hab.: Rivers, coasts, dryland, swamps.

Loc.: Various locations in Australia.

Dur.: 4 – 6 weeks.

Per.: Year round.

L. term: Inquire with organisation.

Age: Min. 18.

Qualif.: Experience and qualifications related to the environment are welcome but not essential.

Lang.: English.

Cost: AUS$1,200 (approx. EUR 700/US$900) for 6 weeks, including food, accommodation and project-related transportation within Australia.

Applic.: Call, write or e-mail CVA National Head Office for information. Applications are accepted on-line.

CVG – Conservation Volunteers Greece

Veranzerou 15,
10677 Athens   Greece
Tel.: ++30 (210) 3825 506
Fax: ++30 (210) 3814 682
E-mail: 1987@cvgpeep.gr / marina@cvgpeep.gr
www.cvgpeep.gr

Desc.: Summer work camps in Greece. These projects usually take place in remote areas of Greece in co-operation with Forestry Departments, Local Authorities, Cultural Associations, etc. Intercultural exchanges and conservation work allow young people to contribute to a hosting community. CVG is also involved in European Voluntary Service (EVS) projects.

Spp.: Various: birds of prey, forest flora and fauna.

Hab.: Mediterranean ecosystems, forests and wetlands.

Loc.: Greece, usually remote areas.

Travel: Contact the organisations for specific projects.

Dur.: 2–3 weeks; fixed dates are provided for every project.

Per.: Summer.

Age: Min. 18.

Work: Nature conservation (forest-fire protection, tree-planting, footpath maintenance, construction and placement of signs), cultural heritage (restoration of traditional buildings, ancient cobbled-stone footpaths and help in archaeological digs) or social benefit (restoration of school buildings, construction of playgrounds). Work is 5 – 6 hours/day, 6 days/week.

Lang.: English.

Accom.: Facilities are modest. Hosting is usually in schools and community or youth centres. Volunteers should bring along a sleeping bag and sleeping mat. Household chores involved.

Cost: Approx. EUR120 (approx. GB£80).

Agents: The Alliance of European Voluntary Service Organisations (www.alliance-network.org).

Applic.: A Volunteer Exchange Form to apply is provided by Alliance partner organisations or CVG web site.

EARTHWATCH INSTITUTE

3 Clock Tower Place – Suite 100, Box 75
Maynard, MA 01754   USA
Tel.: ++1 (978) 461 0081 – (800) 776 0188 (toll free in US/Canada)
Fax: ++1 (978) 461 2332
E-mail: info@earthwatch.org
www.earthwatch.org

Desc.: Earthwatch is an international charity that supports around 140 scientific field research projects in 50 countries. All projects are open to paying volunteers who work alongside leading scientists. Volunteers work as part of a team of people from all corners of the world with one thing in common — a commitment to doing something to protect the environment. From tracking crocodiles in the Okavango Delta, to studying dynamic glaciers in Iceland or to observing dolphin behaviour in New Zealand, Earthwatch has a wide range of projects around the globe. Volunteers can also get a taste of the Earthwatch experience during 'Discovery Weekends'.

Spp.: Jaguars, chimpanzees, mountain lions, dolphins, birds, snakes, rhinos, crocodiles, and many others.

Hab.: Rainforest, desert, savannah, tropical and temperate seas and coasts, arctic, antarctic, sub-arctic, alpine.

Loc.: The Americas, Europe, Africa, Asia, Australia, Antarctica.

Dur.: 3 days to 3 weeks.

Per.: Year round.

Age: Min. 16.

Qualif.: No specific qualifications.

Lang.: English.

Cost: Approx. US$500—3,600, inc. room and board. Earthwatch (Europe) also offers Discovery programmes from GB£130.

Agents: Earthwatch Europe(UK), Australia and Japan (see website).

Applic.: E-mail or call the nearest office for more information.

Notes: Grants are available for students and teachers.

Selected Projects:
Blach Rhino, Kenya
Spanish Dolphins, Spain

THE ECOVOLUNTEER NETWORK

Central Office
Meyersweg 29 7553 AX Hengelo The Netherlands
Tel.: ++31 (74) 250 8250
Fax: ++31 (74) 250 6572
E-mail: info@ecovolunteer.org
www.ecovolunteer.org

Desc.: About 30 projects offer hands-on experience in wildlife conservation and research, assisting in fieldwork, monitoring research and in wildlife rescue and rehabilitation centres. Volunteers work with local conservationists, researchers and rangers and are expected to adapt to local culture and food. Minimum 77% of the price is forwarded to projects.

Spp.: African hunting dogs, wolves, bears, rhinoceros, elephants, gibbons, orang-utans, beavers, otters, dolphins, whales, seals, turtles, birds, rare breeds of dogs, horses and sheep, multiple species in wildlife rescue centres.

Hab.: Ranging from subarctic to tropical rainforest.

Loc.: Worldwide.

Dur.: Min. 1, 2, 3 or 4 weeks, depending on projects.

Per.: Some projects are seasonal, others are year round.

L. term: Possible with many projects, especially for academic research.

Age: Most projects min. 18; some projects min. 20.

Qualif.: Variable. Physically fit and able to work independently.

Lang.: English.

Cost: Variable Starting from EUR325 (approx. GB£235). See Ecovolunteer website .

Agents: Belgium: www.ecovolunteer.be
Brazil: http:// br.ecovoluntarios.org
Britain:www.ecovolunteer.org.uk
France: http:// fr.ecovolunteer.be
Germany: www.oekovolontaer.de or www.ecovolunteer.de
Hungary: www.vadonprogram.co.hu
Netherlands: www.ecovolunteer.nl or www.ecovrijwilliger.nl
Spain: http:// es.ecovoluntarios.org

Applic.: Mail or fax the application form on www.ecovolunteer.org or the Green Volunteers application form to the nearest agency or ask the agency for an appropriate form in the preferred language.

Notes: For projects and new agencies that would like to be included in the Ecovolunteer Network, contact the Ecovolunteer Program, attn.: Roel Cosijn, at the central office.

Selected Projects:
Animal Rescue, Florida
Brown Bear Project, Russia
Elephant Project, Thailand
Monk Seal Project, Turkey
Rhino Rescue Project, Swaziland
River Otter Project, Brazil
Wolf Project, Bulgaria

EUROPARC DEUTSCHLAND

Bundesgeschaftsstelle
Marienstrasse 31
D–10117 Berlin Germany
Tel.: ++49 (30) 2887 8820 – Fax: ++49 (30) 288 7882–16
E-mail: info@europarc-deutschland.de
www.europarc-deutschland.de

Desc.: The German section of the EUROPARC was founded in 1991 to support existing protected areas in Germany. Europarc Deutschland works towards the promotion of environmental education as well as a system's plan of protected areas in Germany so the natural heritage can be preserved for future generations. Each year, there are about 40/60 volunteer placements in protected areas, most of them National Parks, through the project "Praktikum fuer Die Umwelt", supported by the Commerzbank. The project is addressed to students who would like to contribute their knowledge and skills to the Parks.

Hab.: Temperate forest, coastal habitats, lakes, etc.

Loc.: Germany.

Dur.: 3–6 months.

Per.: April to October.

L. term: Up to 6 months.

Age: Min. 18.

Qualif.: Education, geography and biology backgrounds are advantageous. Sometimes field experience and a valid driver license are required.

Work: Environmental education, public relations.

Lang.: German.

Accom.: Provided.

Cost: No contributions, most of the positions are paid.

Applic.: Deadline January. For information see: www.praktikum-fuer-die-umwelt.de; form has to be returned together with a CV.

Notes: Volunteers will be invited to a 4-day workshop in March/April. Mandatory work visa requirements for non-EU residents.

EXPEDITION ADVISORY CENTRE (RGS)

Royal Geographic Society, with The Institute of British Geographers
1 Kensington Gore
London SW7 2AR UK
Tel.: ++44 (20) 7591 3030 – Fax: ++44 (20) 7591 3031
E-mail: eac@rgs.org
www.rgs.org/eac

Desc.: The Expedition Advisory Centre (EAC), founded by the Royal Geographical Society and the Young Explorer's Trust, is primarily concerned with advising those who are planning their own expeditions, with an emphasis on field research projects overseas. The Centre provides information on all aspects of expedition planning and organises the annual Expedition Planning Seminar each November. A wide variety of expedition publications and pamphlets are available including a booklet *Joining an Expedition*, listing 50 organisations that regularly arrange expeditions from environmental research and conservation work to community projects and adventurous training. Guidelines are also given on fund-raising. The Bulletin of Expedition Vacancies lists specific expeditions recruiting members. Those who have a particular skill to offer (either scientific or medical) can be included on a special register of personnel available for overseas projects (send a stamped, self-addressed envelope to the Centre to receive the appropriate form). The Centre is open from 10am–5pm, Monday to Friday. Write for information or ask for an appointment.

Notes: The Centre only provides information and cannot place individuals on any planned expedition.

FRONTIER

50–52 Rivington Street
London EC2A 3QP UK
Tel.: ++44 (20) 7613 2422
Fax: ++44 (20) 7613 2992
E–mail: info@frontier.ac.uk
www.frontier.ac.uk

Desc.: Frontier is a non-profit international NGO, conducting conservation, research and development projects in partnership with host-country institutions, focusing on environmental issues. Current projects are located in Madagascar, Cambodia, Tanzania and Nicaragua and include biodiversity surveys, habitat mapping and socio-economic work in a variety of habitats such as coral reefs, mangroves, savannah grasslands, tropical and arid forests. Volunteers receive full training and can gain unique BTEC qualifications in Tropical Habitat Conservation or Expedition Management (biodiversity research).

Hab.: Rainforests, tropical forests, savannah, mangroves, coral reefs.

Loc.: Cambodia, Madagascar, Nicaragua, Tanzania.

Dur.: 4, 8, 10 or 20 weeks.

Per.: Year round.

L. term: Inquire with organisation.

Age: Min. 17.

Qualif.: To be selected for an expedition, applicants must be enthusiastic and have a commitment to conservation issues in developing countries.

Work: Biodiversity surveys, habitat mapping, socio-economic work with local communities.

Lang.: English.

Cost: Costs start from GB£1,400 (approx. EUR2,000/US$2,675), excluding flights and visa; contact Frontier for details.

Applic.: Contact Frontier for an application form.

GLOBAL SERVICE CORPS

Earth Island Institute
300 Broadway, Suite 28
San Francisco, California 94133–3312   USA
Tel.: ++1 (415) 788 3666 ext.128 – Fax: ++1 (415) 788 7324
E-mail: gsc@earthisland.org
www.globalservicecorps.org

Desc.: Global Service Corps provides opportunities for adult volunteers to live and work on projects in developing nations. Volunteers do village-based community work in Africa and Southeast Asia.

Loc.: Tanzania, Thailand.

Dur.: Mini-projects 2 weeks; short term projects 3–4 weeks; internships 9 weeks.

Per.: Monthly, year round.

L. term: Most long-term volunteers participate on a short-term GSC trip and continue afterwards in their placement. The short-term project provides a good orientation to the country, area, organisations and people. Long-term volunteers pay an additional daily fee that covers room, board and supervision.

Age: Min. 18.

Qualif.: No specific skills needed beyond good English speaking skills.

Work: In Tanzania, volunteers help in implementing an organic farming project and in training local farmers. In Thailand, the work focuses on developing an environmental education programme.

Lang.: English.

Cost: For Thailand 2-week project cost US$2,075 up to US$3,790 for 9 weeks. Tanzania (2–9 weeks) project cost range from US$2,075 to US$3,790. Project fee covers all in-country expenses, except for personal items. Volunteers are required to provide round-trip international airfares for themselves as well as a travel insurance.

Applic.: Download an application form from the GSC website. A CV and a 2–3 paragraph statement must be included with application as well as a US$150 refundable deposit.

GLOBAL VISION INTERNATIONAL

Amwell Farmhouse Nomansland
Wheathampstead St Albans AL4 8EJ UK
Tel.: ++44 (870) 608 8898 (UK) ++1 (888) 653 6028 (toll free USA)
Fax: ++44 (1582) 834 002
E-mail: info@gvi.co.uk
www.gvi.co.uk

Desc.: Global Vision International provides support and funding for long term, pioneering projects in community development and conservation in conjunction with governments, world agencies and NGO's. GVI supplies all science and expedition staff as well as the technical equipment to ensure the validity of these programs well into the future. Current expeditions include Coral reef research and marine conservation in Mexico and the Seychelles, wildlife research in the South African bush, biodiversity studies in the rainforests of Costa Rica and the Amazon, exploration in Patagonia and community development in Mexico. Full training is provided.

Hab.: Rainforests, savannah, coral reefs, glacial areas.

Loc.: Ecuador, Costa Rica, South Africa, the Seychelles, Patagonia and Mexico.

Dur.: 5, 10, 15 or 20 weeks.

Per.: Year round.

L. term: Opportunities are available for who has completed a 10 week expedition, ranging from internships on an expedition or placements in National Parks and protected areas.

Age: Min. 18

Qualif.: No qualifications are necessary as full training in the field is provided. Applicants must be enthusiastic, interested in conservation and able to swim (for Marine Expeditions).

Work: Data collection, biodiversity surveys, wildlife research, scuba diving surveys.

Lang.: English.

Cost: From GB£1,350 (US$2,500), incl. room and board, excl. flights.

Applic. Apply online.

Notes: GVI N.America E-mail: info@gviusa.com www.gviusa.com

GREENFORCE – Careers in Conservation

11–15 Betterton St. Covent Garden
London WC2H 9BP UK
Tel.: ++44 (20) 7470 8888 – (0870) 770 2646 (within the UK)
Fax: ++44 (0870) 712 0153 (within the UK)
E-mail: info@greenforce
www.greenforce.org

Desc.: Greenforce carries out projects to assist developing countries with wildlife resources management. Work includes biodiversity inventory, population estimates and distribution mapping. Results are used for management planning for protected areas. With the co-operation of local experts and students, these long term projects, both terrestrial and marine, fulfil the needs of local management authorities.

Spp : Large and small mammals, reptiles and amphibians, birds, selected invertebrates, coral communities.

Hab.: African savannah, Amazon rainforest, tropical islands.

Loc.: Africa, Ecuador, Nepal, Borneo, Fiji and the Bahamas.

Dur.: Volunteers join for 10-week periods.

Per.: Year round.

L. term: Traineeships are available.

Age: Min. 18.

Qualif.: No scientific knowledge required; full training (including diving training to PADI EFR for marine projects) is provided.

Work: Preparation and identification of specimens, mapping and radiotracking of wildlife resources.

Lang.: English.

Accom.: Traditional stilted house or bure, depending on location. Sleeping bags, mosquito nets and mats required.

Cost: GB£ 2,300 (approx. EUR3,300). The fee includes food and accommodation, visa, local transportation and training in London and in the field. International flight not included.

Applic.: Online application form.

HELLENIC ORNITHOLOGICAL SOCIETY

Vas. Irakleiou 24
GR – 106 82 Athens Greece
Tel.: ++30 (1) 822 8704/822 7937
Fax: ++30 (1) 822 8704
E-mail: birdlife-gr@ath.forthnet.gr
www.ornithologiki.gr

Desc.: Protecting bird fauna and Important Bird Areas of Greece.

Spp.: All endangered species of Greek bird fauna.

Hab.: All habitats of Greece (forests, lagoons, rivers, sealife).

Loc.: Greece.

Travel: Bus, train or plane to the project area.

Dur.: Min. 3 weeks for foreign volunteers; 2 weeks for Greek volunteers.

Per.: May to October (mostly in the summer); some projects year round.

L.term: With project leaders approval.

Age: Min. 18.

Qualif.: Able to work sometimes in difficult conditions, to do manual work, and to be punctual. Able to live and work with people from different countries and cultures and to cooperate with the local communities. Experience in similar projects or studies in biology, environment, ornithology are more than welcome.

Work: Work in the field (constructing & monitoring nests, counting birds, feeding, monitoring of the habitats, etc.) and in public awareness.

Lang.: English, French, German.

Accom.: According to project, either provided by HOS in organized campsites, in rooms rented for the project (tents, sleeping bags and sheets and towels are required) or different accomodation at special low-cost deals .

Cost: A EUR 60 (approx. GB£40) membership fee required. Travel, food and personal expenses are not covered. Expenses needed for work during the project are covered by the HOS.

Applic.: Application form can be found on the HOS website and sent by post, fax or e-mail from March to August.

i to i

Woodside House
261 Low Lane
Horsforth, Leeds LS18 5NY UK
Tel.: ++44 (870) 333 2332 – Fax: ++44 (113) 205 4619
E-mail: info@i-to-i.com
www.i-to-i.com

Desc.: i to i is a volunteer travel & TEFL training organisation, specialising in meaningful conservation work-placements for dedicated travellers aged from 18-80. i-to-i's projects provide inspirational learning opportunities – both for the volunteer and their host community, and all projects aim to preserve the environment, tradition and culture of areas that really need support. Placements include teaching projects in South America,community development in India, shark research in South Africa, elephant conservation in Sri Lanka and also media placements in Ireland. Every year, i-to-i trains over 4,000 volunteers.

Hab.: Forest areas, mountain regions, coastal areas, villages and towns.

Loc.: 25 countries across five continents, including South America, Africa, Asia, Europe and Australia.

Dur.: 2 weeks –12 months.

Per.: Year round.

Age: Min 18.

Work: Teaching English as a Foreign Language (TEFL), Community Development projects (working with underprivileged communities), building, animal and plant species conservation and media placements.

Lang.: English.

Accom.: Hostels, basic hotels or with local families.

Cost: Min GB£495 (approx. US$ 800). Deposit £195 (approx. US$350). Flights not Included.

Applic.: Request brochures and applications by phone or online.

INTERNATIONAL OTTER SURVIVAL FUND

Skye Environmental Centre
Broadford, Isle of Skye
Scotland, IV49 9AQ   UK
Tel./Fax: ++44 (1471) 822 487
E-mail: iosf@otter.org
www.otter.org

Desc.: IOSF works to conserve otters by safeguarding areas of good habitat and supporting people working in research and rehabilitation worldwide. The Fund's mission is to protect 13 species of otter worldwide.

Spp.: Eurasian otter (*Lutra lutra*).

Hab.: Subarctic tundra, boreal forest.

Loc.: Hebridean Islands, Scotland.

Dur.: 1 week.

Per.: April to October.

L. term: Inquire with organisation.

Age: Min. 19, max. 65.

Qualif.: No specific skills needed.

Work: Volunteers learn skills in otter surveying, such as identifying dropping (spraint), footprints, etc. They may also take part in surveying particular islands. Since the otters are nocturnal the chances to observe them are very high (although it is not possible to give any guarantee).

Lang.: English.

Accom.: Volunteers stay in local guesthouses.

Cost: GB£ 240–495 depending on the project. The cost includes Bed & Breakfast, but volunteers pay for the other meals. Transport and equippement (except for peronal camera, binoculars, etc.) are provided.

Applic.: Call or write IOSF for application form.

Notes: IOSF supports several otter conservation projects overseas (for example in Belarus or Vietnam) where occasionally volunteers are needed. Inquire with IOSF for details.

INVOLVEMENT VOLUNTEERS ASSOCIATION INC.
P.O. Box 218, Port Melbourne
Victoria 3207 Australia
Tel.: ++61 (3) 9646 9392
Fax: ++61 (3) 9646 5504
E-mail: ivworldwide@volunteering.org.au
www.volunteering.org.au

Desc.: Involvement Volunteers Association Inc. (IVI) is a non-profit, NGO providing individual programmes for volunteering in 1 or more countries.
Loc.: Over 40 countries worldwide.
Dur.: 2, 6 or 12 weeks, up to 12 months.
Per.: Some projects are seasonal, others all year round.
Age: Min.18.
Qualif.: Suitable qualifications, determination, enthusiasm or experience.
Work: Various conservation related activities.
Lang.: English or Spanish.
Accom.: Various, depending on the project and the location.
Cost: Minimum AU$810 (approx. US$640/EUR490).
Applic.: Contact IVI by e-mail, airmail, fax or telephone.
Note: IVvolunteering is organised to best suit the individual volunteer's needs or the group of individuals taking part.

IUCN – The World Conservation Union

28, rue Mauvernay
1196 Gland Switzerland
Tel.: ++41 (22) 999 0000
Fax: ++41 (22) 999 0002
E-mail: mail@iucn.org
www.iucn.org

Desc.: Founded in 1948, IUCN – The World Conservation Union brings together more than 1,000 governmental and non-governmental members and 10,000 technical and scientific experts in its six Commissions. IUCN's mission is to influence, encourage and assist societies throughout the world to conserve the integrity and diversity of nature and ensure that any use of natural resources is equitable and ecologically sustainable.

Loc.: Refer to www.iucn.org – About IUCN – Offices.

Dur.: Min. 3 months to 1 year.

Per.: Inquire to the appropriate IUCN Regional/Country Office in the preferred location.

L. term: Long-term assignments are preferred.

Age: Min. 21.

Qualif.: Vary according to specific assignments.

Work: Assist in collecting information, desk research and report writing. Organise and facilitate meetings and workshops. Develop project proposals and communication materials. Maintain databases and web-pages.

Lang.: Depends on the location of work (English, French and Spanish are also commonly used).

Cost: Conditions vary according to location and assignment.

Agents: Refer to www.iucn.org - About IUCN – Vacancies – Offices and Members – Directory. Contact the IUCN Regional/Country Office and/or IUCN members in the preferred location.

Applic.: Send CV and information on availability of time to preferred IUCN Regional/Country Office in the preferred location.

LEGAMBIENTE

Via Salaria 403 – 00199 Rome Italy
Tel.: ++39 (06) 862 681 – Volunteer office: ++39 (06) 8626 8324
For SCUBA activities: ++39 (06) 8626 8400
Fax: ++39 (06) 8626 8319
E-mail: volontariato@mail.legambiente.com
www.legambiente.com/canale8/campi/

Desc.: Founded in 1980, Legambiente is a non-profit organisation involved primarily with public awareness and environmental campaigning activities. Volunteer opportunities include work camps and events such as the 'Clean up the World' day. Current projects include restoration and protection camps in small islands near Sicily, underwater archaeology and ecology camps in Sicily, ecological research in the Italian Alps, archeological study in southern Italy and many others.

Spp.: Various species of the different habitats.

Hab.: Mediterranean seas, islands and coasts, temperate forest, lagoons, Alps.

Loc.: National Parks and Reserves, Mediterranean islands, Italian Alps, Germany, Brazil, Japan, France, Wales, Czech Republic, Mexico, Belarus, Turkey, Spain, Denmark, Poland, Belgium, Cuba, South Africa, Swaziland.

Dur.: 10–20 days.

Per.: Year round.

L. term: EU citizens can join the EVS (European Voluntary Service) programme from 3 months to 1 year. See Notes below.

Age: Min.18. Special programmes available for those under 18.

Qualif.: No specific qualifications are required.

Lang.: Italian, English.

Cost: Min. EUR150, max. EUR350 (approx.GB£100–240).

Applic.: Contact Legambiente for information and application forms.

Notes: Legambiente is entitled to offer the EVS programme open to young EU citizens. The programme covers all the expenses of the volunteers for training in languages or in professional skills. For more information contact Paolo Maddonni Tel.:++39 (06) 8626 8324, e-mail: p..maddonni@mail.legambiente.com.

LIPU – Lega Italiana Protezione Uccelli, Birdlife Italy
(Italian League for the Protection of Birds)
Via Trento 49 – 43100 Parma   Italy
Tel.: ++39 (0521) 273 043
Fax: ++39 (0521) 273419
E-mail: info@lipu.it
www.lipu.it

Desc.:	LIPU, founded in 1965, is the Italian representative of BirdLife International. The aim of the organisation is the protection of nature and in particular of birds. It supports bird rescue centres, research programmes for the conservation of endangered species, awareness campaigns and environmental education programmes.
Spp.:	Birds.
Hab.:	Mediterranean coasts and islands, temperate forest, Alps.
Loc.:	Various locations in Italy.
Dur.:	7–10 days or more.
Per.:	April to October.
L. term:	Inquire with organisation.
Age:	Inquire with organisation. Junior and adult camps.
Qualif.:	Previous experience and qualifications are not required. Some camps need expert ornithologists.
Work:	Birdwatching, counts, ringing, data collection, fire prevention, trail maintenance and restoration.
Lang.:	Italian, English.
Cost:	Min. EUR300, max. EUR700 (GB£200–450).
Applic.:	Contact LIPU for information on international application.

MINGAN ISLAND CETACEAN RESEARCH EXPEDITIONS

Mingan Island Cetacean Study, Inc.
378 Rue Bord de la Mer
Longue-Pointe-de-Mingan, Québec, G0G 1V0 Canada
Tel./Fax: ++1 (418) 949 2845
E-mail: mics@globetrotter.net
www.rorqual.com

Desc.: Volunteers join a team of marine biologists conducting cetacean research in Northeastern Quebec (Canada), and in Baja California (Mexico). In the projects, participants spend most of their time on the water; there is no working facility on land at the Quebec site.

Spp.: Blue, fin, humpback and minke whales.

Hab.: Gulf of the St. Lawrence River, Sea of Cortez.

Loc.: Northeast Quebec; Gaspé Peninsula and St. Lawrence Estuary. During winter in Loreto, Baja California, for blue whale studies.

Travel: Airplane to Sept-Iles. For Loreto fly to LA and then to Loreto.

Dur.: 7–14-day sessions.

Per.: June to October in Quebec; February to March in Loreto.

L. term: Possible to stay up to 1 month.

Age: Min. 12.

Qualif.: Be prepared to spend long periods on the water—sometimes up to 12 hours. Recommended a good physical form.

Work: Help collect field data: take notes, observe researchers do biopsies and some photographic work. Assist with organizing daily logistics such as gas, food and boat preparation.

Lang.: English, French, German. Spanish useful in Mexico.

Accom.: B&B, inn or hotel.

Cost: Gaspé, Mingan and blue whale session CAD$1,895 (approx. US$1,600); including transportation, accommodation, food and 7-day session with the biologists. US$1,375 in Loreto; including all activities on the water, hotel and meals; does not include air transportation and transfers to and from the airport.

Applic.: Request from the organisation registration and medical forms.

THE NATIONAL TRUST

Working Holidays Booking office
Sapphire House, Roundtree Way, Norwich NR7 8SQ UK
Tel.:   ++44 (870) 4292429
fax: ++44 (870) 4292427
E-mail: working.holidays@nationaltrust.org.uk
www.nationaltrust.org.uk/volunteering/

Desc.: The National Trust offers 400 working holidays every year. This includes activities from carrying out a conservation survey and herding goats to painting a lighthouse or planting trees and many more.

Loc.: England, Wales, Northern Ireland.

Dur.: 3-14 days.

Per.: Year round.

L. term: Inquire with the organisation. Many opportunities are listed on the website.

Age: Min. 18 (some working holidays 16).

Qualif.: No specific skills required. Some projects need botanists, archaeologists or builders.

Work: Work involves outdoor countryside conservation. On some holidays there are opportunities to learn specific skills such as dry-stone walling, hedge laying etc.

Lang.: English.

Accom.: Basic. Volunteers stay in various types of accommodation; mostly dormitory.

Cost: GB£35-245. Food and accommodation are included.

Agents: Contact the organisation directly.

Applic: On-line application form or to receive an application form call ++44 (870) 429 2429.

Notes: The National Trust has special programmes for young people.

THE NATURE CORPS

3600 Ridge Road
Templeton, California 93465 USA
Tel.: ++1 (805) 434 0299
Fax: ++1 (805) 434 3444
E-mail: info@thenaturecorps.org
www.thenaturecorps.org

Desc.: The Nature Corps recruits volunteers to work on projects in National Parks in California and Hawaii, such as Yosemite, Sequoia, Channel Islands and Hawaii Volcanoes National Park. Projects vary from revegetation and tree planting to species preservation.

Hab.: Rainforest, high sierra.

Loc.: California and Hawaii, USA.

Dur.: 6–8 day excursions.

Per.: May to October.

L. term: Nature Corps will help volunteers make arrangements to stay after the 8–day period.

Age: Min. 18 (12–17 with parents' permission).

Qualif.: No particular skills needed, photography and carpentry skills welcome.

Lang.: English.

Cost: Adults fees start from US$595, including food and camping arrangements. Transportation provided on most excursions. A portion of the adults' contribution goes to supporting the 6–day Youth Expeditions. Youth and students fees are about US$370.

Agents: Contact The Nature Corps directly.

Applic.: Apply on-line at www.thenaturecorps.org or ask for an application form.

Notes: Half of the excursion is devoted to the project and half to guided recreation and education. Further information available from The Nature Corps.

NZTCV – The New Zealand Trust for Conservation Volunteers

Three Streams, 343 S.H.17, R.D.3 Albany
Auckland New Zealand
Tel.: ++64 (9) 415 9336 – Fax: ++64 (9) 415 9336
E-mail: conservol@clear.net.nz
www.conservationvolunteers.org.nz

Desc.: NZTCV is a member of the International Conservation Volunteers Alliance. Projects offer opportunities to visit scenic locations in both the North and South Islands of New Zealand. NZTCV allows overseas visitors to share New Zealand's unique environment and culture. Patrons: Dr. David Bellamy, Stephen King, Sir Paul Reeves & Lady Beverley Reeves.

Spp.: Various species of New Zealand's flora and fauna.

Hab.: Coasts, dryland, National Parks and Reserves, forests, wetlands, natural bush.

Loc.: Throughout New Zealand

Dur.: 1 – 3 weeks (varies).

Per.: Year round.

L. term: Inquire with organisation.

Age: Min. 18.

Qualif.: Experience and qualifications related to the environment are welcome but not essential.

Work: Species monitoring, general maintenance, planting, island revegetation, forest restoration.

Lang.: English.

Cost: Air travel to and from New Zealand. Free accommodation offered with some projects. Food costs for duration of stay and cost of transportation to and from project location are paid by the volunteer. See website for more information.

Applic.: Applications are accepted on-line or write to the address above for information.

OCEANIC SOCIETY EXPEDITIONS
Fort Mason Center, Building E
San Francisco, CA 94123   USA
Tel.: ++1 (415) 441 1106 – (800) 326 7491 (toll free in US/Canada)
Fax: ++1 (415) 474 3395
E-mail: info@oceanic-society.org
www.oceanic-society.org

Desc.:   Founded in 1972, Oceanic Society Expeditions (OSE) is a non-profit organisation that conducts research to protect aquatic environments and promote environmental education. OSE organises over 30 projects classified as 'Natural History Expeditions' (NHE) and 'Research Expeditions' (RE); the latter are designed to accomplish specific scientific objectives. For these projects volunteers work with field biologists, collecting data and logging information.

Spp.:   Dolphins, manatees, corals, seabirds, giant otters, seaturtles.

Hab.:   Tropical seas, temperate seas, rainforest, rivers.

Loc.:   Midway, Baja California, Caribbean, Belize, Bahamas and various locations in Central, South and North America.

Dur.:   4 – 10 days for NHE; 1 week for RE.

Per.:   Year round.

L.term: Inquire with organisation.

Age: Min. 18. Anyone under 18 must be accompanied by a guardian.

Qualif.:   Enthusiasm and willingness to take directions are necessary.

Lang.:   English.

Cost: Approx. US$1,000–3,000 for NHE, US$1,000–2,000 for RE.

Applic.:   Request application form to be returned with a deposit of US$300/person/trip.

Notes: OSE also raises contributions through adopt-a-dolphin, adopt-a-whale and adopt-an-atoll programs.

Selected Projects:
Bottlenose Dolphin Project, Belize
Manatee Research Project, Belize

OPERATION CROSSROADS AFRICA, Inc.

P.O.Box 5570
New York, NY 10027 USA
Tel.: ++1 (212) 289 1949
Fax: ++1 (212) 289 2526
E-mail: oca@igc.apc.org – oca@igc.org
www.oca.igc.org/web/index.html

Desc.: This organisation offers many opportunities for concerned persons with interest in areas such as ecology and environment, traditional medicine, archaeology, reforestation, wildlife, agriculture/farming and teaching.

Loc.: Botswana, Gambia, Ghana, Eritrea, Ivory Coast, Kenya, Senegal, South Africa, Tanzania, Uganda, Zimbabwe.

Dur.: 6–7 week programme.

Per.: Mid-June to mid-August.

Cost: US$3,500, including all expenses (not personal) and airfare from New York. Crossroads assists volunteers in raising funds for their travel and living expenses.

Applic.: On-line applications are available for Volunteers/Interns and Project Directors/Group Leaders. Volunteer information available by e-mail. For Project information, brochure/update, send a request to oca@igc.org. Project Directors/Group Leader applicants must be at least 25 years old with appropriate expertise. To receive the leader packet, send an e-mail message to oca@igc.org, plus include LEADER in the subject field.

Note: Students generally arrange to receive academic credit, typically 7–15 units.

OPERATION WALLACEA

Hope House
Old Bolingbroke, Spilsby, LincolnshirePE23 4EX   UK
Tel.: ++44 (1790) 763 194
Fax: ++44 (1790) 763 825
E-mail: info@opwall.com
www.opwall.com

Desc.: Operation Wallacea (OW) is a series of biological and social science expeditionprojects designed to underpin the achievement of specific wildlife conservation aims. The expeditions have been runnibng for the last 9 years in a remote corner of Sulawesi, Indonesia and in Honduras since 2003 and Egypt from 2005. OW recruits volunteers to join marine, rainforests and desert projects organized by a 75 strong team of scientist from UK, US and other academic institutions.

Spp.: Marine, rainforest and desert, encompassing corals, sponges, fish, birds, bats, butterflies, mammals, macaques, reptiles and amphibians, educational and anthropological projects.

Hab.: Coral reefs, rainforest, deserts.

Loc.: Sulawesi, Indonesia, Honduras and Egypt.

Travel: Airplane to Makassar (Sulawesi), San Pedro Sula (Honduras) and Sharm El Sheikh (Egypt).

Dur.: 2, 4, 6 or 8 weeks.

Per.: June to September.

L. term: Inquire with organisation.

Age: Min. 16.

Qualif.: Enthusiasm and a positive attitude towards the environment are the only qualifications necessary, as full training for diving, jungle survival and field skills are given.

Work: Volunteers work alongside scientists to complete surveys of the endemic species. Both flora and fauna in the marine and rainforest habitats are surveyed.

Lang.: English.

Accom.: Marine volunteers are based in traditional wooden bungalows in Indonesia, tents in Honduras and a research centre in Egypt, whilst the rainforest volunteers are based in village houses or in tents/hammocks at base camps.

Cost: 2 weeks GB£900 (EUR1300/US$1620); 4 weeks GB£1,750 (approx. EUR2,500/US$3,150); 6 weeks GB£2,400 (EUR3,500/US$4,320); 8 weeks GB£2,800 (approx. EUR4,000/US$5,040). Prices include food, accommodation, dive training to PADI OW and internal transfers between sites. Prices do not include flights and insurance.

Applic.: Prospective volunteers need only to contact the UK office; those living in Great Britain have the opportunity to attend some University presentations.

Notes: Dive equipment, excluding wetsuit, may be hired on site. Additional costs include Crewpack/PIC cards, additional dive courses and airport /other taxes.

PERU VERDE

Inkanatura/Peru Verde
Calle Ricardo Palma j-1, Santa Monica, Cusco Peru
Tel.: ++51 (84) 226 392 – Fax: ++51 (84) 224 045
E-mail: postmaster@peruverde.org
www.inkanatura.com – www.peruverde.org

Desc.:   The association offers a 'resident naturalist guide' programme at 4 rainforest lodges, as well as a series of projects ranging from teaching English to local rainforest communities, wildlife observation and mapping fruiting trees and vines.

Spp.:   Over 1,000 birds, 200 mammals and 1,200 insect species.

Hab.:   Amazon rainforest (from cloud forest to lowland rainforest).

Loc.:   Southeastern Peru.

Travel: Lodge reached by plane and then boat ride or by bus.

Dur.:   Min. 3 months for resident naturalist guide volunteers.

Per.:   Dry (April to October) or wet season (November to March).

L. term: Longer period of time at the discretion of the project leader.

Age: Min. 21, max. 65 with rare exceptions.

Qualif.:   A background or strong interest in ecology/biology is essential.

Work: Numerous projects offered with different work times. Guiding guests of the lodges is the main task of resident naturalists.

Lang.:   A working knowledge of Spanish is highly recommended.

Accom.: Bed with mosquito net on open sleeping platform. Bedding must be provided by the volunteer.

Cost: Volunteer Resident Naturalists must cover all airfare and travel costs. Room and board at the project site cost US$10.

Agents: Contact Peru Verde directly, preferably by e-mail. Prospective volunteers can resend an e-mail, or phone or fax, to verify if the application has been received .

Applic.:   Applications for resident naturalist guide volunteers should be received by December for dry season and by July for wet season.

Notes: Prospective volunteers should be aware that work will probably be in hot and humid conditions not experienced before and that lodges are in very remote areas.

RALEIGH INTERNATIONAL

Raleigh House
27 Parsons Green Lane
London, SW6 4HZ   UK
Tel.: ++44 (20) 7371 8585 – Fax: ++44 (20) 7371 5116
E-mail: info@raleigh.org.uk
www.raleighinternational.org

Desc.: Raleigh International, formerly Operation Raleigh, organises expeditions around the world for young people of all nationalities and backgrounds. Volunteer staff with various skills over 25 is also neded to help run the expeditions. Projects may include, scientific research, surveys, community work, building schools or bridges and helping doctors in remote areas.

Hab.: Various.

Loc.: Namibia, Chile, Costa Rica & Nicaragua, Borneo, Fiji.

Dur.: 4,7 and 10 weeks.

Per.: Year round.

L. term: Volunteers (known as Venturers) may continue their involvement with Raleigh at home after the expedition. Volunteers may also continue travelling independently. Two and 3 week projects (in the same areas) are also designed for career gappers over 21. These programmes take the best bits of the longer expeditions and put them into a format suitable for people with only holiday time available.

Age: 17-25 (Ventureers); 25+(Staff on 4,7 and 10 week expeditions).

Qualif.: Volunteers must be physically fit, able to swim 200 metres and speak basic English. An introduction weekend that includes physical and mental challenges is required.

Accom.: Tents. Living conditions during the expeditions are very basic.

Cost: Approx. GB£ 2,995 (EUR 4,200) excluding airfare from the UK. Venturers raise funds for the expedition through sponsorship. With support from the head office, 1,000 young people succeed to take a place on an expedition every year.

Agents: Contact Raleigh International directly.

Applic.: Send a self-addressed, stamped envelope to receive the information and application package. Or visit the website.

RSPB – THE ROYAL SOCIETY FOR THE PROTECTION OF BIRDS

The Lodge, Sandy
Bedfordshire SG19 2DL   UK
Tel.: ++44 (1767) 680 551
Fax: ++44 (1767) 692 365
www.rspb.org/helprspb/volunteering/

Desc.: RSPB Residential Volunteering Scheme operates in 40 reserves around the UK, providing an opportunity for those interested in ornithology and conservation to gain practical experience of the day-to-day running of a RSPB reserve.
Spp.: Birds.
Hab.: Woodland, swamps, ponds, lakes, moorland, coastal lagoons.
Loc.: England, Scotland, Wales, Northern Ireland.
Dur.: Min. 1 week (Saturday to Saturday); max. 1 month.
Per.: Year round.
L. term: Negotiable by arrangement.
Age: Min.16 (18 for international volunteers and in some reserves).
Qualif.: Good physical health.
Work: Duties vary and may include: habitat and estate management, tourist assistance, reception work, survey/research assistance, car park duties, working with stock, grass cutting, bird counts, animal population monitoring. Duties allocated according to volunteer knowledge and experience.
Lang.: English.
Accom.: Chalets, cottages, houses, cabins, caravans or bungalows. May have to share a room with at least 1 other person of same sex. Bedding is provided (except sleeping bag). Cooking facilities available (volunteers must provide and cook their own food).
Cost: Free accommodation. Food and travel expenses not included.
Applic.: The web address above features an on-line brochure and an application form.
Selected Project:
Operation Osprey, Scotland

SANCCOB – The Southern African National Foundation for the Conservation of Coastal Birds

P.O. Box: 1111 6 Bloubergrant, 7443 Cape Town South Africa
Tel.: ++27 (21) 557 61 55
Fax: ++27 (21) 557 88 04
E-mail: carole@sanccob.co.za
www.sanccob.co.za

Desc.: SANCCOB rehabilitates sea birds, mostly from oil pollution, some injured or ill. The species most affected is the African penguin, a bird only found along the southern African coast and classified as 'vulnerable.' The main problem is oil pollution. The South African route is a popular ship-faring route and is very polluted.

Spp: African (jackass) penguin (*Spheniscus demersus*), Cape gannet, Cape, crowned and whitebreasted cormorants, kelp and hartlaub gulls, petrel, tern, albatross.

Hab.: Coastal.

Loc.: 20 km north of Cape Town, South Africa.

Travel: Airplane to Cape Town.

Dur.: Min. 6 weeks.

Per.: May to October is busy but oil spills can happen any time.

L. term: Possible, with project leaders approval.

Age: Min. 16.

Qualif.: Willingness to work hard with wild, difficult birds.

Work: Keeping the centre clean, scrubbing pools and pens daily (cleaning after 30–200 birds), feeding and stabilizing birds, washing birds, and assisting veterinary staff.

Lang.: English.

Accom.: Bed & Breakfast or contact the organisation for other possibilities.

Cost: Volunteers are responsible for food, transport and accommodation costs, approx. US$30–40/day.

Agents: Contact the organisation directly.

Applic.: Fill out application form from the web page.

Notes: Winters can be cold and wet in Cape Town. Old clothes to work in should be brought.

SAN GORGONIO WILDERNESS ASSOCIATION (SGWA)

Volunteer Ranger Program
34701 Mill Creek Road
Mentone, California 92359   USA
Tel./Fax: ++1 (909) 794 1123
E-mail: info@sgwa.org
www.sgwa.org

Desc.: This volunteer programme is open to naturalists, information specialists and persons willing to help with maintenance work, recreation and forest patrolling in the San Gorgonio Wilderness, not far from Los Angeles.

Loc.: The San Gorgonio Wilderness is located on the San Bernardino National Forest, approx. 75 miles east of Los Angeles.

Dur.: Min. 2 days, max. 3 months.

Per.: May to September, primarily on weekends and holidays.

L. term: Inquire with organisation.

Age: Min. 18. Persons under 18 may participate with a guardian.

Qualif.: Volunteers must be able to perform the type of service chosen, be experienced in hiking, backpacking, horseback riding or mountain biking on mountain trails (should the service require it) and have their own equipment. Volunteers are trained.

Work: Naturalists give nature walks and/or present programmes. Information Specialists provide permits, maps and other information to forest visitors. Trail Crew improve trails throughout the National Forest. Recreation Maintenance Crew improve recreation facilities. Forest Patrol day hike, backpack or ride horses or mountain bikes along trails and dirt roads throughout the forest to assist visitors, protect the forest and perform minor trail and camp maintenance.

Lang.: English.

Cost: Volunteers must purchase part (approx. US$30) of Forest Service uniform.

Applic.: Contact SGWA for further information and application form.

SCA – Student Conservation Association, Inc.

P.O. Box 550
Charlestown, New Hampshire 03603 USA
Tel.: ++1 (603) 543 1700
Fax: ++1 (603) 543 1828
E-mail: internships@thesca.org
www.thesca.org

Desc.: SCA is an educational organisation operating volunteer and internship programmes in conservation and natural resource management. The Conservation Internship Programs (CIP) are for anyone 18 or older to serve alongside seasonal staff for public and private natural resource management agencies. The Conservation Crew Program (CCP) allows high school students aged 15–19 to join summer conservation projects.

Loc.: USA: opportunities exist in all 50 states

Dur.: Usually 12–52 weeks for CIP; 3–5 weeks for CCP.

Per.: CIP are available year round, CCP from June to August only.

L.term: Max. 12 months, depending upon project.

Age: Min. 18 for CIP, no upper age limit; 15–19 for CCP.

Qualif.: Good health, enthusiasm, flexibility, fluent English.

Work: Interns work with widlife, in back country patrol, trail building, hydrology and engineering, visitor services and interpretation, environmental education with youth, research, public outreach, and in museum curator positions to name a few.

Lang.: English.

Cost: No cost: CIP Interns receive paid travel (within the US), free housing and related expenses, weekly living allowance of US$50 and free accident insurance. CCP volunteers receive free room and board and equipment but no travel.

Applic.: An application must be submitted with a medical form and at least 2 references. Request by mail or phone or download from SCA's website. Applicants can apply directly on-line. No deadline for CIP; deadline for CCP is March 1, or until all positions are filled. Application fee of US$10–40.

Notes: Listings of positions on website. Searchable database updated weekly; applications can also be filled out on website directly.

SCI – Service Civil International

International Secretariat
St–Jacobsmarkt 82, B–2000 Antwerpen Belgium
Tel.: ++32 (3) 226 5727
Fax: ++32 (3) 232 0344
E-mail: sciint@sciint.org (general)
www.sciint.org (to find all the national contacts)

Desc.: SCI is a voluntary NGO founded in 1920 that aims to promote international understanding and peace. It provides volunteers for projects in communities that cannot afford labour. Every year more than 20,000 volunteers of all nationalities work in over 100 camps.

Loc.: Western and Eastern Europe, United States, Australia.

Dur.: 2–3 weeks.

Per.: Year round, mainly June to September.

L. term: People with workcamp experience can join projects for 3–6 months; short-term volunteers need approval of host in order to stay longer.

Age: Min. 18 for Europe; min. 16 for the United States.

Qualif.: Ability to work as part of a team and live simply.

Lang.: English. For other languages, inquire with local SCI office.

Cost: Volunteers must provide transportation; contributions are US$65 in the United States, EUR120 in Europe, EUR250 in Eastern Europe. Accommodation, food and insurance are provided.

Agents: Local SCI offices listed in the above website. SCI has many branches in the world and cooperates with many organisations: contact the nearest office for information.

Applic.: Standard application; no need to be a member.

Notes: Smallest projects could be for 6 volunteers and largest for 20 volunteers. Usually only 2 volunteers from the same country can join the same project in order to form international teams.

SCI Germany: www.sci-d.de
SCI-IVS USA: www.sci-ivs.org
IVS UK: www.ivsgbn.demon.co.uk
IVP Australia: www.ivp.org.au

TETHYS RESEARCH INSTITUTE

c/o Civic Aquarium
Viale G.B. Gadio 2
20121 Milano Italy
Tel.: ++39 (02)5831 4889/ (02) 7200 1947
Fax: ++39 (02)5831 5345
E-mail: tethys@tethys.org   www.tethys.org

Desc.: This private non-profit organisation is dedicated to the study and protection of marine habitats, focusing on Mediterranean cetaceans. Founded in 1989, TRI is formed by a team of researchers conducting research with the help of volunteers.

Spp.: Cetaceans.

Hab.: Mediterranean Sea.

Loc.: Mediterranean (France, Greece, Italy).

Dur.: 1–2 weeks.

Per.: May to October.

L. term: Biology students or researchers may assist TRI biologists for the duration of projects with the leader's approval.

Age: Min.18. Minors may be accepted if accompanied by an adult.

Qualif.: Volunteers must be enthusiastic and flexible; ability to swim is necessary. Photography and computer skills are helpful.

Work: Assist the researchers with observations, cetacean photo-identification, data entry, operation of hydrophones and recording instruments. Share boat or household duties (shopping, cleaning, cooking).

Lang.: English, Italian.

Accom.: Aboard the 19–metre ketch *Gemini Lab* for research cruises. In house along the coast for dolphin project in Greece.

Cost: Approx. EUR 500–830 (approx. GB£350–580) for 6 or 9 days. Food, membership and insurance included. Travel to and from project not included.

Applic.: Contact TRI for information and application forms.

Selected projects:
Cetacean Sanctuary Research, Ligurian Sea
Ionian Dolphin Project, Greece

TREKFORCE EXPEDITIONS

Community & Conservation Projects
34 Buckingham Palace Road, London SW1W ORE UK
Tel.: ++44 (20) 7878 2275
Fax: ++44 (20) 7878 2276
E-mail: info@trekforce.org.uk
www.trekforce.org.uk

Desc.: Trekforce is a registered UK charity that provides volunteer teams to support conservation, scientific and community projects in the rainforests of Central America and South East Asia. Expeditions offer the opportunity to make a valuable contribution to conservation. All projects are organised by project partners in host countries, and work is also supported by local governments. Projects include construction work, flora and fauna surveys, archaeological surveys and work in national parks, nature reserves and rainforests. Recent projects include working with the Royal Society of South East Asia on a large biodiversity experiment in Sabah, upgrading the infrastructure at several National Parks in Belize and building research centres and visitor centres in nature reserves

Hab.: Rainforest.

Loc.: Central America (Belize, Guatemala), Borneo (Sabah, Sarawak).

Dur.: 2 – 5 months.

Per.: Year round.

L. term: Many 'trekkers' return for more expeditions at discounted rates.

Age: Min. 18.

Qualif.: No specific skills needed.

Lang.: English. Longer programmes involve learning local languages.

Accom.: Hammocks under mosquito nets and waterproof shelters.

Cost: Between GB£2,590 and GB£3,900 (approx. EUR3,800–5,500) depending on expedition length.

Applic.: Apply online for a brochure or a place on an introduction day.

Notes: Prospective volunteers join introduction days where they are offered help and advice on fund-raising and can discuss projects and placements and meet ex-volunteers.

UNITED NATIONS VOLUNTEERS (UNV)

P.O. Box 260–11,
D–53153 Bonn Germany
Tel.: ++49 (228) 815 2000
Fax: ++49 (228) 815 2001
E-mail: information@unvolunteers.org
www.unv.org

Desc.: The United Nations Volunteers programme is open to specialists in various fields. Since 1971 over 30,000 volunteers have joined the programme in about 140 countries (particularly in developing ones), co-operating with local organisations and communities for teaching or offering their professional skills. UNV programmes include: education, environment, peace operations and democracy, humanitarian relief and rehabilitation, technical co-operation and refugee assistance. Today, some 10% of the serving UNVs work with environmental or conservation issues in specific areas such as plant protection, forestry conservation, sanitation/waste disposal, energy engineering, meteorology, coastal erosion, preservation of cultural heritage and tourism. UN Volunteers have been assigned to projects on pandas in a reserve in China or on global warming policy planning in the Maldives.

Loc.: Developing countries throughout the world such as India, Brazil, Mali and Burkina Faso (for the environmental programme).

Dur.: Assignments usually last 2 years. Shorter assignments may be authorized.

Per.: Year round.

L. term: Some assignments can be extended beyond the 2-year period.

Age: Min. 21, but UNV volunteers are usually older than 35, as a professional working experience is necessary.

Qualif.: Volunteers must be professionals or technicians with at least 2 years of experience. Teachers, medical doctors, nurses, mechanical or electrical engineers, geologists, automotive mechanics, librarians, midwives, etc.

Work: Varies depending on programme and location.

Lang.: English, French, Spanish, Arabic, Portuguese. Language ability of selected volunteers will be tested.

Accom.: Simple accommodation provided for volunteer and dependent relatives (spouse and up to 2 children under 21 years of age). Furniture and utilities are normally provided. If these arrangements cannot be made, the paid rent will be reimbursed.

Cost: UNV volunteers receive a monthly living allowance that ranges from US$600–1,400 for single specialists and from US$800–1,900 for specialists with direct dependents. Upon completion of an assignment, a resettlement allowance will also be paid. Life, health and permanent disability insurance is provided free of charge. Return travel to duty station is also provided (includes direct dependents).

Applic.: Write or call for the PHS (Personal History Statement) form (either in French or English), which must be completed and sent in together with 2 photos and reference forms completed by both professional and personal referees. If the PHS is approved by UNV headquarters, the application is added to the roster of candidates. If a volunteer is selected for a particular post, the PHS is submitted for clearance by a UN agency and for approval by the Government requesting the services of a UNV specialist. Submission and selection of candidates may take several months. Candidates who are accepted must begin the assignment within 8 weeks of being notified of final selection.

UNIVERSITY RESEARCH EXPEDITIONS PROGRAM (UREP)

University of California
1333 Research Park Drive, Davis, California 95616 USA
Tel.: ++1 (530)752 8811 – Fax: ++1 (530) 757 8596
E-mail: urep@unexmail.ucdavis.edu
www.extension.ucdavis.edu/urep

Desc.: Founded in 1976, UREP offers a wide range of opportunities to participate in field research around the world, including wildlife, earth sciences, environmental and conservation studies, archaeology, culture and art.

Spp.: Various in the various habitats.

Hab.: Rainforest, alpine, desert, lagoons, tropical seas, grasslands, savannah.

Loc.: Various locations in North, Central and South America, Africa, Europe, Indonesia.

Dur.: Usually 2 weeks.

Per.: Year round.

L. term: Inquire with organisation.

Age: Min.18.

Qualif.: No special academic or prior field experience is required. Curiosity, flexibility and co-operation are essential. Wilderness experience, skills in observation, drawing, photography, diving can be helpful.

Lang.: English.

Cost: From US$1,600, to US$2,400 including food and accommodation.

Applic.: Send application form with US$200 deposit.

Notes: An information catalogue can be obtained by e-mailing or calling the above address.

U.S. DEPARTMENT OF AGRICULTURE - FOREST SERVICE
Volunteering in the National Forests
P.O. Box 96090, Washington, DC 20090 – 6090 USA
or Sidney R. Yates Federal Building
201, 14 Street, SW at Independence Ave., SW Washington, DC
www.fs.fed.us   (then search for 'volunteers')

- Region 1–Northern Region, Federal Bldg., P.O. Box 7669, Missoula, Montana 59807, tel. ++1 (406) 329 3675
- Region 2–Rocky Mountain, P.O. Box 25127, Lakewood, Colorado 80255, tel. ++1 (303) 275 5350
- Region 3–Southwestern, 333 Broadway, SE, Albuquerque, New Mexico 87102, tel. ++1 (505) 842 3292
- Region 4–Intermountain, Federal Bldg. 324, 25th St., Ogden, Utah 84401, tel. ++1 (801) 625 5412
- Region 5–Pacific Southwest, 1323 Club Drive, Vallejo, California 94592, tel. ++1 (707) 562 8737
- Region 6–Pacific Northwest, 333 SW First Avenue, P.O. Box 3623 Portland, Oregon 97208–3623, tel. ++1 (503) 808 2180
- Region 8–Southern, 1720 Peachtree Rd., NW, Atlanta, Georgia 30309, tel. ++1 (404) 347 4191
- Region 9–Eastern, 310 W. Wisconsin Ave., Suite 580, Milwaukee, Wisconsin 53203, tel. ++1 (414) 297 3600
- Region 10–Alaska, Federal Office Bldg., P.O. Box 21628 Juneau, Alaska 99802–1628, tel. ++1 (907) 586 8806
- Pacific Northwest Research Station, 333 SW 1st Avenue, P.O. Box 3890, Portland, Oregon 9208–3890, tel. ++1 (503) 808 2592
- North Central Research Station, 1992 Folwell Avenue, St. Paul Minnesota 55108, tel. ++1 (651) 649 5285
- Rocky Mountain Research Station, 240 W. Prospect Road, Fort Collins, Colorado 80526–2098, tel. ++1 (970) 498 1100
- Northeastern Area State and Private Forestry, 11 Campus Drive, Newtown Square, Pennsylvania 19073, tel. ++1 (610) 557 4200
- International Institute of Tropical Forestry, P.O. Box 25000, UPR Experimental Station, Rio Piedras, Puerto Rico 00928, tel. ++1 (787) 766 6302

Desc.: The Forest Service manages and protects the National Forest System and cooperates with private forest and woodland owners, State and local government agencies and private organisations. It performs research for improving the quality of the forest and forest products. Volunteer service is needed in US National Forests because the Forest Service has a limited budget. The programme goal is to provide fulfilling work experience to volunteers while accomplishing necessary tasks.

Spp.: Various in the United States.

Hab.: Various in the United States.

Loc.: National Forests throughout the United States.

Dur.: Inquire with the National Forest of choice.

Per.: Inquire with the National Forest of choice.

L. term: Inquire with the National Forest of choice.

Age: No age limit. Those under 18 must have the written consent of a parent or guardian.

Qualif.: No specific skills required. Volunteers must be in good health to allow them to perform their duties without risk to themselves or others. A medical examination may be required for some tasks. Persons with disabilities are encouraged to volunteer.

Work: Maintaining and hosting campgrounds, working at visitor centres and ranger stations, planting trees, presenting environmental education programmes, building and repairing structures, taking photographs. Training provided if necessary.

Lang.: English.

Accom.: Housing may be available. Inquire with National Forest of choice.

Cost: Some expenses such as transportation, lodging, subsistence and uniforms may be reimbursed on a case-by-case basis.

Applic.: Write or call the volunteer coordinator of the region of interest. See list in the previous page or from the directory on the website: www.fs.fed.us/intro/directory/orgdir.shtml (or search for 'directory').

U.S. FISH AND WILDLIFE SERVICE
Washington DC   USA
Tel.: ++1 (800) WILD (toll free in North America)
E-mail: volunteers@fws.gov
www.Volunteer.gov/gov or http://volunteers.fws.gov/

Desc.: The United States Fish and Wildlife Service mission is to conserve, protect and enhance fish, wildlife and plants and their habitats. Volunteers work at national wildlife refuges, fish hatcheries, wetland management districts, regional offices or ecological service offices.

Spp.: Migratory birds, fish and all endangered species.

Hab.: Various in the United States.

Loc.: Throughout the United States.

Dur.: From a few days to several months.

Per.: Year round.

Age: Min. 18.

Qualif.: No special skills are required. Experience with the life sciences is preferable. Some positions require teaching, public speaking or other specialized skills. Training provided if necessary.

Lang.: English.

Cost: Volunteers must pay their way to the United States. Assistance is available at times for travel within the US, for US applicants. Travel, food and lodging are usually covered while on duty .

Applic.: Contact the service directly by e-mail, or contact the regional office of your choice. For the list of Regional Offices see menu on top USFWS home page: www.fws.gov

Notes: Non-US citizens must plan well ahead and secure a proper visa or entry papers to enter the US and work as a volunteer. The USFWS does not work with whales and dolphins.

U.S. NATIONAL PARK SERVICE
VIP (Volunteers-In-Parks) Program
National Capital Region
1100 Ohio Dr., SW, Washington, DC 20242 USA
Tel.: ++1 (202) 619 7222
www.nps.gov/volunteer/

Desc.: The United States National Park Service is officially entrusted with preserving more than 350 national parks in the US Through the VIP (Volunteers-In-Parks) Program, anyone can help conserving the parks' natural and historical resources.

Spp.: Various of North America.

Hab.: Various of North America.

Loc.: National parks throughout the United States.

Dur.: Inquire with the park or the field area of choice.

Per.: Inquire with the park or the field area of choice.

L. term: Inquire with the park of choice.

Age: Min. 18. Persons under 18 years of age must have permission of their parents or guardian or be accompanied by adults in a family or group.

Qualif.: Various skills and talents desired. Reasonably good health is expected. A medical examination may be required for some jobs. Disabled individuals are encouraged to volunteer.

Work: Providing information at a visitor centre, accessioning artifacts into a park's archaeological or historic collection, conducting surveys of plant and animal species in the park or doing construction and repair work on hiking trails. Accepted volunteers receive appropriate training and orientation at the beginning of the service.

Lang.: English.

Accom.: Some of the larger parks may provide free housing for VIPs. Arrangements made between the volunteer and the park.

Cost: Some parks reimburse volunteers for some expenses, such as local travel costs, meals and uniforms. Volunteers must cover the cost of travel to and from the park.

Agents: **Alaska Area Region**, 2525 Gambell St., Room 107, Anchorage, Alaska 99503–2892, tel. ++1 (907) 257 2580.

Intermountain Region, 12795 West Alameda Parkway, Denver, Colorado 80225–0287, tel. ++1 (303) 969 2500.

Midwest Region, 1709 Jackson St., Omaha, Nebraska 68102, tel. ++1 (402) 221 3471.

Northeast Region, U.S. Customs House, 200 Chestnut St. Fifth Floor, Philadelphia, Pennsylvania 19106, tel. ++1 (215) 597 7013.

Pacific West Region, One Jackson Center, 1111 Jackson Street, Suite 700, Oakland, California 94607, tel. ++1 (510) 817 1300.

Southeast Region, 100 Alabama St., SW, 1924 Bldg. Atlanta, Georgia 30303, tel. ++1 (404) 562 3100.

Applic.: The website lists hundred of opportunities (click on opportunities) and gives detailed application contacts for each position. Addresses of parks can be obtained from the Regional offices listed above. Ask for a VIP application form. Prospective volunteers can apply to more than 1 park. Selection for summer positions are usually made between February and April.

Notes: Non–US citizens must obtain a work permit or a special student visa to be accepted as park volunteers. The US Immigration and Naturalisation Service considers the reimbursement to cover out-of-pocket expenses and the free housing offered by the parks as a form of payment for work: since it is illegal for a person travelling under a regular tourist visa in the US to work for pay, the INS can send these persons back to their country without allowing them to enter the US. When applying for the VIP programme, be prepared to face the long procedure to obtain the correct permit or visa. There are also insurance requirements for all international volunteers.

VOLUNTEER FOR NATURE

Federation of Ontario Naturalists & Nature Conservancy of Canada
355 Lesmill Road
Don Mills, Ontario M3B 2W8 Canada
Tel: ++1 (416) 444 8419 ext. 222
Fax:++1 (416) 444 9866
E-mail:vfn@ontarionature.org – www.ontarionature.org

Desc.: Together, Ontario NatureFederation of Ontario Naturalists and the Nature Conservancy of Canada (NCC) are creating new conservation volunteering opportunities in Ontario through their Volunteer for Nature (VfN) program. VfN's goal is to provide people with opportunities to learn new conservation skills and participate in hands-on projects including invasive species removal, native seed collection and planting and endangered species monitoring throughout Ontario's spectacular natural areas.

Hab.: Habitats protected through Volunteer for Nature include limestone alvar, oak savannah, tall grass prairie, Great Lakes shoreline, Carolinian forest and northern boreal forest.

Loc.: Ontario, Canada.

Dur.: Min. 1 day, max. 16 days.

Per.: April to October.

Age: Min.16 for Nature Conservation Days; min.19 to join Ontario Nature Volunteers.

Qualif.: No specific qualifications required. Must be reasonably fit.

Lang.: English.

Cost: Nature Conservation Days are free. Ontario Nature Volunteers expeditions have a fee to cover direct expenses, including food and the transit of leaders and tools to the work sites.

Accom.: Accommodations range from basic camping to dormitory style to Park staff houses, lodges, field study centres or bed and breakfasts. All volunteers are responsible for contributing to cooking and general duties at the accommodation.

Applic.: For registration contact Marc Allan at address above.

Notes: See website for full Volunteer for Nature Schedule of Events.

VOLUNTEERS FOR OUTDOOR COLORADO (VOC)

600 South Marion Parkway
Denver, Colorado 80209–2597   USA
Tel.: ++1 (303) 715 1010
Fax: ++1 (303) 715 1212
E-mail: voc@voc.org
www.voc.org

Desc.: This non-profit organisation, founded in 1984, promotes and fosters citizen and visitor responsibility for Colorado's public lands. VOC organises 1-day to week-long conservation and trail construction projects and provides volunteers and training to land management agencies, other non-profits and user groups. The VOC Network serves as a resource opportunity to state, federal and local agencies: with more than 450 volunteer positions in botany, construction, environmental education, recreation, research, wildlife, visitor information and trail work.

Hab.: Urban gardens and parks, streams, lakes, mountains.

Loc.: Urban and natural areas, National Parks, National Forests, State Parks, public lands, Colorado, USA.

Dur.: 1 day to 4 months.

Per.: Year round.

L. term: For projects listed in the VOC Network.

Age: Min. 8 for VOC projects; under16 must be accompanied by an adult. Min. age for Network positions varies with agency.

Qualif.: Desired experience varies from none to skilled.

Lang.: English.

Cost: No cost. Positions may offer room and board.

Applic.: Request application form.

Notes: VOC volunteers can later attend Crew Leader Training, which involves classes, a field weekend and apprenticeship. Contact VOC for information on other volunteer opportunities. The VOC website has an excellent list of links to other volunteering organisations in the US and in Colorado.

VOLUNTEERS SRI LANKA

4/11 Patabendimulla, Ambalangoda Sri Lanka
Tel.: ++94 (91) 225 6621 - 0094 (77) 620 9625
E-mail: info@volunteers-srilanka.com
       nagenahiru@mail.ewisl.net
www.volunteers-srilanka.com

Desc.: An NGO devoted to conservation of threatened species and endangered ecosystems in Sri Lanka. The organisation also helps disadvantaged communities. Conservation projects are locally designed and run under the guidance of experts.

Spp.: Marine turtles, native and migratory birds, temple monkeys, elephants. Medicinal herbs and plants.

Hab.: Coral reef, mangroves, tropical rainforest.

Loc.: Southwestern coast and hill countryside of Sri Lanka.

Travel: Flight to Colombo; airport pickup and local transport arranged.

Dur.: Normally 2 to 12 weeks.

Per.: Year round.

L. term: Long term programs available on request.

Age: Min. 18., 17 with parents' permission.

Qualif.: No previous experience or particular skills needed. Enthusiasm, self reliance, patience and a strong curiosity .

Work: Identifying, measuring and assessing the damages caused to species or ecosystems through biodiversity research and surveys under the guidance of experts. Feeding animals and protecting nesting sites. Promoting community awareness, by teaching conservation issues to adults and children. Assisting in re-forestation and in maintaining plant nurseries.

Lang.: English.

Accom.: Homestay accommodation in single room with fan, electricity, purified water and western style toilet.

Cost: US$550-1,200 from 2 to 12 weeks + US$50 application fee.

Applic.: Form available online or contact the organisation directly.

Notes: Only 4 volunteers per week, working 4 hours a day. During spare time volunteers are free to explore the island. Volunteers Sri Lanka will provide guide and tips.

THE WILDERNESS FOUNDATION

The Oast House
Hankham, Near Pevensey, East Sussex BN24 5AP UK
Tel.: ++44 (1323) 461 730
Fax: ++44 (1323) 761 913
E-mail: info@wilderness-trust.org
www.wilderness-trust.org

Desc.: The Wilderness Foundation promotes self-financed educational journeys and camps into wilderness areas. Programmes focus on conservation, self discovery and teaching wilderness skills for groups of young people and adults. Groups size is from 6 to 8 people.

Loc.: Junior (13–16) trail programmes are available in Wales. Young programmes (16–18 plus) and adult programmes are available in South Africa, Canada and Wales.

Dur.: Min. 7 days, max. 30 days. Junior Programmes 3 – 5 days. Adult Programmes 7, 14 and up to 30 days.

Qualif.: No specific qualifications required. Must be reasonably fit.

Lang.: English.

Cost: Junior Programme from GB£50 (approx. EUR 80). For all other programmes details are available upon request but costs will depend on length of journey, time of year and context.

Accom.: Normally in the open or in remote bush camps for journeys in Africa and Canada. Basic indoor bunk accommodation is provided in Wales.

Notes: Details of programme itineraries and costs available upon request.

WWF Italy

Ecotourism Division
Via Orseolo 12
20144 Milano Italy
Tel.: ++39 (02) 831 33245 – Fax: ++39 (02) 831 33222
E-mail: turismo@wwf.it
www.wwf.it/vacanze

Desc.: WWF Italy is the largest national environmental association, managing about 130 wildlife refuges. Volunteers are recruited for field study projects, restoration activities and fire prevention workcamps.

Spp.: Birds, wolves, sea turtles, whales, dolphins, bears.

Hab.: Mediterranean Sea, mountains, wetlands, lakes.

Loc.: Brazil, Greece, Ireland, Italy.

Dur.: Min. 5 days; max. 2 weeks.

Per.: Summer. Every year programmes are posted on the webpage in March.

L. term: Inquire with organisation.

Age: Min. 18.

Qualif.: Previous experience and specific qualifications are not required.

Lang.: Italian, English.

Cost: Starting from EUR 200 (approx.GB£130), insurance, food and accommodation included.

Agents: WWF has offices in many countries. Contact your national WWF office for information on workcamps in your country or on international volunteering opportunities. For a complete list of national offices see www.wwf.org.

Applic.: Request an application form. Volunteers must be WWF members to participate.

YCI – Youth Challenge International

20 Maud Street, Suite 305
Toronto, Ontario M5V 2M5 Canada
Tel.: ++1 (416) 504 3370
Fax: ++1 (416) 504 3376
E-mail: generalinfo@yci.org
www.yci.org

Desc.: Youth Challenge International combines community development, health promotion and environmental work in adventurous projects carried out by teams of volunteers aged 18–30. Volunteers are accepted from across the world and represent different backgrounds. Conditions are basic and work schedules are demanding. Experienced staff teams ensures projects are dynamic and results oriented. Self-discovery, personal growth and community development are key elements.

Spp.: Rainforest and riverine/coastal fauna.

Hab.: Rainforest, coast, mountains.

Loc.: Costa Rica, Guyana, Vanuatu, Ethiopia, Tanzania.

Dur.: 5, 6, 8, 10 and 12 week projects.

L. term: Placements for field staff are for 4–6 months at a time. Upon review, volunteers can work for another placement period.

Age: Min. 18, max. 30.

Qualif.: No specific qualifications are needed.

Lang.: English.

Cost: Cost range from CDN$2,700 to CDN $3,500 (US$2,200–2,800) plus airfare. Volunteers must pay for inoculations and personal equipment.

Agents: Partner organisations are present in Guyana (Youth Challenge Guyana), Costa Rica (Reto Juevenil) and Australia (Youth Challenge Australia).

Applic.: Participants and field staff can apply at any time; applications can be submitted on-line.

Notes: Due to insurance limitations YCI is unable to accept applications from US citizens.

PROJECT LIST

AMERICAN CONSERVATION EXPERIENCE (ACE)

123 South San Francisco Street, Suite 7
Flagstaff, Arizona 86001
Tel.: ++1 (928) 814 8225
E-mail: annis@conservationvolunteersusa.org
www.conservationvolunteersusa.org

Desc.:	Experience a diverse range of conservation opportunities throughout the Southwest United States. Typical projects include trail reconstruction, habitat surveys and planting, revegetation in remote sections of the Grand Canyon, Zion and other National Parks. Work is physically demanding and production oriented in a supportive multi-cultural atmosphere.
Spp.:	Work with flora and fauna ecosystems ranging from low desert to 3,500 ft (1,200 m) mountains.
Hab.:	Inner canyon, rivers and creeks, Western US desert.
Loc.:	Grand Canyon, Zion and other National Parks and Forests. Home base in Flagstaff, Arizona
Dur.:	4 – 12 weeks (longer terms possible).
Per.:	Year round.
L. term:	Inquire with organisation.
Age:	18 - 35.
Qualif.:	Physically capable of hiking and camping in remote areas. Sense of adventure. Enthusiastic work ethic.
Work:	Trail construction and restoration, planting/revegetation, forest restoration, habitat survey.
Lang.:	English.
Cost:	Air travel to and from Phoenix. Accommodation in Flagstaff on off days, food provided during projects. No costs for volunteers staying 12 weeks or longer. US$50 per week for short term participants. Weekend trips to Las Vegas and other attractions provided at no cost.
Applic.:	Register on line at www.conservationvolunteersusa.org Accepting applications year round.

ACORUS RESTORATION NATIVE PLANT NURSERY, Canada

R.R. 1 Walsingham, Ontario, NOE 1X0 Canada
Tel.: ++1 (519) 586 2603
E-mail: info@ecologyart.com
www.ecologyart.com

Desc.: Acorus Restoration is a Native Plant Nursery on a 95-acre former tobacco farm, which is in the process of being restored.

Spp.: Southern Ontario native vegetation.

Hab.: Carolinian landscape, sandy soils near Long Point World. Biosphere Reserve on Lake Erie.

Loc.: Southwestern Ontario, Canada.

Travel: 2 hours southwest of Toronto, Ontario.

Dur.: Min. 2 months.

Per.: March to November.

L.term: Not at the present time.

Age: Min. 18.

Qualif.: Ability to work long hours and to endure heat or cold, insects, occasional heavy lifting.

Work: Volunteers will participate in all duties in the nursery: from seeding, seed cleaning and collecting to planting and greenhouse maintenance.

Lang.: English. French can be mustered by coordinators.

Accom.: Bunkhouse with cooking facilities and shower.

Cost: No fees. Volunteers must provide own transportation and some food. A small weekly stipend is also provided.

Agents: Contact the project directly with the information provided above.

Applic.: Apply via e-mail, telephone or mail.

Notes: See website for basic information and contact the project for further questions.

ADRIATIC DOLPHIN PROJECT, Croatia

Blue World – Plavi Svjet
Kastel 24 – 51551 Veli Losinj   Croatia
Tel./Fax: ++385 (51) 604 666/8
E-mail: adp@blue-world.org
www.adp.hr or www.blue-world.org

Desc: The Adriatic Dolphin Project is the longest ongoing study of a Bottlenose dolphin population in the Mediterranean. Since 2000 the research has been carried out by a local NGO, Blue World, in cooperation with international researchers. last year a new educational centre was built in Veli Losinj and provides a professional environment in which to study cetaceans. The size of this community has been estimated at around 100–150 individuals, the majority of whom are identifiable. The standard research procedure includes photo-ID and behavioural sampling. Information on dolphin habitat use, association patterns and reproductive rate are also obtained.

Spp.: Bottlenose dolphin (*Tursiops truncatus*). Other marine species occasionally observed include: marine turtles, blue sharks, tuna, cormorants, seagulls, terns and other marine birds.

Hab.: Coastal waters.

Loc: Cres–Losinj archipelago, northern Adriatic Sea (Croatia).

Travel: The island of Losinj can be easily reached by bus, via Rijeka, from Trieste (Italy), Zagreb (Croatia) and Ljubljana (Slovenia), or (during the summer) by ferry from Venice or hydrofoil from Trieste (Italy); all these cities have major train and flight connections.

Dur.: 12 days. Up to 4 volunteers can participate in each shift.

Per.: May to September.

L. term: Extra days beyond the initial 12 can be arranged.

Age: Min.18.

Qualif.: Interest in the research and positive motivation is required. Volunteers must be physically fit and able to endure long hours, possibly in hot sun or in harsh sea conditions on a small boat.

the team cooperates in data handling and analysis. Slide projections and lectures are organised and volunteers are also free to visit the island and enjoy its sights.

Work: Behavioural observations and photo-ID of the dolphins from the inflatable boat. With good weather researchers and volunteers conduct boat surveys. With bad weather volunteers may work in the centre, entering and analysing data and matching the catalogued slides. Lectures on the dolphin biology are also carried out by the researchers.

Lang.: English. Italian and German are also spoken by researchers.

Accom.: Shared rooms in a house in Veli Losinj. Volunteers take part in cooking and housekeeping.

Cost: Min. EUR600, max. EUR700 (approx. GB£ 400–470), depending on the season. Volunteers must confirm that they have personal insurance. The contributions of volunteers are used to defray part of the research costs and food. Fees do not include travel expenses. All tourists coming to Losinj are required to pay the local tourist fee (about EUR1/day for the duration of the programme).

Applic.: Write, e-mail, phone or refer to the website for further information. A downloadable application form is available on the website. Given the limited availability of places and the high number of applications, early booking is suggested.

Notes: From 2–3 researchers reside at the field station with the volunteers. Safety gear for on the boat is provided. Volunteers must be aware that they are participating in scientific research rather than a vacation programme.

AFRICAN CONSERVATION TRUST, South Africa

P.O.Box 310, 3652 Linkhills South Africa
Tel.: ++27 (31) 201 6180
Fax: ++27 (31) 201 6180
E-mail: info@projectafrica.com
www.projectafrica.com

Desc.: The African Conservation Trust has initiated a multi work/ research project at Dqae Qare Bushmen Community Game Farm in Botswana.

Spp.: Multiple species will be radio collared and tracked.

Hab.: Kalahari Desert.

Loc.: D'Kar, Botswana.

Travel: Flight to Maun, where volunteers are met.

Dur.: From 2 weeks up to 1 year.

Per.: Year round, this is a permanent project.

L. term: Will accept long term volunteers.

Age: Min. 18.

Qualif.: Volunteers must have good physical health, a very flexible attitude, be able to withstand long working hours on various tasks and in a remote environment.

Work: Radio track various species on the farm. Undertake a tracking course. Alien plant eradication. Fence line maintainance.

Lang.: English.

Accom.: Volunteers must provide their own tents.

Cost: GB£450 per month.

Applic.: Request application form.

Notes: The trust has other projects in South Africa.

AMIGOS DE LAS AVES, Costa Rica

Flor de Mayo, 600m norte Super Santiago, Rio Segundo, Costa Rica
Apdo 2306 - 4050 , Alajuela, Costa Rica.
Tel.:/Fax: ++ (506) 441 2658
E-mail: richmar@racsa.co.cr
www.hatchedtoflyfree.org

Desc.: Amigos de las Aves is a Costa Rican non profit organization dedicated to the conservation of the two endangered species of macaws found in Costa Rica. Activity is concentrated on breeding macaws and introducing them into their native habitat at designated release sites. Recently, for the first time, a pair of captive bred macaws have produced two youngsters in the wild! The Organisation also runs a refuge with various endemic birds and an education program for schools in the local areas.

Spp: Scarlet macaw (*ara macao*), great green macaw (*Ara ambigua*), 4 species of Amazon parrot and 2 of Toucan.

Loc.: Central Valley: 10 minutes from San Jose airport, 40 minutes from San Jose city, 5 minutes from Alajuela town.

Dur.: Minimumone month at the Breeding Centre - two in the 'field'.

Per.: Year round.

L.term: No long term limits.

Age: Min.18.

Qualif.: No qualifications necessary - but 'bird' experience would be a help. Students in the field of biology preferably for 'field' work.

Work: Breeding Centre: feeding the birds, aviary maintenance, educational program (basic knowledge of Spanish needed) perching, cleaning, making toys, playing with babies. In the field: working with biologist in field research program.

Lang: English, Spanish helpful in the field.

Accom.: Shared facilites or private room and shower in a family home.

Cost: Breeding Centre: US$12-15 per day for accommodation, 3 meals and laundry. In the field: basic facilities and meals.

Applic.: Via email or by telephone.

Notes: Field research opportunities are available, as are gardening, educational and fund raising opportunities upon application.

ANIMAL RESCUE PROJECT, Florida

The Ecovolunteer Network
Meyersweg 29 7553 AX Hengelo The Netherlands
Tel.: ++31 (74) 250 8250
Fax: ++31 (74) 250 6572
E-mail: info@ecovolunteer.org
www.ecovolunteer.org

Desc.: An animal sanctuary and educational facility dedicated to the adoption of confiscated, retired, abused or otherwise homeless animals.

Spp.: Tigers, cougars/pumas, lynx, black bear, buffalo, emu, miniature burro, horses, leopard, jungle cat, capuchins, tamarinds, spider monkey, owl, skunk, egyptian fruit bats, peacock, sugar gliders.

Hab.: Wildlife rescue center.

Loc.: Central Florida, USA.

Travel: Flight to Tampa or Orlando International Airports; from there it is a one-hour drive or on request a transfer to the project can be arranged.

Dur.: Min. 2 weeks.

Per.: Year round.

L.term: Long-term is possible.

Age: Min. 18.

Qualif.: Good health and physical condition, tolerate heath. In order to work with primates, a Tuberculosis test is required with a medical declaration of a negative test result.

Work: Participation in the daily chores directly and indirectly related to the care of the animals. Volunteers will learn to work without risk of injury and will be exposed to the experience needed to care for the different species at the sanctuary.

Lang.: English

Accom.: In a comfortable campground near the sanctuary. Food is prepared at the sanctuary and included in the fee.

Cost: US$597 or US$298, for two weeks or extra weeks respectively.

Agents: The Ecovolunteer Network at www.ecovolunteer.org.

Applic.: The Ecovolunteer Network (see Organisation list).

ARFA – ASOCIACION DE RESCATE DE FAUNA, Venezuela

Calle La Vista, Edif. La Vista, Apto. 11–B, Colinas de Los Caobos,
Caracas 1050   Venezuela
Tel.: ++58 (212) 782 4182
Fax: ++58 (212) 793 4421
E-mail: lucyalio@cantv.net
www.geocities.com/arfavenezuela/index.html

Desc.: ARFA is an NGO devoted to the conservation of wildlife in Venezuela, through educational programmes and its centre where animals of the central plains are rescued and rehabilitated.

Spp.: Capuchin and howler monkeys (*Cebus olivacea,Allouata sealicus*), aquatic turtles and terrapins, parrots, macaw (*Ara spp.*). Occasionaly deer, ant eating bear, iguana, alligator, some birds of prey and many other bird species from the area.

Hab.: Plains or flatlands, 'llanos' (similar to savannah), rainforest.

Loc.: Flatlands of the Edo.Cojedes, between the towns of Las Vegas and Tirado, Central Venezuela.

Travel: Airplane to Caracas , car or bus from Caracas to project area. Transportation from Caracas to project area will be provided.

Dur.: 3 months.

Per.: Year round.

L. term: 3 months limited by visa requirements.

Age: Min. 22.

Qualif.: Veterinary, biologist or related careers and good physical condition.

Work: Feeding the animals, facility maintenance, assistance with the ecological educational programmes, wildlife record keeping and observation, assistance on wildlife rehabilitation.

Lang.: Spanish.

Accom.: Private room in a house with indoor bathroom and shower.

Cost: Room, accommodation and simple meals are provided. There is a charge of US$300.

Applic.: Via e-mail with the subject heading: 'Volunteer program'. In the text, include CV, letter of intentions and possible dates.

Notes: Web page has other volunteers' experiences. Health insurance and vaccinations (yellow fever, tetanus and rabies) mandatory.

AYUTTHAYA ELEPHANT CAMP, Thailand

Ayutthaya Elephant Palace & Royal Kraal and Elephant Care
Assembly – Pathon Rd., Ayutthaya Historical Park
Phranakornsri Ayutthaya province, 13000 Thailand
Tel.: ++66 (35) 211 001/321982 – Fax: ++66 (35) 328 685
E-mail: elephant@ksc.th.com – ayutthaya_elephant@hotmail.com
www.saveelephant.com

Desc.: Asian elephants are an endangered species. The Ayutthaya Elephant Palace & Royal and Elephant Care Assembly is striving to help the elephants survive into the future in a sustainable way. The importance of the elephant in Thai Culture and the unique life-time relationship that the Mahout creates with the elephant are other important aspects that the project tries to preserve.

Spp.: Asian elephant (*Elephus maximus*).

Hab.: Tropical rainforest.

Loc.: Ayutthaya Elephant Palace & Royal Kraal World Heritage Site in Ayutthaya province.

Travel: 1 hour drive north from Bangkok International Airport.

Dur.: Min.1 week, max. 3 months.

Per.: Year round.

L.term: Only after initial period and approval by project manager.

Age: Min. 18 in good physical health.

Qualif.: No particular skills needed. Veterinarians are especially welcome as are specialists in animal science or other relevant fields.

Work: Volunteers must take initial training with the elephants and an examination to receive a certificate before working with the elephants. Volunteers learn also about Thai rural culture.

Lang.: English.

Accom.: Bunkhouse and communal facilities.

Cost: US$1500/month (includes accommodation); inquire for details.

Applic.: Send e-mail to request an application form.

Notes: Health insurance is needed. The Project has 2 satellite projects: the Kanchanaburi Elephant Camp in Kanchanaburi province and the Koh Chang Elephant Camp in Trad province.

BIMINI LEMON SHARK PROJECT, Bahamas

Bimini Biological Field Station
c/o RSMAS University of Miami
9300 SW 99 Street, Miami, Florida 33176 – 2050 USA
Tel./Fax: ++1 (305) 274 0628
E-mail: sgruber@rsmas.miami.edu
www.miami.edu/sharklab/

Desc.: Study of the feeding, predator-prey relations, growth, survival, movements and community relations of the lemon shark using field techniques and computer modelling/simulations. Disciplines of systems ecology, bioenergetics, life history studies, population genetics, ethology and sensory biology involved.

Spp.: Lemon shark, (*Negaprion brevirostris*) and its prey organisms, primarily mojarra fish, (*Gerres spp.*).

Hab.: Coastal reefs, mangrove forest, seagrass meadows.

Loc.: Bimini Bahamas, 85 km east of Miami across the Florida straits.

Travel: Flight to Fort Lauderdale International Airport; taxi to Fort Lauderdale Executive Airport for Bimini Island Air charter.

Dur.: Min. 1 month.

Per.: Year round.

L. term: With project leader's approval.

Age: Min.20, max. 38.

Qualif.: Students or graduates with a biology background are given priority, preferably with an interest in graduate school. Also necessary some boating skills, swimming and computer literacy.

Work: Field research on boats in shallow water all hours of the day; cooking, household and mechanical maintenance, etc.

Lang.: English.

Accom.: Wood frame, air-conditioned house with bunk beds for 4 persons in small dorm rooms.

Cost: Room and board approx. US$575/month. Transportation not included. Return flight to Bimini approx. US$220.

Applic.: Contact Dr. Samuel H. Gruber or Marie Gruber.

BIRDS OF TORTUGUERO, Costa Rica

Caribbean Conservation Corporation
4424 NW 13th Street, Suite A–1
Gainesville, Florida 32609   USA
Tel.: ++1 (352) 373 6441 – Fax: ++1 (352) 375 2449
E-mail: resprog@cccturtle.org
www.cccturtle.org

Desc.: Tortuguero is the most important site in Costa Rica for resident and migratory neotropical birds. Caribbean Conservation Corporation (CCC) is working to gather information on the status of the bird populations and the number of species residing or migrating here (up to 300).

Spp.: Resident and migratory neotropical birds.

Hab.: Tropical coast.

Loc.: Tortuguero, Costa Rica.

Travel: Airplane to San José, where participants are met.

Dur.: 1, 2 or 3 weeks.

Per.: March to June and August to November.

L. term: Volunteers can stay longer than 3 weeks with prior approval.

Age: Min. 18.

Qualif.: Volunteers must be in good physical condition, able to live in a rustic setting and tolerant of harsh weather.

Work: Assist researchers in mist netting, point counts, identification and transects.

Lang.: English.

Accom.: Dormitory style with shared baths in research station.

Cost: US$1,399 for 1 week; US$1,864 for 2 weeks; US$2,099 for 3 weeks. Cost includes 2 nights in San José, transfers to Tortuguero, all room and board at CCC station in Tortuguero.

Agents: Contact the organisation directly.

Applic.: On-line application form to be submitted with a US$200 deposit.

BLACK HOWLER MONKEY PROJECT, Argentina

Refugio del Caraya
Tiu Mayu, La Cumbre, CP: 5178, Prov. Cordoba Argentina
E-mail: carayaproject@yahoo.com.ar
www.refugiodelcaraya.com.ar

Desc: The centre works to rescue and rehabilitate ex-pet monkeys. The monkeys are re-educated and kept in the sanctuary. The centre conducts also environmental education programmes.

Spp.: Black howler monkey (*Alouatta caraya*).

Hab.: Mountain forest.

Loc.: La Cumbre, Cordoba, Argentina.

Travel: Airplane to Cordoba, then bus or taxi to La Cumbre and the sanctuary.

Dur.: Min. 3 weeks.

Per.: Year round.

L. term: Volunteers can stay as long as they want.

Age: Min. 21.

Qualif.: Ability to work with cold, snowy, rainy or hot days, and with other animals like pumas, or farm animals, in a very rustic environment. Free-ranging animals observations are often done on foot.

Work: Feeding the monkeys, cleaning the cages of the monkeys in rehabilitation, care of the orphans, observation and study of the free-ranging groups. Volunteers have the possibility of working on weekends in the local zoo with an NGO called Guardazoo.

Lang.: Spanish, English.

Accom.: A bedroom separated from the main house.

Cost: Approx. US$ 420/month for room and board.

Applic.: By e-mail.

BLACK RHINO, Kenya

Earthwatch Institute (Europe)
267 Banbury Road
Oxford OX2 7HT   UK
Tel.: ++44 (1865) 318 831 – Fax: ++44 (1865) 311 383
E-mail: projects@earthwatch.org.uk
www.earthwatch.org/europe

Desc.: The number of Black Rhinos in Kenya has declined from an estimated 20,000 in 1970 to about 500 today. The principal reason for this decline is unrelenting poaching—the rhino is sought for the medicinal and decorative use of its prestigious horn. This project is in the enclosed 100 km² Sweetwaters Black Rhino Reserve, which has an healthy and well protected rhino population. But new concerns have arisen: competition with other large herbivores, predatation of calves by hyenas and lions and an excessive concentration of rhinos. Only an accurate study of these factors can help preserving the balance of the ecosysitem.

Spp.: Black rhino (*Diceros bicornis*), zebra, impala, kudu, lion, leopard, hyena, wild dog, giraffe, elephant, wildebeest, buffalo.

Hab.: Savannah with acacias.

Loc.: Sweetwaters Black Rhino Reserve, Nanyuki, Kenya.

Travel: Airplane to Nairobi then bus to Nanyuki.

Dur.: 12 days.

Per.: January, February, August, September.

L. term: No long-term volunteer opportunities available.

Age: Min. 16.

Qualif.: No special skills required.

Work: Volunteers observe rhinos and other large mammals and gather data on vegetation and feeding preferences of the competing species. Acacia trees damage is also assessed.

Lang.: English.

Accom.: Confortable single rooms in the Reserve Research Centre.

Cost: Approx. US$ 2,695.

Agents: Earthwatch Institute (Europe, see organisation list).

Applic.: Apply online at www.earthwatch.org/europe.

BLACK SHEEP INN, Ecuador

Andres Hammerman & Michelle Kirby
P.O. Box 05–01–240 Latacunga, Cotopaxi Ecuador
Tel.: ++593 (3) 2814 587
Fax: ++593 (3) 2814 588 (call ahead)
E-mail: info@blacksheepinn.com
www.blacksheepinn.com

Desc.: A small Ecological Lodge in the Ecuadorian Sierra. It grows its organic vegetables, uses composting toilets, gray water systems and a recycling programme. Volunteers learn how low impact sustainable tourism works. A small reforestation programme is also carried out with native tree species. Lodge managers also help the local community and in conservation work in the Iliniza Ecological Reserve.

Spp.: The Reserve has over 172 species of birds; it also hosts the endangered Andean spectacled bear (*tremarctos ornatus*).

Hab.: High Andean Sierra and Andean Cloud Forest.

Loc.: Western Cordillera of Central Ecaudor, Cotopaxi.

Travel: Flight to Quito, bus Quito to Chugchilan and to the Inn.

Dur.: Min. 6 weeks.

Per.: Year round.

L. term: Long term welcome after initial period.

Age: Min. 25, no max.

Qualif.: Volunteers must be fit and physically active. No allergies, to animals: dogs, llamas, sheep, chickens and ducks. Useful skills are: small business administration, farm work, trip leading, hotel service, computer skills and construction.

Work: Volunteers help in the lodge and in taking care of guests needs (hiking and travel information, etc.) general maintenance, gardening, cooking and cleaning, animal care and participating in all the hikes, horseback rides and excursions.

Lang.: English is essential, Spanish helpful.

Accom.: Comfortable private room at the Inn with full bedding.

Cost: First 2 weeks (trial period) volunteers pay US$8/day for room and board. After trial week, room and board are usually free.

Applic.: Send e-mail or visit website for more information.

BLUE-FRONTED PARROT PROJECT, Argentina

Secc. Ornitología
D.pto Vertebrados Museo de Ciencias Naturales de La Plata
Fac. de Ciencias Naturales y Museo - Universidad Nacional de La Plata
La Plata Argentina
E-mail: aaestiva2002@yahoo.com.ar or voluntarios@loreros.com.ar
www.loreros.com.ar

Desc.: The objective of this long-term project is to obtain information on the reproductive ecology of the blue-fronted parrot in order to conserve and sustainably manage the species in the Gran Chaco, Argentina. Volunteers have the opportunity to visit a remote part of Argentina while gaining experience in a variety of field ornithology methodologies and learning about the local relevant issues, such as poaching and the pet trade.

Spp.: Blue-fronted parrot or loro hablador (*Amazona aestiva*).

Hab.: The Dry Chaco, a thick thorny forest known as the "Impenetrable", with over 300 species of birds and mammals such as jaguar, anteaters, brocket deer and armadillo.

Loc.: Blue-fronted Parrot Natural Reserve, Chaco Province, Argentina.

Travel: By bus from Buenos Aires to Castelli, Chaco Province.

Dur.: 2–3 months.

Per.: September to February.

L. term: Volunteer periods are specific terms as required for the project.

Age: Min. 18.

Qualif.: Responsible, self-disciplined, tolerant to extreme weather and insects, willing to work in group and able to stay at a remote place without long distance communication such as telephone or internet. Bird handling experience preferred but not required.

Work: Daily nest-checking assistance (tree-climbing), territory spot mapping, banding, blood and diet sampling, parrot point counts, behavioral observations, fruit censuses and data entry.

Lang.: Spanish, English also spoken.

Accom.: Camping, conditions are very basic.

Cost: Approx. US$85/week. Lodging and equipment provided.

Applic.: Send cover letter and CV with references to Berenice Charpin.

Notes: Web page includes other volunteers' experiences.

BOHOROK ENVIRONMENTAL CENTRE, Indonesia

Jl. Wahid Hasyim No 51, Medan 20154
Sumatera Utara Indonesia
Tel./Fax: ++62 (61) 451 4363/451 4360
E-mail: lawang@indosat.net.id or mail@paneco.ch
www.sumatranorangutan.org
www.paneco.ch

Desc.: The Centre originates from a programme started in 1995 to help control the environmental impact of tourism on the Orangutan Rehabilitation Station of Bohorok. The Centre has input in the town planning process and in environmental management programmes (such as water pollution control/ waste water treatment). Other goals include environmental education in general and development of eco-tourism.

Spp.: Orangutan/environmental education.

Hab.: Tropical rainforest.

Loc.: Bukit Lawang, Bohorok, Langkat, North Sumatra, Indonesia.

Travel: Airplane to Medan, then bus to Bukit Lawang.

Dur.: Min. 2, max. 4 months.

Per.: Year round.

L. term: Inquire with the organisation.

Age: Min. 21.

Qualif.: Specific skills are required depending on the topic. Teamwork capacities and interest in Indonesian culture are important.

Work: Development of the Centre: environmental education (school programme), ecotourism, environmental management (waste, water bio-filtration). No work at the Orangutan Quarantine Station.

Lang.: English. Bahasa Indonesian would be helpful.

Accom.: Simple local accommodation. Free housing food not included.

Cost: US$500 for students, US$1,000 for persons with regular income, travel and insurance are covered by the volunteer.

Agents: PanEco Foundation, Ms. Cornelia Jenny, Chileweg 5, CH–8415 Berg am Irchel, Switzerland, tel.: ++41 (52) 318 2323, fax: ++41 (52) 318 1906, e-mail: mail@paneco.ch

Applic.: Download and mail the application form, from www.paneco.ch

BOTTLENOSE DOLPHIN PROJECT, Belize

Oceanic Society Expeditions
Fort Mason Center, Building E
San Francisco, CA 94123   USA
Tel.: ++1 (415) 441 1106 – (800) 326 7491 (toll free in N.America)
Fax: ++1 (415) 474 3395
E-mail: info@oceanic-society.org www.oceanic-society.org

Desc.:   The Oceanic Society has been studying the behavioural ecology of free-ranging bottlenose dolphins in Belize since 1992 at its Blackbird Caye research station in the pristine waters of coral reef-ringed Turneffe Atoll. This is the first long-term study of dolphins in such a diverse ecosystem. The objective is to examine foraging patterns and social behaviour, as well as continue long-term baseline monitoring of dolphin distribution. Participants work directly with researchers in small teams, from small boats inside the atoll. There will also be some free time for snorkeling and birdwatching.

Spp.:   Bottlenose dolphin (*Tursiops truncatus*).

Hab.:   Tropical coastal waters.

Loc.:   Turneffe Atoll, Belize, Central America.

Travel: Airplane to Belize City.

Dur.:   8 days.

Per.:   Year-round.

L. term: Inquire with organisation.

Age: Min. 18.

Qualif.: Volunteers must be able to swim.

Work: Assist researchers with fieldwork such as collecting environmental data, searching for dolphins, recording behaviour, and identifying dolphins individually through natural markings.

Lang.:   English.

Accom.: Beachfront cabanas with porches, double rooms with private bath.

Cost: US$1,490, excluding flight.

Applic.: Request application form to be returned with a deposit of US$300.

BOTTLENOSE DOLPHIN PROJECT, Italy

CTS – Centro Turistico Studentesco e Giovanile – Sezione Ambiente
Via Albalonga 3
00183 Roma Italy
Tel.: ++39 (06) 6496 0306 – Fax: ++39 (06) 6496 0335
E-mail: ambiente@cts.it
www.ctsambiente.it

Desc.:   The goals of this research project are to study and protect the bottlenose dolphin in Italy. Research activities include: mapping the distribution of bottlenose dolphins in Italy; determining health status of these dolphins; examining the impact of tourism and fishing activities; and outlining a strategic plan.

Spp.:   Bottlenose dolphin (*Tursiops truncatus*).

Hab.:   Coastal sea waters.

Loc.:   Italian islands of Sardinia. Lampedusa (a little island the southern coast of Sicily).

Travel: The island of Sardinia is easily reached by boat from Civitavecchia (Rome) and Livorno and by plane from all the principal Italian cities. Direct flights to Lampedusa leave from Rome, Milan and Palermo.

Dur.:   7–10 days.

Per.:   June to September.

L. term: Inquire with the organisation.

Age: Min. 18 (16 if authorised by a parent).

Qualif.:   No particular skills are needed except being able to swim.

Work: Volunteers will undergo a short training period before being involved in data gathering on the behaviour of this marine mammal.

Lang.:   Italian, Spanish or English.

Accom: In tents or guestrooms.

Cost: EUR250–700 (approx. GB£160–450) excluding food and transportation.

Agents: CTS regional offices in Italy (see Organisation list).

Applic.:   Request application form. Membership to CTS required.

BROWN BEAR PROJECT, Russia

The Ecovolunteer Network
Meyersweg 29, 7553 AX Hengelo The Netherlands
Tel.: ++31 (74) 250 8250
Fax: ++31 (74) 250 6572
E-mail: info@ecovolunteer.org
www.ecovolunteer.org

Desc.: Orphan bear cubs are rescued from hunters with the aim of raising them and returning them back into the wild. The cubs need to be fed for approximately 3 months. In the spring, one-year old bear cubs are released and some are equipped with radio-collars, and their dayly movements are recorded.

Spp.: Brown bear (*Ursus arctos*).

Hab.: Typical southern taiga.

Loc.: Isolated biological station approx. 400 km west of Moscow.

Travel: Airplane to Moscow then train to Staraya Toropa, meeting is at the train station. Private transportation by car from Moscow can be arranged for an extra cost of EUR110.

Dur.: Minimum one month commitment.

Per.: February – October.

L. term: Inquire with the organisation.

Age: Min. 18

Qualif.: February – April: some practice and experience of animal handling is preferred.
May – October: be very fit, long and strenuous walking may be required.

Work: February – April: preparing food for and feeding of brown bear orphan cubs.
May – October: radio-tracking dayly movements of released one-year old bear cubs.

Lang.: English or Russian.

Accom.: Simple rooms at a biological station.

Cost: Volunteers booking at least 90 days have a special rate of EUR25/day.

Agents: The Ecovolunteer Network at www.ecovolunteer.org.

Applic.: The Ecovolunteer Network (see Organisation list).

CANO PALMA BIOLOGICAL STATION, Costa Rica

Tortuguero Costa Rica SJO 1882 Tel.: ++(506) 381 4116
COTERC, Canadian Organization for Tropical Education
and Rainforest Conservation
P.O. Box 335, Pickering, Ontario L1V 2R6, Canada
Tel.:++1 (905) 831 8809 – Fax: ++1 (905) 831 4203
E-mail: info@coterc.org   www.coterc.org

Desc.: The station serves as a facility for visiting biologists and student groups interested in studying various aspects of neotropical lowland forest biology. The station also supports a volunteer programme.

Spp.: Over 300 bird species, 120 mammal species, 100 reptile and amphibians.

Hab.: Lowland Atlantic tropical wet forest.

Loc.: 9 km north of the village of Tortuguero and Tortuguero National Park, in northeastern Costa Rica.

Travel: Tortuguero is accessible only by bus then boat, or by small airplane from San José. There are no roads nearby. Contact station staff for travel details 2–3 days prior to arrival.

Dur.: Min. 2 weeks.

Per.: Year round.

L. term: Applicants with useful skills will be taken into consideration.

Age: Min. 18.

Qualif.: Volunteers should be enthusiastic, self-starting, in good physical condition and able to fit in with remote field station conditions.

Work.: Participation in the station's activities, including grounds and equipment maintenance, helping out in the kitchen, etc. Assisting visiting researchers.

Lang.: English, Spanish.

Cost: US$100 or colone equivalent per week, in cash. No travellers cheques or personal cheques. Tortuguero has no banks.

Accom.: A 4-bedroom dormitory with bunks capable of sleeping 20 persons. Bedding is provided, but volunteers should bring mosquito nets. Conditions are basic but clean and comfortable.

Applic.: Contact COTERC in Canada.

CAPE TRIBULATION TROPICAL RESEARCH STATION, Australia

PMB 5, Cape Tribulation
Qld. 4873   Australia
Tel.: ++61 (7) 4098 00 63 – Fax: ++61 (7) 4098 0147
E-mail: austrop@austrop.org.au
www.austrop.org.au

Desc.: An independent field research station (in a World Heritage site) open to all researchers interested in working in the area, funded through the Australian Tropical Research Foundation. Station staff conduct research on a wide range of issues, from radio-tracking bats to researching alternative technology.

Spp.: About 12 microbats and 5 mega bats; figs: at least 12 species; angiosperm plant species, many rare and locally endemic. Captive colony of 9 flying foxes (*Pteropus* spp.) at the Station.

Hab.: Rainforest and tropical coastal communities.

Loc.: Australia (far north Queensland).

Travel: Contact the station for travel details (hugh@austrop.org.au).

Dur.: After initial 2 weeks volunteers can negotiate a longer stay.

Per.: Year round.

L. term: Encouraged; duration is negotiable after the first stay.

Age: Over 23 preferred.

Qualif.: Any skills; carpenters, botanists, computer programmers, etc. Researchers must provide a proposed research summary.

Work: From routine maintenance to assisting with research projects.

Lang.: English.

Accom.: The station has bunkhouse accommodation and 2 air-con labs.

Cost: US$15/day for food and accommodation. Researchers and assistants pay more depending on the external funding available. Rates are negotiable for overseas volunteers.

Applic.: Applications should be sent via e-mail (be prepared to send reminders) to the Station director. Also send a brief CV with photo and a statement of research interests. Faxes can only be received during working hours (recognise time differences).

Notes: The climate and conditions can be difficult in this remote area. (from October to April).

CARETTA RESEARCH PROJECT, USA

Savannah Science Museum
P.O.Box 9841
Savannah, Georgia 31412 USA
Tel.: ++1 (912) 447 8655 – Fax: ++1 (912) 447 8656
E-mail: wassawCRP@aol.com
www.carettaresearchproject.org

Desc.: Since 1973, the Savannah Science Museum, in co-operation with the U.S. Fish and Wildlife Service and the Wassaw Island Trust has been conducting a research and conservation programme on the endangered loggerhead sea turtle. The program's purpose is to learn more about population levels, trends, and nesting habits of loggerheads. It also hopes to enhance the survival of eggs and hatchlings and to involve the public in this effort.

Spp.: Loggerhead sea turtle (*Caretta caretta*).

Hab.: Coastal barrier island.

Loc.: Wassaw Island, about 10 miles south of Savannah.

Travel: Bus or airplane to Savannah, then boat to Wassaw. The island is accessible only by boat.

Dur.: 1 week.

Per.: May to September.

L. term: Inquire with organisation.

Age: Min. 15.

Qualif.: No previous experience required.

Work: Volunteers patrol the beaches in search of female turtles, tag and measure the animals, record data, monitor the nests and escort hatchlings to the sea.

Lang.: English.

Accom.: Rustic cabins (dormitory style).

Cost: US$600/week. Most of the registration fee is tax-deductible (for US citizens) and includes lodging, meals, leadership/ instruction and transportation to and from the island.

Applic.: Full payment must accompany the application (refund is granted if cancellation takes place at least 60 days prior to departure).

Notes: Academic credit may be available.

CATS OF ROME, Italy

Torre Argentina Cat Sanctuary
Via Marco Papio 15
00175 Rome Italy
Tel./Fax: ++39 (06) 687 2133
E-mail: torreargentina@tiscali.it
www.romancats.com

Desc.: An international group of volunteers, working together to raise the quality of life of Rome's abandoned cats. Approximately 600 cats get abandoned annually at the Sanctuary, which shelters anywhere from 250 to 450 cats. The Sanctuary promotes spay/neuter, proper animal care, adoptions and education projects through public relations events. All funding comes from the 8,000 tourists who visit every year.

Spp.: Domestic cat.

Loc.: Center of Rome, Italy, in the archaeological ruins.

Dur.: Minimum one week with a full or part time schedule.

Per.: All year round.

L.term: Inquire with the sanctuary.

Age: No age limits.

Qualif.: No particular qualifications other than strong motivation, flexibility and love of animals, especially cats.

Work: Everyday jobs include cleaning cages, distributing food and treating sick cats, clerical work such as stuffing envelopes, making photocopies and various other administrative tasks. People who are able to speak to the many tourists who visit, give a tour of the sanctuary (mostly in English) and eventually ask for contributions.

Lang.: English, other languages useful but not necessary.

Accom.: Housing is available for approximately EUR 350-420 (approx. US$450-550) a month. This usually consists of a nice room in someone's apartment with private bath.

Cost: Volunteers are responsible for travel, housing, food and personal expenses.

Applic.: Prospective volunteers must send a resumè with a short letter about themselves.

CENTRE FOR REHABILITATION OF WILDLIFE (CROW), South Africa

P. O. Box 53007, Yellowwood Park
4011Durban, Kwa-Zulu Natal   South Africa
Tel: ++27 (31) 462 127 – Fax:+ +27 (31) 462 9700
E-mail: info@crowkzn.co.za
www.crowkzn.co.za

Desc.: CROW is a non-profit organisation that takes care of South Africa's indigenous wildlife, both injured and orphaned. CROW is the only rehabilitation centre of its kind in KZN. It has approximately 400 animals under its care at any given time, all of which are wildlife indigenous to Natal, from birds and mammals to raptors and reptiles, and many primates. The main objective is to rescue, rehabilitate and release these animals either back into the wild, or into sanctuaries.

Spp.: All wildlife indigenous to Natal: from blue vervet monkeys, to tortoises, bushbuck, genet, garden birds, fish eagles, vultures, owls, crocodiles, zebra, lemurs, baboon, mongoose, etc.

Hab.: Tropical forest, tropical beach, mangrove coastal wetland.

Loc.: In the outskirts of Durban, about 10 minutes from the airport, next to the Kenith Stainbank nature reserve.

Travel: Airplane to Durban.

Dur.: Minimum of 5 day's (as training is involved).

Per.: Year round, peak is from November to March (baby season).

L.term: Volunteers can stay for as long as they want.

Age: Min. 18.

Qualif.: No specific skills required for volunteers.

Work: Volunteers help cleaning cages and feeding and caring for the animals. Special projects may include: observing animals in the rehabilitation area, building cages, animal releases, etc.

Lang.: English.

Accom.: The volunteer house is quiet and very comfortable, sleeps 10 people and has ample entertainment areas (TV, books).

Cost: R150 (approx. US$25) per person/day. Includes 3 basic meals.

Applic.: Online application form.

CERCOPAN, Nigeria

4 Ishie Lane, Housing Estate
P.O. Box 826, Calabar, Cross River State Nigeria
Tel.:/Fax: ++234 (87) 234 670 – Mob.: ++234 (802) 827 5428
E-mail: cercopan@compuserve.com
www.cercopan.org

Desc.: An NGO dedicated to tropical rainforest conservation through primate rehabilitation, education and research.

Spp.: Red-capped mangabey (*Cercopithecus torquatus*) and forest guenons (*Cercopithecus spp.*).

Hab.: Tropical rainforest.

Loc.: Southeast Nigeria (close to Cameroon border).

Travel: Flight to Lagos; internal flight Lagos-Calabar.

Dur.: Short-term volunteers: min. 4 weeks, max. 3 months.

Per.: Any time of the year. Rainy season is June to September.

L. term: Min. 1 year with coordinator's permission (possible stipend).

Age: Short-term volunteers min. 21; long-term volunteers min. 25.

Qualif.: Short-term (paying) volunteers skills: field experience (ecology, primatology), building skills, biological surveying. Long-term volunteer skills: veterinary, building skills; environmental education, community development/communication skills, biological research (ecology, animal behaviour, botany).

Work: Varies with skills and needs of the project.

Lang.: English.

Accom.: At forest site: bush sheds with tent/mosquito net, solar power for evening lighting, fridge, outdoor showers and toilets. In Calabar: shared house/room, electricity and running water.

Cost: Short-term volunteers: room and board (approx. GB£ 100-150/week). Long-term volunteers: room and board provided. International travel, medical insurance and visa are responsibility of the volunteer.

Agents: Prospective volunteers may also contact the UK based trustee: Bob Baxter, 13 Prestbury Crescent, Banstead, Surrey ++44 (784) 102 1147, e-mail: bob.baxter1@ntlworld.com

Applic.: Send letter of interest with C.V. (including 3 referees with tel. no.) by snail mail or e-mail without attachments to Cercopan.

116

CETACEAN RESEARCH & RESCUE UNIT (CRRU), Scotland

P.O. Box 11307,
Banff AB45 3WB, Scotland UK
Tel: ++44 (1261) 851 696
E-mail: volunteer@crru.org.uk
www.crru.org.uk

Desc: The CRRU is a small charitable research organisation dedicated to the understanding, welfare, conservation and protection of cetaceans (whales, dolphins and porpoises) in Scottish waters through scientific investigation, environmental education and the provision of professional veterinary assistance to sick, stranded and injured individuals.

Spp.: Primarily the bottlenose dolphin (*Tursiops truncatus*) and minke whale (*Balaenoptera acutorostrata*).

Hab.: Marine, coastal.

Loc.: Moray Firth, Northeastern Scotland.

Travel: By plane, bus or train to Aberdeen, then bus to Banff.

Dur: 12 days.

Per.: May to October.

L. term: Possible for outstanding volunteers.

Age: Min. 18.

Qualif.: Commitment to wildlife conservation and positive attitude towards living and working in a small group of enthusiastic people from different backgrounds and cultures is essential.

Work: Counting animals, recording behaviour, determining geographical positions and taking photographs under scientific supervision from a 5.6 m inflatable boat. On shore, identifying animals, cataloguing slides, and inputting data into the computers (full training provided). Opportunities to train in marine mammal rescue techniques will also be available.

Lang.: English;

Accom.: Researchers and volunteers will be accommodated together in 1 of 2 furnished houses.

Cost: GB£650 (approx.EUR900) for 12 days including food.

Applic.: By e-mail or post.

CETACEAN SANCTUARY RESEARCH

Tethys Research Institute
c/o Civic Aquarium, Viale G.B. Gadio 2
20121 Milano Italy
Tel.:++39 (02) 5831 4889/72001947 — Fax:++39 (02) 5831 5345
E-mail: tethys@tethys.org
www.tethys.org

Desc.: "Cetacean Sanctuary Research" is a long term project on the ecology and conservation of cetaceans in the western Ligurian Sea. Research is carried out in two main habitats: the continental slope zone and the pelagic environment. In the continental slope the focus is on odontocetes such as sperm whales, beaked whales and dolphin species including Risso's dolphins, striped dolphins, long-finned pilot whales and bottlenose dolphins. In the pelagic environment the research focuses on fin whales. The study area includes the waters of the Pelagos Sanctuary for the Conservation of Mediterranean Cetaceans. Through a multidisciplinary approach, the researchers investigate different aspects of cetacean biology and ecology (distribution, abundance and population dynamics, stock discreteness, behaviour, social organisation) and the impact of human activities like unregulated whale watching, in order to suggest effective conservation measures.

Spp.: Fin whale (*Balaenoptera physalus*), striped dolphin (*Stenella coeruleoalba*), Risso's dolphin (*Grampus griseus*), sperm whale (*Physeter macrocephalus*), long-finned pilot whale (*Globicephala melas*), Cuvier's beaked whale (*Ziphius cavirostris*), short-beaked common dolphin (*Delphinus delphis*), common bottlenose dolphin (*Tursiops truncatus*)

Hab.: Pelagic and coastal waters.

Loc.: Ligurian Sea, Mediterranean Sea.

Travel: Departure and arrival is in San Remo, Italy. Airplane to Nice, Genoa or Milan, then train to San Remo.

Dur.: 6 nights on board.

Per.: June to October.

L. term: Consecutive cruises can be booked with a discount. Discount also granted to students less than 26 years old.

Age: Min. 18 years.

Qualif.: No qualifications required. Volunteers should be able to swim. Flexibility, enthusiasm and willingness to help with all research and household activities are necessary.

Work: Volunteers will be trained at the beginning of the cruise and then will assist with research activities (data collection, observations, photo-ID, etc.). Lectures and slide projections on cetacean biology and research methods are carried out by the researchers. Preliminary photo-identification analysis are also scheduled. In bad weather conditions the boat stays in a safe harbour; volunteers may decide to stay on board, helping researchers entering and analysing data and matching digital photos, or visit the area.

Lang.: Italian, English.

Accom.: On board the 19-metre ketch *Gemini Lab*, participants will be hosted in 3 double and 1 quadruple cabin, with bunk beds. Sleeping bags required. There are 2 showers and 2 toilets.

Cost: Costs range between EUR 720—820 (approx. GB£ 500—570) for a 6—day cruise, depending on the season. Food (except for the first evening), fuel, membership and insurance are included. Travel to San Remo is not included.

Agents: Tethys Research Institute (see Organisation list).

Applic.: Request a standard application form to be completed and returned to the Tethys Research Institute. Early booking is suggested.

Notes: Participants gain insight into research methods and the management of a field research project.

CHARLES DARWIN FOUNDATION, Galapagos

External Relations Unit Charles Darwin Research Station
P.O. Box 17–01–3891
Quito   Ecuador
Tel.: ++ (593) 5526 146/147 or ++ (593) 527 013/014 (ext.119)
E-mail: vol@fcdarwin.org.ec or volunteer@darwinfoundation.org
www.darwinfoundation.org

Desc.: In 1971 the Charles Darwin Foundation (CDF) began the National and International Volunteer Programme. Its purpose is to collaborate with the training of university and undergraduate students, who focus their careers in biology and conservation science and those who want to improve their skills through field experience in the Galapagos Islands.

Spp.: Terrestrial and marine flora and fauna of the Galapagos.

Hab.: Various marine and terrestrial habitats of the Galapagos.

Loc.: Galapagos Islands, Ecuador. Stations on 4 different Islands.

Travel: Flight to Quito or Guayaquil, then Puerto Ayora, Galapagos.

Dur.: Min. 6 months.

Per.: Year round.

L. term: Duration is set by the project: 6 months minimum.

Age: Min. 20.

Qualif.: Qualifications vary according to position available. Volunteers must be at least a second year undergraduate.

Work: The CDF has 4 different areas of investigation : vertebrate ecology monitoring, invertebrate research, botany and marine investigation and conservation. Non-scientific areas include communication, participation, education and institutional development. Volunteers can participate in any of these areas.

Lang.: English and Spanish. Fluency not essential.

Accom.: Dormitory in the Station or apartment or hotel in town.

Cost: International volunteers cover all their expenses: a 50% discount is awarded on the flight Continent/Galapagos. Food approx. US$8–10/day. Room approx. US$10/day.

Applic.: Application form to be downloaded and sent with specified documentation via regular mail at least 2 months in advance.

Notes: For information of available openings see website.

CHEETAH CONSERVATION FUND, Namibia

P.O. Box 198072
Cincinnati, Ohio 45219-8072 USA
Tel.: ++1 (513) 487 3399
Fax: ++1 (513) 487 3398
E-mail: ccfinfo@iway.na
www.cheetah.org

Desc.: CCF sponsors scientific research and education programmes in areas such as cheetah population biology, ecology, health and reproduction and human impacts; and works with stakeholders.

Spp.: Cheetah *(Acynonix jubatus)*.

Hab.: Semi-arid, bush-encroached savannah.

Loc.: Central Namibia, Southwest Africa.

Travel: Flight to Windhoek International Airport; shuttle bus or taxis to city centre. Transport from Windhoek (at volunteer's cost) to Otjiwarongo (3 hours) can be arranged prior to arrival.

Dur.: 2 – 4 weeks.

Per.: Year round.

L. term: Depending on the needs of CCF, the volunteers qualifications and commitment and on the CCF Director's approval.

Age: Min. 20.

Qualif.: No particular skills required.

Work: Cheetah collecting, feeding and care; habitat monitoring of game and vegetation; assisting with data input, mapping, radio tracking; assisting with goat, sheep and livestock guarding dog healthcare and education programmes.

Lang.: English.

Accom.: Two-person thatched huts with beds: detached latrine block. All bedding is provided.

Cost: US$3,000 for 2 weeks, US$5,000 for 4 weeks.

Agents: Earthwatch Institute or African Conservation Experience, for UK students, (see Organisation list).

Applic.: Contact the organisation at the above address or the agents.

CHEETAH CONSERVATION, Botswana

Mokolodi Nature Reserve, Private Bag 0457
Gaborone,   Botswana
Tel: ++ (267) 3500613 Fax: ++ (267) 3165488
Email: info@cheetahbotswana.com
www.cheetahbotswana.com

Desc: CCB is a long term monitoring program, including research into behaviour and population status; with an essential focus on community participation/education, working with rural communities to encourage coexistence of these elegant, endangered cats. Botswana is one of the last hopes for this species' survival.

Spp: Cheetah (*Acinonyx jubatus*).

Hab: Savannah and bush lands.

Loc: Jwaneng Game Reserve, Southern Botswana.

Travel: Airplane to Johannesburg, then plane to Gaborone, then by vehicle to Jwaneng.

Dur: Min. 1 month, max. 3 months.

Per: Year round.

L.term: Possible opportunities of longer term stays as research assistants, for keen volunteers who have already completed a term of volunteering with the project.

Age: Min. 18.

Qualif: Wildlife background useful but not required. Strong passion for conservation essential. Desire to learn new skills. Ability to work long days, often in heat during summer, or cold during winter. Ability to live in the bush with a small group of people.

Work: Assisting with radiotracking cats, spoor surveys, camera trapping, possible capture and release, community visits, school presentations, data input, camp maintenance, etc.

Lang: English, Setswanan.

Accom: Small chalets for 2 people sharing. Electricity and lights. Separate kitchen and bathroom facilities.

Cost: Approx. US$1500/ month for room and board.

Applic: By e-mail or by mail.

COCHRANE ECOLOGICAL INSTITUTE (CEI), Canada

P.O.Box 484, Cochrane, Alberta, T4C 1A7, CANADA
Tel.: ++1 (403) 932 5632
Fax: ++1 (403) 932 6303
E-mail: cei&nucleus.com
www.ceinst.org

Desc.: CEI is an NGO devoted to the conservation of wildlife in Alberta, Canada, through captive breeding for reintroduction, endangered species reintroduction, habitat inventories, educational programmes, wildlife rescue, rehabilitation and release.

Spp.: Swift fox (*Vulpes velox*) and other wildlife of the Great Plains.

Hab.: Foothills of the Rockies, short, mixed grass, and fescue prairie.

Loc.: Town of Cochrane, between Banff and Calgary, Alberta.

Travel: Airplane, bus or train to Calgary. Transportation from Calgary to project area will be provided.

Dur.: Min. 1 month.

Per.: Year round.

L. term: There is no limit of time for long-term stays.

Age: Min. 20.

Qualif.: High school diploma, veterinary or biology studies helpful but not necessary and good physical condition.

Work: Feeding the animals, facility maintenance, assistance with the ecological educational programmes, wildlife record keeping and observation, assistance on wildlife rehabilitation.

Lang.: English.

Accom.: Rustic.

Cost: Room, accommodation and simple meals are provided.

Applic.: By e-mail with the subject heading: 'Volunteer program'. In the text, include CV, letter of intentions and possible dates.

Notes: Webpage has other volunteers' experiences. Health insurance and clean international driving license mandatory.

COMUNIDAD INTI WARA YASSI, Bolivia

Parque Machia
Villa Tunari
Chapare, Cochabamba Bolivia
Tel.: ++ 591 (44) 136 572
E-mail: intiwarayassi@hotmail.com
www.intiwarayassi.org

Desc.: A community project that rescues and rehabilitates native wild animals taken from unsuitable captive environments. Aims of the project include confiscation of animals from illegal markets, rehabilitation where possible and education and awareness to prevent the illegal trading of wild animals is.

Spp.: Wild cats - including pumas and ocelots. Monkeys - including Capuchins and black spiders, tropical birds and reptiles.

Hab.: Tropical rainforest.

Loc.: Chapare region of Bolivia, South America.

Travel: Plane to La Paz or Santa Cruz, Bolivia, then bus to project.

Dur.: Minimum 2 weeks. Staying at least 1 month is encouraged.

Per.: Year round.

L.Term.: Long-term volunteers are encouraged.

Age: Min.18, due to strenuous work and basic living conditions.

Qualif.: No set qualifications required. Experience with animals is advantageous, as well as carpentry and building skills. Volunteers must be hard working and committed.

Work: Work includes maintenance such as building cages and fences and clearing forest areas, care and supervision of animals and basic husbandry tasks such as preparing food and cleaning. Working days can be long and in a humid climate.

Lang.: English, Spanish an advantage.

Accom.: Basic shared rooms, with communal bathroom and kitchen areas. Personal sleeping bag and mosquito net required.

Cost: Volunteers pay all transport expenses to and from the project. Accommodation is US$70 for the first 15 days, then US$2.5 daily thereafter. Food is approx. US $5 daily.

Applic.: No official application required. Volunteers should verify the website for full details. Work is allocated on arrival.

CONSERVATION PROJECT UTILA IGUANA (CPUI), Honduras

Department Herpetology Senckenberganlage. 25,
D-60325 Frankfurt am Main,   Germany
Iguana Station Utila, Iguana Road, Island Utila
Islas de la Bahia, Honduras
E-mail: volo@utila-iguana.de
www.utila-iguana.de

Desc.: CPUI runs a research and conservation center which includes an environemental education programme in local schools, ecological field work, public awareness work and practical conservation work aswell as nature reserve development.

Spp.: Various iguana species: Utila iguana (*Ctenosaura bakeri,* endemic), *Norops bicaorum, Norops utilensis* and others.

Hab.: Mangrove forest, Carribean dry forest, sandy and rocky beachshores as breeding grounds.

Loc.: Utila Island, in the Caribbean coast of Honduras.The Iguana Station is located in the center of the island.

Travel: Airplane to La Ceiba via San Pedro Sula. Via Ferry or Airplane to the Utila island. Meeting at the dock or airport.

Dur.: Min. 3 Weeks.

Per.: Year round.

L. term: There is no limit of time for long-term stays.

Age: Min. 18.

Qualif.: Motivation and willingness to dedicate time and work.

Work: Feeding the animals, facility maintenance, assistance with the ecological educational programmes, wildlife record keeping and observation, assistance on wildlife rehabilitation.

Lang.: English (primary language on the Bay Islands), Spanish (additionally) for schoolwork or official communication.

Accom.: Two bed rooms at the first floor of the wooden station building.

Cost: EUR100/Month: room, accommodation, use of kitchen is provided. Food and bevareges are not included

Applic.: Via e-mail please refer to website.

Notes: Health insurance and vaccinations (hepatitis, tetanus) mandatory.

DOLPHIN RESEARCH CENTER, Florida

Volunteer and Internship Program
58901 Overseas Highway
Grassy Key, Florida 33050–6019 USA
Tel.: ++1 (305) 289 1121 ext. 230   Fax: ++1 (305) 743 7627
E-mail: drc-vr@dolphins.org
www.dolphins.org

Desc.: Dolphin Research Center (DRC) is a non-profit organisation dedicated to marine mammal research and education. It offers volunteers unique opportunities for learning about dolphins and various aspects of the daily operations of a marine mammal care facility. DRC also offer Internships involving concentration in a specific department. For individuals desiring a more interactive programme, see DolphinLab in Notes.

Spp.: Bottlenose dolphin, California sea lion.

Loc.: Grassy Key, Florida, USA.

Travel: Flights to Miami then by bus to Marathon.

Dur.: 1 – 4 months for volunteers; 3 – 4 months for internships.

Per.: Year round.

L. term: Available for local residents.

Age: Min. 18.

Qualif.: Good physical shape (able to lift 30 lbs/15 kg).

Work: Assist in animal food preparation, monitor visitors and answer questions, assist staff in conducting public interactive programmes, perform various facility maintenance tasks and provide administrative support. Interns duties vary depending upon the specific internship (Animal Care & Training, Dolphin-Child Therapy, Research, Education and Visual Communications.

Lang.: English fluency is a requirement.

Accom.: Not provided, DRC assists with house sharing information.

Cost: Living expenses can be as much as US$1500/month.

Applic.: Application available on website or mailed upon request.

Notes: Individuals desiring a shorter, more interactive learning experience may be interested in the week-long DolphinLab class. See website or contact for info: drc-ed@dolphins.org.

DOLPHINS & SEA LIFE AROUND THE MALTESE ISLANDS
The Biological Conservation Research Foundation (BICREF)
P.O. Box 30, Hamrun Malta
Tel./Fax: ++(356) 3290 3049
E-mail: avel@cis.um.edu.mt
http://sites.keyworld.net/bicref

Desc.: Boat and aerial research surveys undertaken in the region throughout the year to analyse the associations between environmental variables and observe different marine organisms. Boat surveys take 1 day, but 3-day research cruises are planned when weather permits.

Spp.: Bottlenose dolphin (*Tursiops truncatus*), common dolphins (*Delphinus delphis*), sea turtles (*Caretta caretta*), sea birds, such as cory shearwaters, large fish, manta rays.

Hab.: Mediterranean coastal and pelagic waters.

Loc.: Maltese Islands.

Travel: Fly to Luqa International Airport, Malta, or ferry from Sicily.

Dur.: Negotiable, inquire with the organisation.

Per.: Year round; summer is most intense.

L. term: Possible, but ask more information to the project.

Age: Min. 18, max. 45.

Qualif.: A background in biology. Sea-faring stamina and interest or experience in marine research and conservation required. Training on basic survey techniques and applications of research is provided.

Work: Observation and data recording during research surveys. Organise information and data after the surveys.

Lang.: English or Italian.

Accom.: Hotels, hostels, etc., are available in Malta. During 3-day trips, volunteers will sleep on board of the sailing or survey boat.

Cost: Contact the organisation for information.

Applic.: Send a brief CV, letter of interest and application form 6–4 months prior to the volunteering period.

Notes: Any special needs should be stated in the application letter.

DONKEY SANCTUARY, Netherlands Antilles

P.O.Box 331
Bonaire Netherlands Antilles
Tel.: ++ (599) 9510 7607
Fax: ++ (599) 788 9111
E-mail: donkeyshelp@telbonet.an
www.Donkeysanctuary.org

Desc.: Donkey Sanctuary Bonaire is a non-profit foundation taking care of the wild donkeys of the Island of Bonaire, particularly the abused and motherless donkeys who lost their mothers in car accidents. There are about 325 donkeys to care for at the sanctuary and they can not be released in the wild, because of the possible car accidents.

Spp.: Donkeys.

Hab.: Caribbean Island farmland.

Loc.: The Sanctuary is 100ha estate, located in the middle of the island.

Travel: Airplane to Bonaire, airport pick up is available.

Dur.: Min. 2 months.

Per.: Year round.

L. term: There is no limit of time for long-term stays.

Age: Min. 20.

Qualif.: No particular qualifications required, just a strong motivation and love for animals. Veterinary medicine students are welcome. Good physical condition is important.

Work: Feeding the animals, facility maintenance, assistance with the educational programmes for school kids, record keeping and observation of the donkeys, cleaning stables, care of injured animals.

Lang.: English or Dutch.

Accom.: Private small house on the compound, with kitchen, shower and toilet.

Cost: Accommodation and lunch is provided at no cost.

Applic.: Via e-mail with the subject heading: 'Volunteer program'. In the text, include CV, letter of intentions and possible dates.

Notes: Personal medical insurance required.

ECOLODGE SAN LUIS & RESEARCH STATION, Costa Rica

Apdo. 108, Santa Elena de Monteverde, Puntarenas Costa Rica
Tel.: ++ (506) 645 8049
Fax: ++ (506) 645 8050
E-mail: jillparsell@ecolodgesanluis.com
www.ecolodgesanluis.com

Desc.: The Ecolodge San Luis & Research Station, which is affiliated with the University of Georgia, is dedicated to research, education, ecotourism, conservation and the community. Field courses, academic programmes and the public are served. Volunteers include Interns and Resident Naturalists.

Spp.: Cloud forest flora and fauna, crop species.

Hab.: Tropical cloud forest, tropical agricultural landscape.

Loc.: San Luis de Monteverde, Northwestern Costa Rica.

Travel: Bus from San Jose to Monteverde; then taxi to the Ecolodge.

Dur.: Interns: min. 3 months. Resident Naturalists: min. 5 months.

Per.: Year round.

L. term: Preferred for Resident naturalists (9 months or longer).

Age: Min. 20.

Qualif.: Interns: excellent physical condition, able to interact with scientists, students and the public. Resident Naturalists: BS, tropical experience, natural history background, Spanish.

Work: Working as part of a team in: leading hikes, horseback tours, birdwalks, slide shows, community service; helping with logistics; designing educational programmes; participating in research, education, ecotourism and conservation missions.

Lang.: English; conversational Spanish is essential for Resident Naturalists. Intensive language study can be arranged on site at $280/week, including homestay.

Accom.: Bunkhouse or rustic one-room casitas. Bedding provided.

Cost: Interns pay initial US$450; Resident Naturalists pay no fee. All volunteers receive free room and board.

Applic.: Send e-mail to request application form and further details.

Notes: Intensive training in flora and fauna, language, culture, is provided. Good research potential. University credit possible.

ECOLOGY & CONSERVATION OF DEER IN PATAGONIA

Deerlab
JoAnne Smith-Flueck, PhD
C.C. 176 8400 S.C. de Bariloche   Argentina
Tel./Fax: ++54 (944) 467 345
E-mail: joannesmith@baritel.com.ar
www.patagonianfauna.org

Desc.: The project objectives are to estimate population density and determine the reproductive status, health condition, predation by puma and habitat use of red deer in southern Patagonia. Population surveys of endangered deer are conducted as well.

Spp.: Andean huemul deer (*Hippocamelus bisulcus*), naturalised red deer (*Cervus elaphus*).

Hab.: Mountainous temperate rainforest and edge of steppe.

Loc.: Southwest Argentina.

Travel: Airplane to Buenos Aires, then airplane or bus to Bariloche.

Dur: 2–5 weeks.

Per.: November to March.

L. term: Only with project leader's approval after regular period.

Age: Min. 18.

Qualif.: Good backpacking and camping experience in mountainous wilderness.

Work: Research includes: herd counts, radio-telemetry work of red deer, habitat surveys, morphometric analysis, use of topographic maps and GPS units. Direct observations with binoculars and scopes. A telemetry study on predation by puma is pending funding.

Lang.: English or Spanish (German also spoken).

Accom.: Sleeping bags and tents during field work. Hostel in town.

Cost: Contact leader for information. Room and board in Bariloche is approx. US$20/day.

Agents: Contact project leader directly.

Applic.: A short CV with a letter of introduction is required.

Notes: The climate is harsh and unpredictable even in summer. Expect windy, rainy and even snowy conditions. Supportive hiking boots, warm clothing, rain gear, sleeping bag and tent are required.

ELEPHANT NATURE PARK, Thailand

23-25 Charoenpratet Road, Soi 6
Chiang Mai 50100 Thailand
Tel.: ++66(53) 818 932/818 754/818 7442
Fax: ++66 (53) 818 755
E-mail: info@elephantnaturepark.org
www.thaifocus.com/elephant/

Desc.: Thailands Elephant population is struggling for its very survival with existing numbers down to some 3,000. Land encroachment as the population grows is the main problem facing both wild and domesticated elephants. This majestic gentle giant is finding it harder to find places to live without exploitation by humans. The Park, founded in 1966, provides a home for 17 elephants. The location, in a valley surrounded by jungle mountains and bordered by a river, is the ideal setting and natural habitat for elephants.

Spp.: Asian elephant (*Elephus maximus*), dogs and cats.

Hab.: Tropical rainforest.

Loc.: Northern Thailand, 60km from the city of Chiang Mai.

Travel: About one hour from Chiang Mai. Transport from Chiang Mai is provided. No public transportation available.

Dur.: Min. 1 week, max. 1 month (12 volunteers at a time).

Per.: Year round.

L.term: Only after initial period and approval by project manager.

Age: Min. 18 in good physical health. Children may participate if accompanied by their legal guardian.

Qualif.: No particular skills needed. Constant instruction and supervision by park staff is provided.

Work: Volunteers help with a variety of tasks including basic elephant health care and park duties.

Lang.: English.

Accom.: Simple bamboo tree huts, with toilet and shower, in the center.

Cost: US$260/week (includes lodging, food, local transport).

Applic.: Send e-mail to request an application form.

Notes: Health insurance is required.

ELEPHANT PROJECT, Thailand

The Ecovolunteer Network
Meyersweg 29   7553 AX Hengelo The Netherlands
Tel.: ++31 (74) 250 8250 – Fax: ++31 (74) 250 6572
E-mail: info@ecovolunteer.org
www.ecovolunteer.org

Desc.: Volunteers can help in caretaking of and offering an alternative for the domesticated elephants to live in a clean, close-to-nature environment with a fresh approach under a sustainable setup.

Spp.: Asian elephants (*Elephas maximus).*

Hab.: Elephant camp.

Loc.: 160 Kilometers south from Bangkok.

Travel: Flight to Bangkok; on request a taxi-transfer from Bangkok to the project can be arranged.

Dur.: Min. 1 week.

Per.: Year round.

L.term: Long-term encouraged; price decreases for longer stays.

Age: Min. 18.

Qualif.: Good health and physical condition, abilty to work in the heat.

Work: Hands-on work with the elephants, washing, cleaning them and their night enclosures. Volunteers help educate visitors about the need to conserve the elephants and accompany the elephants to the forest for foraging. They also help preparing the night enclosures for the elephants that return late afternoon from the mountains with fresh food and water.

Lang.: English

Accom.: Simple bungalows, European-style toilet & shower; lunch & dinner areprepared by a Thai cook.

Cost: EUR325, 234, 234, 156, for first, second, third and every extra weeks respectively

Agents: The Ecovolunteer Network at www.ecovolunteer.org.

Applic.: The Ecovolunteer Network (see Organisation list).

ENVIRONMENTAL VOLUNTEER PROGRAMME, Murcia

Regional Ministry of Environment and Land use.
DG of Natural Environment. Nature Protection and Conservation Service
C/ Catedrático Eugenio Ubeda Romero, 3, 3ª Pl. 30071 Murcia Spain
Tel: 968.22.88.31 ó 625148489 – Fax: ++34 (968) 856 066
e-mail: voluntariadoambiental@listas.carm.es
www.carm.es/cma/dgmn/mnatural/voluntar/indice.htm

Desc.: Nature protection and conservation in ten different projects. Encompassing training, trekking, biological research on the regional natural areas network. Birdwatching and tagging, reforestation and greenhouse work, environmental restoration of degraded landscapes, river watershed conservation.

Hab.: Semi arid sea and landscapes, Mediterranean forests (up to 1000 m). Inland and coastal wetlands.

Loc.: SE of Spain, near Alicante, Murcia, 250 km from Valencia .

Travel: By Plane to Alicante or San Javier (Murcia Airports) . 60 km to Murcia By motorway A30.

Dur.: From a few weeks to a few months.

Per: From April to December.

Age: Mín. 18.

Qualif.: No special qualification is required. Volunteers have to accept to live in simple rural life style conditions.

Work: Participation in maintenance, visitors' information, biological surveys activities and education. Teams work with local volunteers and fieldworkers, and receive basic training on management on protected areas.

Lang: Spanish

Accom.: Basic facilities can be available, such as houses for rangers. In some coastal areas camping is possible.

Cost: Volunteers must pay for their room, board, and travel to Murcia. Low cost lodging and local transportation can be arranged.

L-Term.: To be arranged by the Environmental Volunteer Programme Coordination Secretary E-mail: voluntatyenp@telefonica.net

Applic.: Online application form to be sent in with a letter explainig interest and motivation. At least 2 projects must be selected according to motivation and experience.

FAUNA FOREVER MANU PROGRAMME, Peru

CREES - The Rainforest Education and Resource Centre
Calle San Miguel 250, Cusco   Peru
Tel: ++51 (84) 262 433
E-mail: info@crees-manu.org
www.crees-manu.org   or   www.faunaforever.org

Desc.:	The programme, based in the Peruvian Amazon, is designed to develop future leaders in biodiversity assessment and tropical natural resource investigation. Consists of both training and practical components dealing with Neotropical wildlife monitoring, as well as leadership and project management.
Spp.:	Tropical rainforest and high Andean species.
Hab.:	Tropical rainforest, cloud forest and high Andean grassland.
Loc.:	Manu Biosphere Reserve (MBR), southeastern Peru.
Travel:	Airplane to Cusco, then by bus and river boat to the MBR.
Dur.:	Min. 2 weeks, max. 3 months.
Per.:	Year round. Applicants should arrive 2 days earlier to acclimatise and be trained from instructors and field biologists.
L. term:	Outstanding participants may be asked to stay as long-term assistants on the programme for 12 months.
Age:	Min. 20.
Qualif.:	Undergrads and grads in natural sciences with an interest in gaining field research experience and project leadership skills.
Work:	Assistants will learn data collection techniques and will subsequently undertake wildlife monitoring of mammal, bird, plant and aquatic fauna populations at 3 locations in the MBR.
Lang.:	English, Spanish not essential.
Accom.:	Shared room in facilities at research stations and lodges.
Cost::	From US$ 350 per person/week, includes accommodation food, local transport, professional training, research permit and equipment costs. Participants chosen to become long-term assistants will have all their in-country costs covered.
Applic.:	Online at: www.crees-manu.org or via e-mail.
Notes:	Participants and assistants may also be able to undertake their own research during their stay in the MBR.

FOREST RESTORATION, USA

National Park Service, Rock Creek Park
3545 Williamsburg Ln, NW
Washington, DC 20008 USA
Tel.: ++1 (202) 895 6077 – Fax: ++1 (202) 895 6075
E-mail: sue_salmons@nps.gov
www.nps.gov/rocr/

Desc.: This project focuses on exotic plant management, Dutch elm disease management, gypsy moth mitigation and vegetation mapping. Projects depend upon the season. Researchers may also write grant proposals and use Global Positioning software.

Spp.: *Celastrus orbiculatus, Ampelopsis brevipedunculata*, American elm, etc.

Hab.: Eastern deciduous forest.

Loc.: Mid-Atlantic of North America.

Travel: Airplane to Washington DC, USA.

Dur.: Variable.

Per.: Year round.

L. term: Inquire with organisation.

Age: Min. 18.

Qualif.: Familiarity with botany and computer knowledge is welcome. Must be in good shape and fluent in English. Participation or completion in a college level programme required.

Work: Integrated pest management may include vine cutting and work with herbicides, monitoring rare, threatened and endangered species, as well as vegetation plot monitoring and data entry.

Lang.: English.

Accom.: Group housing may be available. Bring sheets or sleeping bag. A small stipend for lunch may be available.

Cost: If a room cannot be provided, the cost will vary, depending on the type of accommodation. Hostels range from US$14–35/day. Volunteers must pay for transportation.

Agents: Contact Sue Salmons at the above address directly.

Applic.: Send CV, 3 references and copy of school transcript.

GENESIS II CLOUDFOREST PRESERVE AND WILDLIFE REFUGE, Costa Rica

Apdo. 655
7050 Cartago Costa Rica
Tel./Fax: ++ (506) 381 0739
E-mail: info@genesis-two.com
www.genesis-two.com (click on 'more options')

Desc.: This 47-hectare preserve was established to protect endangered cloud forest habitat. Volunteers assist with planting native trees and trail construction and maintenance.

Spp.: Birds, trees, epiphytes, ferns, butterflies/moths.

Hab.: Cloud forest, recovering pastureland.

Loc.: Central Talamanca mountains of Costa Rica; altitude 2,300 m.

Travel: Airplane to San José, then bus to project site.

Dur.: Min. 4 weeks; max. 9 units of 4 weeks each.

Per.: January to November.

L. term: Possible for specially qualified or highly motivated volunteers.

Age: Min. 21.

Qualif.: Volunteers must be physically fit and motivated; an interest in environmental concerns is especially welcome.

Work: July to October: planting native trees. November to June: constructing and maintaining trail system. Other projects include reforestation, T-shirt design, topographical mapping, bird frequency and observations. In the 4-week commitment, volunteers work for 2, 10-day periods (6 hours/day), with 4 days off after each period.

Lang.: English. Spanish is useful.

Accom.: Facilities are simple; electricity is 120-volt alternating current; there is a short-wave radio, but no TV.

Cost: Min. US$150/week, including room, board and laundry.

Applic.: Request application form to be returned with a deposit of US$150. Balance is due 1 month before joining the project.

Notes: June to December is wet season: expect cool, rainy conditions. Sunburn is possible owing to the high altitude.

GIBBON REHABILITATION PROJECT

The Wild Animal Rescue Foundation of Thailand (WAR)
65/1 Sukhumvit 55, Wattana
Bangkok 10110 Thailand
Tel. ++ 66 2 712 9515 – Fax. ++ 66 2 712 9778
Email: volunteer@warthai.org
www.warthai.org

Desc.: "The first gibbon project in the world." The sanctuary is located on the remote area of Phuket which currently houses over seventy gibbons. The aim of this project is the rehabilitation of gibbons back to their natural habitat additionally providing ongoing care to those unsuitable for repatriation, some of which are infected with communicable diseases. GRP is the oldest and most famous for volunteers of all WAR projects which houses a sanctuary dealing exclusively with gibbons many of whom have come to us by various means, from situations of abuse and cruelty. The GRP provides a refuge for these unfortunate animals that through no fault of their own have fallen victims to uncaring thoughtless humans. The sanctuary was created in the late nineteen eighties by people concerned about the large number of gibbons being exploited in bars and restaurants in the Phuket area. As they were being kept illegally the idea was to have them confiscated, houses them at the sanctuary then releases them into the forest.

Spp.: White-handed gibbon (*Hylobates lar*).

Hab.: Tropical rainforest.

Loc.: Bang Pae Waterfall, Khao Phra Thaew National Park, Phuket, Thailand.

Travel: Airplane to Bangkok for an orientation then a domestic flight to Phuket.

Dur.: Min. 3 weeks.

Per.: Year round.

L. term: Students and graduates in biology, anthropology and veterinary medicine are especially welcome to stay for long periods. Interesting opportunities also exist for those with an education in tourism or public relations.

Age: Min. 18.

Qualif.: Good physical condition, enthusiastic and able to work without assistance. Experience with animals or skills in construction, tourist assistance, public relations, etc., can be very helpful. Experience can be a criterium for selection.

Work: Volunteers work 6 days a week, day off can enjoy themselves at the beach. Quarantine and Rehabilitation Site: this involves food preparation, feeding, cage maintenance, cleaning and enrichment and observation (health check, vaginal check). Reintroduction Site: this involves forest feeding, mapping and trail maintenance, follow up and data collection. Conservation Education and Fund-raising: volunteer will give talk to tourists, educating them about the problems gibbon faces and selling merchandise. Other: this could be teaching English in the local primary school, etc.

Lang.: English.

Accom.: Bungalows for 2 or more persons located close to the sanctuary, with toilet, shower and cooking facilities.

Cost: $US 1,020 for the first 3 weeks and $US 105 for each additional week. Or $US 945 for the first 3 weeks and $US 105 foe each additional week. Or $US 2,500 for 6-month stay.

Agents: The Wild Animal Rescue Foundation of Thailand at www.warthai.org or the Ecovolunteer Network at www.ecovolunteer.org.

Applic.: Through The Wild Animal Rescue Foundation of Thailand or Ecovolunteer Network.

Notes: The Centre can accommodate 8–12 people at a time; couples and groups can be accommodated depending on season and number of volunteers.

GOLDEN BOOMERANG LANDCARE, Australia

594 Sunny Corner Road
Touron Springs
Via Bthurst 2795 Australia
Tel.: ++61 (263) 377 279 – Mob.: ++61 (401) 093 005
E-mail: earthfix@optusnet.com.au
www.earthfix.org.au

Desc.: Rejuvenating 125 acres of Australian farmland.

Spp.: Several subtropical plant species.

Hab.: Australian scrubland.

Loc.: Turon Springs in the Central Tablelands, 200 km northwest of Sydney.

Travel: Contact the project for information about travel.

Dur.: Negotiable, there are no set periods.

Per.: Year round.

L. term: Volunteers can join for short or long periods.

Age: Min.18.

Qualif.: No special skills required. Anyone is welcome to join and apply their skills and interests.

Work: The projects considers landcare as care and survival for everyone. The focus is community care, entertainment and land repair.

Lang.: English.

Accom.: In a bunkhouse situation: shared cooking, cleaning, etc. Sometimes sleeping outdoors in tents and swags.

Cost: No cost. Food and expenses are shared: no more than AUS$15 (approx.US$8) per day.

Applic.: An initial membership fee is required. All volunteers become members and are covered by insurance. Apply with expressions of interest by e-mail.

GREAT WHALES IN THEIR NATURAL ENVIRONMENT, Canada

ORES – Foundation for Marine Environment Research
Postfach 1252, 4502 Solothurn, Switzerland
Tel./Fax.: ++41 (32) 623 6354
E-mail: utscherter@ores.org
www.ores.org

Desc.: The coastal ecosystem in the St. Lawrence River estuary in Eastern Canada is known for the near-shore abundance and diversity of its marine life forms, especially of baleen whales. ORES marine biologists, with the help of volunteers, study their feeding behaviour, distribution, abundance and habitat utilisation applying minimally intrusive research methods. During the course, volunteers not only will have daily encounters with different species and are actively involved in data collecting, they also will learn what the whales are doing and why. Research results, conservation issues and general knowledge on whales are shared on the water and during several slide and film presentations.

Spp.: Harbour porpoise, beluga, sperm whale, minke, humpback, finback and blue whale, several seal species.

Hab.: Ocean-river estuary in protected marine waters.

Loc.: Province of Québec, Canada, Les Bergeronnes (220 km east of Québec City), St. Lawrence and Saguenay River confluence.

Travel: Airplane to Toronto, Montreal or Québec City, then by bus (or car) to Les Bergeronnes.

Per.: July to September.

Dur.: Two programmes are offered: the General Interest Course (GIC) of 2 weeks to broaden knowledge of the ocean generally and of whales in particular (students-degree or diploma credit available); the Internship Course (ISC; medium-term 6 weeks, long-term 12 weeks) is open to anybody who has completed the introductory course and who would like to gain deeper insight into the ongoing studies.

L. term: See previous section.

Age.: Min. 18.

Qualif.: No particular skills or knowledge are needed. ORES volunteers should show strong interest in field work, team work, outdoor activities and must be able to spend 4–6 hours on an open boat.

Work: Observation and data gathering daily (weather permitting) by small research teams from open inflatable boats. Protected waters offer encounters with whales without any seasickness. Studies carried out among others: feeding strategies and techniques, ventilation recording, spatial and temporal distribution, photo-identification. Volunteers help collect data on the water and quickly learn to distinguish species and to identify individual animals.

Lang.: English. The language in the province of Québec is French. ORES personnel also speak French and German.

Accom.: Stay at the well-equipped Bon Désir Campground overlooking the St. Lawrence. Sleeping tents with wooden floors, cooking tent and infrastructure are provided. Lectures and lab work take place at the nearby research centre, where Internship students will be accomodated in simple cabins with 4 beds.

Cost: Fee for GIC (incl. accommodation, exposure suits, on-water and land transportation, lectures and excursions; excl. travel and food) is US$1,150 (approx. EUR950/GB£630). Fees for ISC on request. Volunteers individually organise their travel to and from the Centre.

Agents: The Ecovolunteer Network at www.ecovolunteer.org.

Applic.: Apply directly via e-mail to receive detailed information and an application form. Due to the high demand, it is recommended to contact ORES early in the year. After enrolment, participants will receive a comprehensive booklet on the project.

GREY WHALES RESEARCH EXPEDITIONS, Canada-Mexico

Coastal Ecosystems Research Foundation
General Delivery, Dawson's Landing
British Columbia, VON IMO   Canada
Tel.: ++44 7745 130 873 – Fax: ++1 (815) 327 0183
E-mail: info@cerf.bc.ca   www.cerf.bc.ca

Desc: The Coastal Ecosystem Research Foundation conducts research on the distribution, abundance and movements of grey whales and their environment in British Columbia and Baja California. Projects include: population census, home-range determination, micro-habitat use, prey dynamics, social behaviour on the summering grounds and feeding behaviour on the wintering grounds. Graduate student research currently includes work on the migration of grey whales between summering and wintering grounds and a study of the underwater behaviour of the whales in relation to the bottom topography and distribution of their prey. Studies on other marine mammal species include abundance, distribution and association patterns of humpback whales, river otters, harbour seals and killer whales. In some years, depending on funding and staffing, research is also conducted on the biodiversity of the intertidal, subtidal and coastal forest ecosystems.

Spp.: Marine mammals: grey whales (*Eschrichtius robustus*), killer whales (*Orcinus orca*), humpback whales (*Megaptera novaeangliae*), river otters (Lutra Canadensis).

Hab.: Northern Pacific coastal waters, temperate rainforest coast in BC, desert coast in Baja.

Loc.: Central coast of British Columbia, Canada, and west coast of baja California, Mexico.

Travel: BC. Participants will be met in Port Hardy, BC, for the day-long boat trip to CERF's research base at Duncanby Landing, Rivers Inlet. Baja: participants will have to make their own way to the town of San Ignacio, where they will be met by project staff.

Dur.: 6 days (Sunday to Friday).

Per.: June to September.

L. term: Possible with approval. Subject mostly to space and funding.

Age: Min. 15.

Qualif.: No particular skills required. Volunteers must be willing to spend long hours at shore stations or on boats. Previous experience with boat handling and photography is an asset, but not necessary.

Work: Volunteers are incorporated into the research team for the duration of their stay, and will participate in all of the research, including: boat handling (training provided), photo-ID (taking photos of the animals and identifying individuals by pigmentation patterns), data collection (behaviour, distribution, micro-habitat use, and movements) and ROV (mini-submarine) operations. Short talks are given every morning on research methods and evening lectures provide a background for the work.

Lang.: English, French, German - Spanish and Italian on some trips.

Accom.: BC: double rooms (bunks) with shared facilities at Duncanby Landing. Single rooms available at additional price. Once a week overnight aboard ship. Baja: camping.

Cost: Adults: CAD$1,395 (approx. US$900); students: CAD$1,275 (approx. US$850). All food and accommodation provided. Baja: $200 USD per day. Participants must provide their own transportation to Port Hardy or San Ignacio. The organisation can help arrange details at time of booking.

Applic.: Deposit of CAD$250 (approx. US$200) is due at time of booking, balance is due 60 days before trip date.

Notes: Max. group size is 12.

GREY WOLF PROJECT, USA

Wolf Education and Research Center (WERC)
517 Joseph Ave, P.O. Box 217, Winchester, Idaho 83555 USA
Tel.: ++1 (208) 924 6960
Fax: ++1 (208) 924 6959
E-mail: werced@camasnet.com
www.wolfcenter.org

Desc.: Public information, education and research concerning endangered species, with an emphasis on the grey wolf, its habitat and ecosystem in the northern Rocky Mountain region. WERC cares for a captive pack of wolves: "The Sawtooth Pack: Wolves of the Nez Perce". WERC is in partnership with the Nez Perce Tribe, which currently handles the wolf management and reintroduction for Idaho.

Spp.: Grey timber wolf (*Canis lupus*).

Hab.: Camas prairie, timber.

Loc.: North-central region of Idaho; near the borders of Idaho, Washington and Oregon, USA.

Travel: From Lewiston, ID take Highway 95 south to Winchester, ID. Follow signs for the Winchester Lake State Park. The centre is approximately 1 mile past the State Park.

Dur.: Varies with prior agreement between individual and WERC.

Per.: Year round; the need is greater from June to September.

L. term: Possible: inquire with the project.

Age: Min.18.

Work: Volunteers are involved in maintenance and/or construction, building, staffing the visitor centre; providing educational programmes, assisting with membership documentation and generally helping where needed.

Lang.: English.

Accom.: Local off-site lodging facilities can be recommended.

Cost: Max. US$20/day; excluding meals and transportation to/from Winchester.

Applic.: Request information and application form via e-mail or mail.

GRIFFON VULTURE CONSERVATION PROJECT, Croatia

Eco-center Caput Insulae – Beli
E Beli 4, 51559 Beli Croatia
Tel./Fax: ++385 (51) 840 525
E-mail: info@caput-insulae.com
       caput.insulae@ri.htnet.hr
www.caput-insulae.com

Desc.: The griffon vulture has disappeared from many European countries and is declining in its southeastern European range. The Croatian population includes approximately 100 breeding pairs. The objective of this project is to study griffon vulture biology and ecology to determine the critical factors for their survival on the islands and to develop new conservation strategies in order to maintain the present breeding population.

Spp.: Griffon vultures (*Gyps fulvus*), golden eagle (*Aquila chrysaetos*), short-toed eagle (*Circaetus gallicus*), peregrine falcon (*Falco peregrinus*), eagle owl (*Bubo bubo*), shag (*Phalacrocorax aristotelis*).

Hab: Mediterrannean sea-cliffs, oak forests and grasslands.

Loc.: Kvarner Archipelago, Northeast Adriatic, Croatia.

Travel: Airplane to Zagreb; bus or train to Rijeka; bus to Cres.

Dur.: Min. 1 week.

Per.: Year round.

L. term: Possible, for extremely motivated and qualified volunteers.

Age: Min. 18 years (16 with parent's permission).

Qualif.: Good physical health.

Work: Recording griffon vulture colonies, noting all sightings and behaviour on the cliffs, documenting visible wing-markers, etc.

Lang.: English, Italian.

Accom.: Eco-center: 26 beds, 2 bathrooms, hot showers, fully-equipped kitchen (volunteers help cook and housekeep).

Cost: From EUR80–125 (approx.GB£55–85) for 1 week. Food not included (approx. EUR5/day).

Agents: The Ecovolunteer Network at www.ecovolunteer.org.

Applic.: Application form on website.

Notes: Volunteers can also participate in other activities: interpretation for tourists and locals, dry stone wall or trail reconstruction, etc.

GRUPO LOBO, Portugal

Faculdade de Ciências da Universidade de Lisboa
Bloco C2 – 3º Piso, 1749-016 Lisboa   Portugal
Telf: ++351 (21) 750 0073 or ++351 (261) 785 037 (IWRC)
Fax: ++351 (21) 750 0028 or ++351 (261) 785 037 (IWRC)
Email: globo@fc.ul.pt
http://lobo.fc.ul.pt/

Desc.: Grupo Lobo is a non-profit association, founded in 1985, to work on wolf conservation and its habitat in Portugal, where the wolf is in danger of extinction. One of the objectives is to spread accurate information about this misunderstood and persecuted predator. The Iberian Wolf Recovery Center (IWRC) was created by GL with the aim of providing a suitable environment in captivity for wolves that can no longer live in the wild. At the same time it allows the public to understand the species' biology and conservation problems.

Spp.: Wolf (*Canis lupus*).

Hab.: Atlantic ecosystem.

Loc.: Malveira, 25 km north of Lisbon, Portugal

Travel: Airplane to Lisbon and then by bus or car to Malveira.

Dur.: Minimum of 15 days.

Per.: Volunteers are accepted year round.

L.term: Volunteers can stay for as long as 1 month.

Age: Min. 18.

Qualif.: Ability to work as part of a team. Anyone is welcome to join and apply their skills and interests.

Work: Several tasks can be performed by volunteers: monitor the captive wolves; help feeding the wolves; take part in the daily activities of the center; take part in the reforestation project; during the summer assist in pratolling the area for fire control.

Lang.: English or Portuguese (preferably).

Accom.: In volunteer house is fully equiped. Own sleeping bag needed.

Cost: Volunteering costs depend on the lodging availability at the IWRC. Contact IWRC for information.

Applic.: Online application form.

Notes: Accident and health insurances is mandatory.

HAWAIIAN FOREST RESTORATION PROJECT, USA

Kokee Resource Conservation Program c/o Natural History Museum
P.O. Box 100, Kekaha, Hawaii, 96752 USA
Tel.: ++1 (808) 335 9975 – Fax: ++1 (808) 335 6131
E-mail: rcp@aloha.net – kokee@aloha.net
www.krcp.org

Desc.: In the isolated Hawaiian Islands over 1,000 plant species evolved, and the forests of Kokee State Park contain many species found nowhere else in the world. However, because of invasive weed species introduced to the islands in the last 2 centuries, Hawaii also contains over 50% of the US Federally listed endangered plant species. This programme removes invasive weeds from selected areas of the mountain state park in order to restore those forested areas to their native state.

Spp.: Weed species: strawberry guava, blackberry, kahili ginger.

Hab.: Mesic montane Koa-dominated forests, wet montane Ohia-dominated forests, mixed-bog communities.

Loc.: Kokee State Park, Kauai, Hawaii.

Travel: Airplane to Kauai.

Dur.: 1 week to 1 month.

Per.: Year round.

L. term: Possible, inquire with organisation.

Age: Min. 21, or enrolled in an environmentally oriented degree.

Qualif.: Must be physically fit. Volunteers are trained and supervised. Priority is given to volunteers with a degree and/or experience in ecology, conservation or botany.

Work: Supervised by programme staff, volunteers use herbicides and hand weed to maintain the nearly native state containing unique, rare and endangered plant species. Volunteers work 8-hour days, often involving strenuous hiking in mountainous areas.

Lang.: English.

Accom.: Rustic housing in historic camp (bunk beds).

Cost: Volunteers pay for their own food and must rent a car.

Applic.: Request application form to Ellen Coulombe or Katie Cassel.

Notes: Groups are welcome but space is limited to parties of 14.

HELLENIC WILDLIFE HOSPITAL, Greece

Hellenic Wildlife Hospital
PO. Box 57
18010 Aegina Greece
Tel.: ++30 (229) 702 8367/++30 (697) 723 1983
ekpaz@ekpaz.gr – volunteer@ekpaz.gr
www.ekpaz.gr

Desc.: Founded in 1990, is the oldest and largest wildlife rehabilitation center in Greece dedicated to rehabilitation of wildlife, education and information of the public on wildlife protection issues, protection of endangered species, research on threats to wildlife and wildlife rehabilitation (illegal shooting & trapping, poisoning & pollution, habitat degradation and destruction) and taking preventative action, cooperation with public authorities, national and international NGO's with similar goals

Spp.: Indigenous and exotic species (may be rare or threatened).

Hab.: All the animals are found in Greece, but can be migrating birds or illegally transported animals from all over the world.

Loc.: Island of Aegina, 10km from Aegina near Pachia Rachi

Travel: Fly to Athens, then by ferry to Aegina from Piraeus

Dur.: Min. 20 days, max. one year

Per.: All year around.

Age: Minimum 18.

Qualif.: No special skills required. Team work. All skills are welcome, especially veterinarian, wildlife expertise.

Work: Cleaning of outdoor and indoor (also where the animals are treated), food preparation, feeding and watering, maintenance and construction work, help in treatments, work in the information booth of the Aegina Island and other special duties depending on experience. Training opportunities for veterinarian, biology or administration students or graduates.

Lang.: English.

Acc.:: There is a house for volunteers in the center.

Cost: No fees, volunteers pay own living costs and travel expenses.

L.term: Long-term is welcome with a maximum duration of one year.

Applic.: Application and agreement forms can be found in the website.

HUMPBACK RESEARCH PROJECT, Brazil

The Ecovolunteer Network
Meyersweg 29   7553 AX Hengelo The Netherlands
Tel.: ++31 (74) 250 8250 – Fax: ++31 (74) 250 6572
E-mail: info@ecovolunteer.org
www.ecovolunteer.org

Desc.: The Humpback Research Project carries on humpback research cruises in the Abrolhos Marine National Park. Humpbacks winter in this area for reproduction, between July and November. The research focuses on monitoring the humpack whale population and on behavioural studies on humpbacks.

Spp.: Humpback whale.

Hab.: Marine habitat with coral reefs and islands.

Loc.: Caravelas, Bahia and the Abrolhos Archipelago, Brazil.

Travel: Travel to Caravelas, Bahia, Brazil. Meet at airport or bus terminal.

Dur.: 2 – 3 weeks.

Per.: July to November.

L.term: Not possible.

Age.: Min. 18.

Qualif.: No particular skills needed. Volunteers must be in good health.

Work: Volunteers search for whales, operate the GPS and register whale behaviour. Scientists and volunteers participate in all activities, including processing data, computer work, operating the outboard motor, cooking, cleaning and other household duties. Volunteers may be asked to assist in other research projects of the National Park, such as monitoring tourism, protecting seaturtles or counting birds.

Lang.: English.

Accom.: Shared rooms in a hotel or on the research vessel.

Cost: US$1,295 for 2 weeks; US$325 for 1 extra week.

Agents: The Ecovolunteer Network at www.ecovolunteer.org.

Applic.: The Ecovolunteer Network (see Organisation list).

INTAG ANDEAN BEAR RESEARCH PROJECT, Ecuador

Fundación Espíritu del Bosque
Barcelona 3-11 y Tolosa, La Floresta, Quito Ecuador
Tel.: ++593 (2) 239 703
E-mail: volunteerbears@yahoo.com
www.espiritudelbosque.com

Desc.: This is the only project in the world that radiotracks Andean bears in the wild. The research is conducted as part of ongoing efforts to expand protected areas and prevent the extinction of the species. The primary purpose of this study is to determine the use of the habitat, activity patterns and size of home range and core area of the Andean bear.

Spp.: Andean Spectacled Bear (*Tremarctos ornatus*).

Loc.: Intag region, north western Ecuador.

Travel: Airplane to Quito. Transportation to project area provided.

Dur.: Min. 4 weeks.

Per.: Year round.

L.term: Volunteers can stay for as long as they want.

Age: Min. 18 years.

Qualif.: There are no special qualifications to participate in the project. However, volunteers should have a good level of fitness as the work can be strenuous.

Work: Volunteers follow roads or trails, listening for signals from the bears by means of radio-telemetry equipment. Volunteers may also be required to clear trails to be used for tracking, help collect samples and record marking behaviour.

Lang.: English or Spanish.

Accom.: Traditional Andean house with electricity, running water. Volunteers sleep in a large dormitory room.

Cost: Approx. US$350 for the first month, US$275 per month thereafter. Includes three meals per day, accommodation, transportation to project site. Transport costs at project site not included (approx. $15-20 per month).

Appl.: A simple application via e-mail. Include CV and possible dates.

INTERNATIONAL CONSERVATION VOLUNTEER EXCHANGE, Nevada

Mailstop 099 - University of Nevada Reno
Reno, Nevada 89557 USA
Tel.: ++1 (775) 784 1192 – Fax: ++1 (775) 327 2307
E-mail: powellj@unr.edu
www.greatbasininstitute.org click on "International Volunteering"

Desc.: Volunteers construct and maintain trails in various wilderness areas. Work includes a variety of techniques to design minimum impact trails and control erosion. Volunteers may learn the art of dry stone masonry, and other responsibilities will include recreating tread surface to allow proper trail run-off and also removing encroaching vegetation. Wilderness Road Removal and Desert Restoration: include a variety of restoration practices from removing illegal roads to restoring the native vegetation. Volunteers will decompact illegal ORV roads and transplant native vegetation to the area. Native plant restoration will involve the removal of non-native invasive plants, and the transplanting of native plant seedlings.
Loc.: Projects in locations throughout the state of Nevada.
Travel: By plane to Reno or San Francisco (bus or train from S.F.).
Dur.: 1-6 months.
Per.: Year round (see website for specific dates).
L. term: Inquire with the organisation.
Age: 18-35
Qualif.: No qualifications required.
Work: 10 hour work days. 4 days in the field, with 3 days off or 8 days in the field with 6 days off. ICVE is not recommended for people with conditions that limit physical activity.
Accom.: Camping during field work dormitory style cabin when off-time.
Cost: Volunteers pay for travel and travellers' insurance. Food while in and out of the field is provided.
Applic: Contact Joshua Powell, ICVE Program Coordinator.
Notes: This program is open only to International Volunteers, US volunteers can find other opportunities with Nevada Conservation Corps (NCC) www.greatbasininstitute.org

IONIAN DOLPHIN PROJECT, Greece

Tethys Research Institute
c/o Civic Aquarium, Viale G.B. Gadio 2
20121 Milano Italy
Tel.: ++39 (02) 5831 4889/7200 1947 – Fax:++39 (02) 583 15345
E-mail: tethys@tethys.org
www.tethys.org

Desc.: This is the first long-term project on cetaceans in Ionian Greece, initiated in 1993 by the Tethys Research Institute (see Organisation list), with the goal to study the socio-ecology of common and bottlenose dolphins that live in the coastal waters around the island of Kalamos. Common dolphins are now declining in the Mediterranean, owing to overfishing, by-catch and habitat degradation. By monitoring this community, researchers are promoting proper conservation measures. Methods of investigation include systematic surveys, individual photo-identification and behavioural sampling of free-ranging dolphins.

Spp.: Common dolphin (*Delphinus delphis*), bottlenose dolphin (*Tursiops truncatus*); sea turtles (*Caretta caretta*) swordfish (*Xiphias gladius*), manta rays (*Mobula mobula*) and monk seals (*Monachus monachus*) may be also observed.

Hab.: Coastal waters of the central Ionian Greece.

Loc.: Island of Kalamos, Greece.

Travel: Airplane to Athens or Preveza, then bus or taxi to Mytika. Transfer to Kalamos is provided by the researchers. Igoumenitsa and Patra can also be reached by ferry from the Italian ports of Venice, Ancona or Brindisi.

Dur.: 6 or 9 days.

Per.: May to September.

L. term: Consecutive shifts can be booked with a discount. Discount also granted to students less than 26 years old.

Age: Min. 18.

Qualif.: No particular skills are required. Volunteers should be interested and very motivated.

Work: The work consists of observations from inflatable craft during surveys at sea and long-lasting observations of dolphin groups found in two study areas (the area around Kalamos and the Amvrakikos Gulf). With bad weather volunteers stay at the base, entering and analysing data and matching digital photos. Trips can also be organised. Daily lectures on dolphin research methods and conservation strategies are carried out by the researchers.

Lang.: English, Italian.

Accom.: The base is located in the village of Episcopi, on the island of Kalamos. The house has 4 bedrooms, 1 of which is for the volunteers. Everyone takes part in cooking and housekeeping. The base is equipped with computers, a basic scientific library, research archives, telephone-and fax.

Cost: EUR500–830(approx. GB£350–580) for 6-9 days, depending on the season, including food, membership and insurance. Fees do not include travel.

Agents: Tethys Research Institute (see Organisation list).

Applic.: Request a standard application form to be completed and returned to the Tethys Research Institute. Early booking is suggested.

Notes: Only 4-6 volunteers can participate in each shift, depending on period. From 3–4 researchers reside at the field station with the volunteers. The small size of the boat and the low-noise engine allow an easy approach of the dolphins and their following at close range without modifications of their behaviour.

IRACAMBI ATLANTIC RAINFOREST RESEARCH AND CONSERVATION CENTER, Brazil

Fazenda Iracambi, Rosário da Limeira
36878–000 Minas Gerais Brazil
Tel.: ++55 (32) 3721 1436 – Fax: ++55 (32) 3722 4909
E-mail: iracambi@iracambi.com
www.iracambi.com

Desc.: Iracambi is committed to making the preservation of the rainforest more attractive than its destruction. Its members are seeking ways that will not only arrest the rate of destruction, but reverse it, whilst providing at the same time a higher standard of living for the local farmers.

Spp.: Inventories of flora and fauna are being carried out.

Hab.: Semi-deciduous rainforest.

Loc.: Southeastern Brazil in the State of Minas Gerais.

Travel: Fly to Rio de Janeiro, bus to Muriaé and Rosário da Limeira.

Dur.: Minimum 1 month.

Per.: Year round.

L. term: Visa allows max. 180 days. Longer stays require special visa.

Age: Min.18, no max.

Qualif.: General hands with no skills are welcome. IT, GIS and mapping specialists, carpenters, teachers (in Portuguese), tropical botanists and zoologists are especially needed.

Work: The work falls into 5 areas: land use management, forest restoration, community understanding and engagement, income generating alternatives and work to improve the capacity of the centre. There is a wide range of projects within each area, so plenty of room is available for people offering some skills and their enthusiasm. A role will be sorted out for every motivated applicant.

Lang.: Portuguese and English.

Accom.: Shared room in traditional farm cottages.

Cost: US$370 for first month, US$340 for the second month and US$310 for third and subsequent months.

Applic.: Send CV via e-mail. No deadlines or forms to fill in.

Notes: Full information from the volunteer page on the website.

ISCHIA DOLPHIN PROJECT

DELPHIS Mediterranean Dolphin Conservation
Via Zaro 22
80075 Forio d'Ischia (NA) Italy
Tel./Fax: ++39 (081) 989 578 – Mob.:(on board) ++39 (349) 5749927
E-mail: info@delphismdc.org
www.delphismdc.org

Desc.: The submarine canyon of Cuma is an important habitat where a particular pelagic fauna can be found very close to the coast. The presence of whales and dolphins, pelagic fishes and marine birds is related to the geological and ecological characteristics of the area. Primary research concentration is of a relic population unit of endangered short-beaked common dolphins. The island of Ischia was noted as 'critical habitat' for the species in the Mediterranean Sea by the IUCN. Pollution, prey depletion and by-catch are the main threats for cetaceans. Delphis MDC works to include the canyon into the perimeter of the future Marine Protected Area of Ischia, procida and Vivara Islands proposed by the Italian Ministry of the Environment. The canyon represents a hot spot for other cetacean species, like striped, bottlenose and Risso's dolphins, pilot, sperm and fin whales. Management measures to protect cetaceans in this key area are urgently needed.

Spp.: Common dolphin (*Delphinus delphis*), striped dolphin (*Stenella coeruleoalba*), bottlenose dolphin (*Tursiops truncatus*), Risso's dolphin (*Grampus griseus*), pilot whale (*Globicephala melas*), sperm whale *(Physeter macrocephalus),* fin whale (*Balaenoptera physalus*).

Hab.: Coastal and pelagic Mediterranean waters, submarine canyon.

Loc.: Mediterranean sea, Ischia Island, Italy.

Travel: Airplane or train to Naples, then bus to Beverello, then ferry or hydrofoil to Ischia island.

Dur.: 1 week.

Per.: June to October.

L. term: Maximum stay is 2 weeks with project's leader's approval.

Age: Min. 16.

Qualif.: No particular skills required, just good physical health.

Work: Lectures on cethology (evolution, adaptation to the sea, classification, bio-acoustic, social behaviour, interactions with fisheries; practical lessons on cetacean watching; during sightings volunteers carry out precise tasks, such as timing the divings or photo-identifying the animals. The underwater audio system allows volunteers to get confidence with cetaceans' vocalisations and noises in the sea. Cooking, dish washing, cleaning, steering and watching shifts are shared among the volunteers.

Lang.: English or Italian/French/Spanish.

Accom.: On board of 'Jean Gab', a 17.70 m wooden cutter built in 1930 in Marseille, transformed in a laboratory on the sea, the boat is provided with a 13-year database and a recording system to collect bio-acoustic data and underwater videos. Available on board are books and scientific literature on cetaceans.

Cost: EUR720-820 (approx. GB£500–570). Price inlcudes: food and beverages, accommodation, insurance, fuel for the research vessel and the inflatable craft, port fees, lectures and training by Delphis researchers, membership fee, certificate of attendance. Travel and the first dinner are not included.

Agents: Delphis MDC.

Applic.: Send and e-mail to above address. A 50% deposit to reserve the place is needed with the application.

Notes: Delphis MDC works in the area since 1991 thanks to the volunteers' help.

JATUN SACHA, Ecuador

Fundación Jatun Sacha
Eugenio de Santillán N34 –248 y Maurián
Casilla 17–12–867 Quito   Ecuador
Tel.: ++593 (2) 243 2173 – Fax: ++593 (2) 243 2240
E-mail: volunteer@jatunsacha.org
www.jatunsacha.org

Desc.:	Jatun Sacha Foundation is an Ecuadorian NGO whose main objective is conservation of the environment. Jatun Sacha has 10 biological stations located in different areas of Ecuador: Amazon, coast and highlands, Galapagos Islands.
Spp.:	Various species of Ecuadorian fauna and vegetation.
Hab.:	Andean cloud forest, tropical rainforest, dry forest, premontane forest, humid forest, mangrove forest.
Loc.:	Ecuadorian coast, highlands and Amazon, Galapagos Islands.
Travel:	By airplane to Quito, bus or truck from Quito to the stations.
Dur:	Min. 15 days.
Per.:	Year round.
L.term:	Possible, inquire with the organisation.
Age:	Min. 18.
Qualif.:	Volunteers must be dynamic and interested in conservation.
Work:	Reforestation, agroforestry, organic agriculture and farming, community extension projects, general mainteinance, meteorological and other environmental data collection, trekking, visits to communities, aquaculture work.
Lang.:	English, basic Spanish is highly recommended, but not required.
Accom.:	Shared cabins, in some cases without electricity, with toilets outside.
Cost:	Application fee US$35. Food and accommodation US$395 per month.
Applic.:	Send by regular mail: CV, a cover letter, 2 passport size photos, medical certificate, police record, and a US$35 application fee.

LEATHERBACK SEATURTLE TAGGING PROGRAMME, Grenada

Ocean Spirits Inc.
P.O. Box 1373, Grand Anse, St.George's, Grenada West Indies
Tel.: ++ (473) 403 2282
E-mail: volunteer@oceanspirits.org
www.oceanspirits.org

Desc.: Ocean Spirits Inc. is a non-profit NGO dedicated to the conservation of marine life and the marine environment. Through 3 programmes: Education, Research and Conservation and Community Development, the NGO is working to change attitudes towards the sustainable use of resources in Grenada.

Spp.: Leatherback sea turtle (*Dermochelys coriacea*); Hawksbill sea turtle (*Eretmochelys imbricata*).

Hab.: Tropical beaches.

Loc.: Grenada, Caribbean.

Travel: Plane to Grenada, volunteers are met at the airport.

Dur.: Volunteers must commit for a minimum period of 3 weeks.

Per.: April to August.

L. term: Volunteers may stay for more than1 period at reduced cost.

Age: Min. 18.

Qualif.: Previous experience of field work and data collection is an advantage but not essential. Good physical condition as the work involves long hours and in variable weather conditions. Must be enthusiastic and flexible.

Work: Night patrols for nesting turtles, applying tags and collecting other data. Morning beach surveys to determine other turtle nesting activity. Conducting educational field trips and school summer camps. Assist in accomodation mainteinance.

Lang.: English.

Accom.: Dormitory style accommodation, sheets and towels needed.

Cost: From GB£795/US$1,470 for 3 weeks. Price includes accommodation, food and airport transfers.

Applic.: Application form available via e-mail or website. Apply no later than 6 weeks before departure.

LEATHERBACK TURTLE PROJECT, Costa Rica

Estación Las Tortugas
Matina, Region Mondonguillo, Costa Rica
Tel.: ++ (506) 396 0268 (in Costa Rica, during nesting season)
    ++ 44 (1903) 244 134 (in the UK before nesting season)
E-mail: estacionlastortugas@yahoo.co.uk
www.estacionlastortugas.org or http://tortuga.is.dreaming.org/pub

---

Desc.:   Each year the leatherback turtle visits the Caribbean coast of Costa Rica to nest. The biological station, Estación Las Tortugas is one of their most important nesting beaches. Since 2000, the project has been focusing on the conservation and protection of this now critically endangered species.

Spp.:   Leatherback turtle (*Dermochelys coriacea*).

Hab.:   Secondary coastal rainforest.

Loc.:   Caribbean coast of Costa Rica (30 km north of Puerto Limon).

Travel: Airplane to San Jose, Costa Rica. Volunteers will be picked up at the airport and taken to Matina.

Dur.:   1 month.

Per.:   March-June.

L.term: Long term opportunities might be available for research.

Age :   Min. 18.

Qualif.: No specific skills required, just enthusiasm, willingness to work and ability to live in basic conditions and high humidity levels.

Work: Volunteers will assist researchers. Long distance walking without assistance is required, as 4-hour beach patrols will be carried out each night. Leatherback nests will be collected and translocated, together with environmental data. A few hours is also carried out in the day time.

Lang.:   English or Spanish.

Accom.: Basic accommodation with rooms of 4-6 people and shared showers. Basic food of rice and beans provided 3 times a day.

Cost: US$750 which includes accommodation, 3 meals a day, transport from airport and first night accommodation in San Jose. Flights and travel insurance are not covered in the cost.

Applic.: Contact Stamie at the above address for further information and application forms.

LEOPARDS OF PHINDA, South Africa

Dept. of Biological Sciences, Monash University
P.O. Box 18. Victoria, 3800 Australia
Tel.: ++61 (3) 9905 5602
Fax: ++61 (3) 9905 5613
E-mail: luke.hunter@sci.monash.edu.au
www.wildaboutcats.org/internship.htm

Desc.: The research investigates the conservation ecology of leopards in a region where land-use varies from wildlife reserves (where protection is strict) to livestock farms where leopards are heavily persecuted. The research will provide data essential to ensure the species survival in the region.

Spp.: Primarily leopards; additional monitoring of lions, cheetahs and spotted hyaenas as well as counts of prey species.

Hab.: Woodland-savannah mosaic.

Loc.: Northern KwaZulu-Natal province, South Africa.

Travel: Airplane to Johannesburg then to the field site by a 90-minute flight in a light passenger plane.

Dur.: 2 weeks.

Per.: Year round.

L. term: Outstanding applicants will be considered for longer-term placements at minimal cost.

Age: Under 18 must be accompanied by a guardian. No upper limit.

Qualif.: No particular skills needed but volunteers must be physically fit and be able to work long hours in demanding field conditions.

Work: Volunteers assist in live-capture of wild leopards to fit with radio-collars and to collect data on physical measurements, weight, tissue sampling. Long hours are spent radio-tracking and observing leopards. Monitoring of other carnivore species (lions, cheetahs and spotted hyaenas), intermittent counts of prey species and entering data onto computer databases.

Lang.: English.

Accom.: Accommodation is in a large comfortable farmhouse.

Cost: US$2,660; includes room, board and inland flight from Jo'burg.

Applic.: Contact Dr. Luke Hunter for an application form.

Notes: Only 2 volunteers can join each expedition.

LIBANONA ECOLOGY CENTRE, Madagascar

BP 42, Fort Dauphin–614 Madagascar
Tel.: ++ 261 (20) 922 1242
E-mail: libanonaecology@hotmail.com
www.andrewleestrust.org.uk/libanona.htm

Desc.: The Libanona Ecology Centre (LEC) is a Malagasy NGO working in the field of conservation and training in Southeast Madagascar. Current projects are themed on: community forest management, GIS, conservation education, applied biodiversity, anthropological research and community tourism.

Spp.: Various species of Malgasy flora and fauna.

Hab.: Malagasy spiny forest, littoral forest, humid forest, transitional forest, coastal ecosystem.

Loc.: Madagascar, off the coast of Africa.

Travel: Flight to Antananarivo and internal flight to Fort Dauphin.

Dur.: From a few weeks to 8–9 months.

Per.: Year round.

L.term: Possible, inquire with organisation.

Age: Min. 18, no max.

Qualif.: Depend on particular placement and project. An ability to work in extremely challenging conditions is a must.

Work: In the following skill areas: GIS, eco tourism, conservation education, TEFL, apiculture, forestry, biodiversity research. Placements are designed with specific volunteers in mind.

Lang.: English, French required for field and office activities.

Accom.: Very basic. Ranges from rough camping to rooms in wooden huts to a comfortable house in LEC. No hot water.

Cost: Depends on placement, concrete contribution to a LEC development project is requested (financing materials for local development associations, or for the lab and library) as a goodwill gesture. Volunteers should be self financing.

Applic.: Send CV and letter of interest via e-mail to Sylvia Ravelonjatovo. Specify area of expertise, availability and theme of interest.

LIFELINE CAT RESEARCH AND REHABILITATION CENTRE, Belize

P.O. Box 86 San Ignacio
Cayo   Belize
E-mail: catsbze@direcway.com – lifelinebelize@yahoo.co.uk
www.li-feline.com

Desc.: A Belizean non-profit, NGO dedicated to the conservation of endangered wild cats, with special emphasis on the rehabilitation of confiscated cats to the wild.

Spp.: Jaguar, puma, ocelot, margay, jaguarundi.

Hab.: Broadleaf forest, tropical pine forest.

Loc.: Central Belize, Central America.

Travel: By air to Belize International Airport then by minibus to LiFeline.

Dur.: Volunteer placements are usually for 28 days.

Per.: Year round.

L.term: 3-, 6- or 12-month periods for outstanding volunteers.

Age: Min. 18.

Qualif.: Ability to work in tropical rainforest, clean driving licence. Must have reasonable standard of physical fitness. A degree in zoology or associated subject would be an advantage.

Work: Helping build and maintain cat enclosures, monitoring released cats by radio telemetry, behavioural studies. Caring for rescued cats (feeding them and helping with veterinary procedures). Occasionally act as guide to visiting school parties.

Lang.: English, some Spanish useful.

Accom.: On-site, meals are included in the cost.

Cost: US$900 for 28 days, excluding flights.

Applic.: Request application form via e-mail.

Notes: See website for more information.

LOGGERHEAD SEA TURTLES IN LINOSA, Italy

CTS – Centro Turistico Studentesco e Giovanile – Sezione Ambiente
Via Albalonga 3
00183 Roma Italy
Tel.: ++39 (06) 6496 0306 – Fax: ++39 (06) 6496 0335
E-mail: ambiente@cts.it
www.ctsambiente.it

Desc.: Loggerhead sea turtles come to nest on the island of Linosa, south of Sicily. Their survival in the Mediterranean is threatened by water pollution, habitat destruction and human activities. CTS researchers, with funding from the EU, are trying to protect the rare nesting beaches by collecting data, patrolling these areas and informing tourists and local people about the importance of habitat and species protection. Monitoring and tracking of turtles by advanced satellite technology are among the activities carried out.

Spp.: Loggerhead sea turtle (*Caretta caretta*).

Hab.: Mediterranean coast.

Loc.: Island of Linosa, Sicily, Italy.

Travel: Airplane to Palermo and Lampedusa or ferry from Agrigento.

Dur.: 8 days.

Per.: June to September.

L. term: Inquire with organisation.

Age: Min. 18 (16 with parent's authorisation).

Qualif.: Volunteers must be flexible and willing to work during the night.

Work: Participants will observe and count nesting females, nests, eggs or hatchlings and rescue injured animals. Volunteers will also give information to local people and tourists. Lectures on flora, fauna and geology of the island and excursions are scheduled.

Lang.: Italian, Spanish accepted.

Accom.: Apartment with kitchen.

Cost: EUR 280–350 (approx.GB£ 180–230), food and travel not included.

Agents: CTS regional offices in Italy (see Organisation list).

Applic.: Request application form. Membership to CTS required.

MANAGEMENT PLAN FOR PILOS LAGOON, Greece

Hellenic Ornithological Society (HOS)
Vas. Irakleiou 24, 10682 Athens   Greece
E-mail: mkalouli@ornithologiki.gr
www.ornithologiki.gr

Desc.: The goal of the project is the implementation of a management plan for the Pilos lagoon. The goals are wetland restoration, providing visitor facilities and educating local people about the value of the site. A very important and sensitive section of the project is the research and protection of the African chameleon, found exclusively in this region.

Spp.: African chameleon (*Chamaeleo africanus*).

Hab.: Mediterranean coastal lagoon.

Loc.: Greece, southwestern coast of the Peloponnese peninsula.

Travel: Airplane to Athens or by ferry from Italy to Patras; bus, train or airplane to Kalamata or Kiparissia; bus to Pilos.

Dur.: 1–2 months.

Per.: June to October.

L. term: Only with project leader's approval after regular period.

Age: Min. 20, max. 40, depending on the experience.

Qualif.: No particular skills required.

Work: Beach patrolling to prevent collection and disturbance of the chameleons and helping with field research. Running information kiosk.

Lang.: English, Greek.

Accom.: In tents in a private campsite. Volunteers can bring their own tent. Sleeping bag and mat are a must.

Cost: Prticipation fee EUR60 (approx. GB£40).

Agents: Contact project leader Marilia Kalouli.

Applic.: An application form needs to be filled out.

Notes: Field work and beach patrolling is hard work, especially during the summer. Volunteers must be motivated.

MANATEE RESEARCH PROJECT, Belize

Oceanic Society Expeditions
Fort Mason Center, Building E
San Francisco, CA 94123 USA
Tel.: ++1 (415) 441 1106 – (800) 326 7491 (toll free in N.America)
Fax: ++1 (415) 474 3395
E-mail: info@oceanic-society.org www.oceanic-society.org

Desc.: The goal of this project is to collect biological data necessary for manatee protection and habitat management. The research objectives are to determine distribution and abundance of manatees at Turneffe Atoll, their behavioural ecology, and environmental parameters of microhabitats used consistently.

Spp.: Manatee (*Trichechus manatus*).

Hab.: Tropical sea.

Loc.: Turneffe Atoll, Belize.

Travel: Volunteers can reach Belize by airplane using group airfare from some US gateway cities (Houston, Los Angeles, Miami).

Dur.: 8 days.

Per.: June, July.

L. term: Inquire with organisation.

Age: Min. 18.

Qualif.: No particular skills required.

Work: By small boat, volunteers visit zones of manatee concentration, map positions, note individual markings, and log behavioural information.

Lang.: English.

Cost: US$1,490.

Accom.: Beachfront cabanas with porch, double rooms with private bath.

Applic.: Request application form to be returned with a deposit of US$300.

Notes: Max. group size is 8. Volunteer can have free time for beach snorkelling.

MANGA DEL MAR MENOR RESTORATION AND RESEARCH PROJECT, Spain

ICSA & Amigos de la UNESCO
C/Sagasta n°13, 1° izq. 30004, Murcia Spain
Tel.: ++34 (902) 113 792 – Fax: ++34 (902) 113 792
E-mail: unesco@ctv.es or calblanque@ono.com www.ctv.es/USERS/
murban/volunt.htm – www.icsanet.com/volunt.htm

Desc.: The project includes cultural and natural resource restoration and research in different zones in the Manga del Mar Menor; ecological research in the coastal landscapes and wetlands of the Calblanque Park; prehistoric and archaeological research in the Cueva Victoria, antiquities site; coastwatching and research activities around the wetlands.

Spp.: Seabirds, raptors, marine mammals, endemic species.

Hab.: Coastal Mediterranean wetland.

Loc.: La Manga del Mar Menor, Spain.

Travel: A brochure with information will be provided upon request.

Dur.: 15 days to 3 months.

Per.: July to September.

L. term: Max. 3 months.

Age: Min.16.

Qualif.: No special qualifications required. Volunteers must have a strong motivation to work for nature conservation.

Work: Activities include data collection, cleaning caverns, filming videos, observation of submarine zones and plants, informing the visitors to the park, environmental education with children.

Lang.: Spanish, English, French. Other languages are welcome. Spanish lessons can be provided.

Accom.: Tents in First Touristic Camping, tents in the park.

Cost: 15 days without accommodation cost EUR145; tents in the park and meals cost EUR375; tents in a First Class Camping cost EUR330 without meal (in both cases participants must provide their own tent and sleeping bag). Fees include transportation from the airport, half board and insurance.

Applic.: Request application form, or download it from the website.

THE MARINE MAMMAL CENTER (TMMC), California

Marin Headlands, GGNRA
Sausalito, California 94965 USA
Tel.: ++1 (415) 289 7325 /979 4357 (volunteer inquiries)
Fax: ++1 (415) 289 7333
E-mail: volNteer@tmmc.org
www.tmmc.org – www.marinemammalcenter.org

Desc.: The Marine Mammal Center is a leading rescue, rehabilitation and release facility for marine mammals. It treats almost 600 animals a year. Volunteer crews work on a 6-12 hour shift, both day and evening, 365 days a year.

Spp.: Marine mammals, primarily pinnipeds.

Hab.: Pacific coast.

Loc.: Northern California (San Francisco).

Travel: Airplane to San Francisco, then by car.

Dur.: Flexible.

Per: Volunteers are accepted year round but are most needed during high season (March to August).

L. term: Volunteers can remain as long as they like.

Age.: Min. 18.

Qualif.: Ability to work as part of a team and with wild animals.

Work: Volunteers prepare food, feed animals, restrain animals for tube feeds and physical exams, clean pens, wash dishes, do laundry, administer medication, weigh animals and chart all observations. The shifts run from 6–12 hours depending on the season. Training is provided.

Lang.: English.

Accom.: No accommodation available.

Cost: Volunteers must provide accommodation, food and transportation. There is no public transportation to the site. Volunteers can reach the site by bicycle.

Applic.: After admission volunteers must attend an orientation upon arrival and complete a liability waiver.

Notes: This physically demanding work requires good health and a current tetanus shot is recommended.

MARINE TURTLES ADRIATIC ARCHE' PROJECT, Italy

A.R.C.H.E'. Research and Educational Activities for Chelonian Conservation
Via Mulinetto, 40/A-I   44100 Ferrara Italy
Tel.:/Fax: ++39 (0532) 767 852 – Mob.: ++39 (349)393 7924
E-mail: archeturtle@tiscali.it
http://archeturtle.org

Desc.: The research project focuses on interactions between marine turtles and fishing methods, tagging and recapture, rescue of stranded animals, education program for fishermen, education program for tourists on marine turtles.

Spp.: Loggerhead seaturtles (*Caretta caretta*).

Hab.: Mediterranean coast.

Loc.: Porto Garibaldi (Italy) Northwestern Adriatic Sea.

Travel: Train from Bologna to Ostellato, then bus to Porto Garibaldi.

Dur.: Min. 1 week.

Per.: June, July, September.

L. Term.: There is no limit for long-term stays.

Age: Min. 18.

Qualif.: No special qualifications, other than enthusiasm, adaptability, love for animals and willingness to work long hours.

Work: Volunteers will carry on educational activities among tourists on the beach, collect data on stranded animals. Data on marine turtles accidentally captured by fishing nets are collected at the harbour. Depending on fishing boats' availability, volunteers and researchers will go on board to experience a fishing day (for 12/14 hours).

Lang.: English, basic Italian useful.

Accom.: In shared rooms, sleeping bag required.

Cost: EUR300/week (approx.GB£ 210), with a reduction of 5% for students. Food, accommodation and insurance are included. Travel and personal expenses are not inlcuded.

Applic.: Via e-mail or by completing the online application form.

MARINE TURTLE & YOUTH ENVIRONMENTAL EDUCATION, Mexico

Grupo Ecologico de La Costa Verde
827 Union Pacific
PMB 078–253, Laredo, Texas 78045–9452   USA
Tel.: ++52 (311) 258 84100
E-mail: grupo-eco@project-tortuga.org   www.project-tortuga.org

Desc.: Grupo Ecologico de la Costa Verde is a Mexican non-profit, Civil Association dedicated to the protection of the natural environment, with special interest in the protection of the marine turtles and in Youth Environmental Education.

Spp.: Olive Ridley (*Lepidochelys olivacea*); leatherback (*Dermochelys coriacea*); eastern Pacific green turtle (*Chelonia agassizi*).

Hab.: Marine, tropical, coastal.

Loc.: Central Pacific coast of Mexico.

Travel: By airplane to Puerto Vallarta, where volunteers are met, or bus from Puerto Vallarta, to San Francisco or San Pancho.

Dur: 1 month, although 2 would be ideal.

Per.: July 1 to November 15.

L. term: Possible for outstanding volunteers.

Age: Min. 18.

Qualif.: No special skills are required to work within the marine turtle program, although volunteers should be willing to work 6 to 7 nights a week in occasional heavy rain, and operate a Wolkswagen dune buggy over rough, muddy roads. Youth education instructors must speak Spanish. Volunteers must be enthusiastic, able to work in a team and to deal with the public.

Work: Collect marine turtle nests between 9am–6pm; maintain records on relocation and/or collection of nests, temperatures, hatchlings released and nest cleaning; teaching and lectures.

Lang.: English. Spanish useful for turtle work (required for teaching).

Accom.: Volunteers rent their own, from a shared room to a house.

Cost: There are no fees. Volunteers pay for accomodation and living expenses. Room US$80-100/month, or single home US$200-300/month. Food: approx. US$165/month.

Applic.: By e-mail only on www.project-tortuga.org/volunteers.htm

MONK SEAL PROJECT, Turkey

The Ecovolunteer Network
Meyersweg 29   7553 AX Hengelo   The Netherlands
Tel.: ++31 (74) 250 8250
Fax: ++31 (74) 250 6572
E-mail: info@ecovolunteer.org
www.ecovolunteer.org

Desc.: The Mediterranean monk seal is 1 of the 12 most endangered species in the world and needs immediate protection. In the Aegean Sea there are only 150–180 individuals left. This project was initiated in 1993 with help from WWF and AFAG, a Turkish nature conservation organisation.

Spp. Mediterranean monk seal (*Monachus monachus*).

Hab.: Mediterranean Sea.

Loc.: Foca, 80 km north of Izmir, Turkey.

Travel: Airplane to Izmir, then transfer to Foca.

Dur.: Min. 2 weeks.

Per.: Year round.

Age: Min. 18, max. 40.

Qualif.: Volunteers must speak English, be in good physical health, able to walk on difficult ground and swim well. Diving and boating experience, knowledge of biology and other languages is useful. Volunteers with birdwatching experience can contribute to the inventory of bird species.

Work: Volunteers assist biologists in surveys of caves, land observations, collecting data on animals, plants and weather conditions and help in public awareness activities (slide shows, T-shirt sales, daily talks on tour boats).

Lang.: English, knowledge of other languages is welcome.

Accom.: Small pension or campsite depending on the period.

Cost: EUR727 (approx. GB£ 480) for 2 weeks; EUR39 (approx. GB£25) for every additional day.

Agents: The Ecovolunteer Network at www.ecovolunteer.org.

Applic.: The Ecovolunteer Network (see Organisation list).

THE MONKEY SANCTUARY TRUST, England

Looe
Cornwall PL13 1NZ   UK
Tel./Fax: ++44 (1503) 262 532
E-mail: info@monkeysanctuary.org
www.monkeysanctuary.org

Desc.: The Monkey Sanctuary is home to a colony of woolly monkeys and rescued capuchins. It was founded in 1964 as a reaction against the pet trade in primates. The Sanctuary is open to the public during the summer and the main emphasis is to encourage an attitude of caring and respect toward primates and the environment. The Sanctuary gardens and meadows contain many native species of plants and animals.

Spp.: Woolly monkeys (*Lagothryx lagothricha*) and capuchins.

Hab.: N/A.

Loc.: Looe, Cornwall, UK.

Dur.: 2–4 weeks.

Per.: Year round.

L. term: Invitation to stay long term if the initial visit proves successful.

Age: Min. 18.

Qualif.: No specific skills required, although applicants should have an interest in the field and practical skills are always welcome.

Work: Maintaining and cleaning the enclosures, preparing food for the animals, providing information to the public.

Lang.: English.

Cost: A voluntary donation for room and board is requested. Volunteers must provide transportation to the Sanctuary.

Applic.: Write for further details (please enclose international postage coupon or stamped SAE for UK residents), then fill out an application form. Owing to the large number of applicants, please apply at least 6 months in advance.

MONTE ADONE WILDLIFE PROTECTION CENTRE, Italy

Via Brento, 9
40037 – Sasso Marconi (BO) Italy
Tel./Fax: ++39 (051) 847 600
E-mail: info@centrotutelafauna.org
www.centrotutelafauna.org

Desc.: A voluntary non-profit institution working in the rescue and rehabilitation of wild animals found injured. Emergency service is active 24hrs/day. The Centre also takes care of different exotic animals found abandoned or others that have been confiscated from Government authorities. Guided visits for schools and families also play an important socio-educational role in the Centre's activities.

Spp.: Local wildlife (ungulates, mammals, raptors) and exotic fauna (primates, felines, reptiles, etc.).

Hab.: Temperate mountain woodland.

Loc.: Monte Adone, Sasso Marconi, near Bologna, Italy.

Travel: From Bologna by train to Pianoro or to Sasso Marconi.

Dur.: Min. 20 days, after a 1-week trial period.

Per.: Year round, busiest months during the spring (April to June).

L. term: To be arranged with Centre's Director after intial period.

Age: Min. 20.

Qualif.: A true love for animals, attitude to live and work in community, willingness to work in close contact with animals, goodwill and spirit of adaptation, sense of responsibility.

Work: Work (8–10hrs/day) depends on the season. Feeding, cleaning and caring of animals. Day and night rescuing operations of wounded fauna. Maintenance and building activities. Volunteers will give a little help in the housekeeping.

Lang.: Italian, English is also spoken by centre coordinators.

Accom.: In shared rooms in the Centre.

Cost: A EUR80 (approx. GB£55) payment is required to cover food and insurance for the first trial week. The Centre will offer free full board for the remaining period. Travel not included.

Notes: Anti-tetanus and B hepatitis vaccinations are required.

MORAY FIRTH WILDLIFE CENTRE, Scotland

Research, Education & Conservation
WDCS - The Whale and Dolphin Conservation Society
Spey Bay, Moray, Scotland IV32 7PJ   UK
Tel.: ++44 (1343) 820 339 – Fax: ++44 (1343) 829 065
E-mail: wildlifecentre@wdcs.org
www.wdcs.org/wildlifecentre

Desc.:	Volunteering opportunities are extremely varied at WDCS's Wildlife Centre. Tasks include interpretation at the Wildlife Centre, helping with events, school visits, guiding wildlife-watching holidays & dolphin research (boat and shore-based).
Spp.:	Bottlenose dolphin (*Tursiops truncatus*).
Hab.:	North Sea coast.
Loc.:	Northeast Scotland.
Travel:	Airplane (or bus or train) to either Aberdeen or Inverness; bus or train to Fochabers. Spey Bay lies 5 km north of Fochabers.
Dur.:	Min. 1 month.
Per.:	Year round.
L. term:	Long term volunteering preferable; accomodation and living expenses preferrable.
Age:	Min. 18.
Qualif.:	Biology background preferred. Experience working with the public useful. Ability to work as part of a team.
Work:	Project officer: photo-ID work, update records, supervise volunteers, public interpretation. Support volunteers: assist project officer; shore monitoring and estuary wildlife surveys.
Lang.:	Excellent written and spoken English essential. Other languages (especially German) helpful.
Accom.:	House on-site at the Wildlife Centre.
Cost:	Longer term volunteers get accomodation and living expenses paid.
Applic.:	Send CV by email and give details of preferred length of stay.
Notes:	More opportunities during summer months (March-September).

MUNDA WANGA WILDLIFE PARK AND SANCTUARY, Zambia

P.O. BOX 38267, Kafue Rd,
Lusaka   Zambia
Tel.: ++260 (1) 278 456 – Fax: ++260 (1) 278 529
E-mail: environment@zamnet.zm
www.mundawanga.ccom

Desc.: Munda Wanga is a wildlife park and sanctuary. In the 1990s, due to the lack of funds and poor management, the estate, including the botanical gardens, was left to decay. Many animals died in their cages. In 1998 the estate was taken on by the new Munda Wanga Trust. Five years on and the wildlife park and sanctuary have been rehabilitated, the gardens reshaped and an education programme developed that addresses environmental education. The facility now contributes to conservation efforts, both *in-situ* and *ex-situ*.

Spp.: A variety of African birds and mammals, including wild dogs, lions, antelope and primates. Exotic species like tigers or bears.

Hab.: Wetland, woodland and grassland. A river runs through the area.

Loc.: Approx.15km outside of Lusaka, the capital of Zambia.

Travel: Airplane to Lusaka, volunteers are met at the airport.

Dur.: 3 weeks. Volunteers can stay for longer or shorter periods.

Per.: Year round.

L. term: Possible at reduced rate after approval of the project manager.

Age: Min. 18, no max.

Qualif.: No particular skills needed other than enthusiasm to work hard.

Work: Designing enrichment material, monitoring animals, giving tours, working with school groups, fundraising, hand-rearing orphaned animals, cleaning enclosures, giving out flyers, construction, etc. Work is 6 days/week, 8 hours/day.

Lang.: English.

Accom.: Basic dorm style room, with bathroom and cooking area.

Cost: US$750 (approx. GB£ 420) includes accommodation, trips to wildlife ranches, airport pick-up and a stipend for the food.

Applic.: Request via e-mail, fax or mail a standard form to fill in.

Notes: Volunteers' contributions help projects undertaken at the time.

NAUCRATES CONSERVATION PROJECT, Thailand

Naucrates 'Conservation Biology'
Via Corbetta 11
22063 Cantù (CO)   Italy
Tel.: ++39 (333) 430 6643 – Fax: ++39 (031) 716 315
E-mail: naucrates12@hotmail.com – naucrates12@tiscalinet.it
www.naucrates.org

Desc.:	The Conservation project focuses on sea turtles' nest protection, reef and mangrove forest survey, educational programming for the local community and on conservation awareness activities for visitors.
Spp.:	Olive ridley (*Lepidochelys olivacea*), leatherback (*Dermochelys coriacea*), green (*Chelonia mydas*) and hawksbill (*Eretmochelys imbricata*) turtles, reefs and mangroves.
Hab.:	Tropical coast.
Loc.:	Phra Thong Island, Phang-Nga province, Thailand.
Travel:	Airplane to Phuket Island or to Ranong (via Bangkok), then bus or car to Kura Buri pier and boat to Phra Thong Island.
Dur.:	Min. 10 days.
Per.:	December to April.
L. term:	Inquire with the organisation.
Age:	Min. 18.
Qualif.:	Volunteers must be prepared for long walks in hot and humid conditions on the beach. Research assistant position (unpaid) available based on academics and experience.
Work:	Beach patrols (day or night) for turtle nest monitoring. Visits to the local schools for the educational programme. Lectures on biology and conservation are given to tourists. Rescuing turtles caught in fishing nets.
Lang.:	English, Italian.
Accom.:	In huts on the beach at the Golden Buddha Beach resort.
Cost:	EUR 760 (approx. GB£520) in huts for 2 weeks including 3 meals per day. Travel expenses and insurance not included.
Agents:	The Ecovolunteer Network (see organisation list).
Applic.:	Contact the organisation or the Ecovolunteer Network (www.ecovolunteer.org) for an application form.

NOAH'S ARK, Greece

Crete-wide Animal Welfare Organisation Noah's Ark
Giamboudaki 30, GR 73134 Chania, Crete   Greece
opp. Supporters' Association Noah's Ark (reg.char.) Germany
Neritzer Weg 6, D 23867 Sulfeld
E-mail: rschmid@archenoah-kreta.com
www.archenoah-kreta.com

Desc.: Noah's Ark is the name of the first animal shelter on Crete, as well as the supporters' association in Germany and the Crete-wide animal welfare organisation, operating on donations and small foreign grants only. The project is aimed at rescuing, treating, caring for and re-homing animals, as well as information and education programs for the locals and island-wide castration actions.

Spp.: Domestic cats and dogs as well as donkeys.

Hab.: Mediterranean.

Loc.: Western Crete, Greece.

Travel: Plane to Chania airport (20 minutes from the shelter), Heraklion (2 hours away) or Athens (then night boat to Chania).

Dur.: 2 weeks to 1 year.

Per.: Year round.

L. term: Long-term encouraged, inquire with organisation.

Age: Min.16, max. 60.

Qualif: Volunteers should love animals and be strong enough to handle the sight of animal cruelty, starvation, illness.

Work: Nursing cleaning, feeding, diet control, treating small animals under supervision.

Lang.: English, German, Greek.

Accom.: Local accommodation at reasonable rates.

Cost: Volunteers pay for accommodation. Noah's Ark will assist in obtaining accommodation and local transportation.

Agents: Contact Ms. Regina Schmid at: rschmid@archenoah-kreta.com.

Applic.: No official form needed, send letter of inquiry.

Notes: High summer is very hot; winter months are wet and muddy.

THE OCEANIA RESEARCH PROJECT

The Oceania Project
P.O. Box 646
Byron Bay NSW 2481 Australia
Tel.: ++61 (2) 668 58128 – Fax: ++61 (2) 9225 9176
E-mail: expedition@oceania.org.au
www.oceania.org.au

Desc.: The Oceania Project is a non-profit research and education organisation dedicated to raising awareness of Cetacea and the Ocean Environment through research and education. The Oceania Project is in the twelfth year of a long-term study of the abundance, distribution and behaviour of humpback whales in the Whale Management & Monitoring Area of the Hervey Bay Marine Park, off the northeast coast of Queensland, Australia. The study is being undertaken in conjunction with the Queensland Department of Environment & Heritage. The Hervey Bay research is conducted from a 12-metre power catamaran during 10 weeks of the annual humpback migration from August to October. Paying Eco-volunteers/Interns who join the expedition for a week at a time fund the research platforms. As well as participating in the on-board research programme, expedition participants are provided with in-depth interpretation and education programmes about cetaceans.

Spp.: Humpback whale (*Megaptera novaeangliae*), brydes tropical whale (*Balaenoptera edeni*), minke-piked whale (*Balaenoptera acutorostrata*), common dolphin (*Delphinus delphis*), bottlenose dolphin (*Tursiops truncatus*), Indo-pacific humpback dolphin (*Sousa chinensis*).

Hab.: Tropical coast/ocean bay/ancient sand island.

Loc.: Hervey Bay/Fraser Island, northeast coast of Queensland, Australia.

Travel: Airplane to Brisbane (capital of Queensland). The expedition departure point is Urangan Boat Harbour, Hervey Bay (approx. 400 km north of Brisbane, with access by car or daily bus, train or intrastate airline).

Dur.: 1–10 weeks, Sunday to Friday.

Per.: July to October.

L. term: Eco-Volunteers/Interns can join the expedition for a max. of up to 10 weeks.

Age: Min. 14.

Qualif.: No particular skills needed, previous field experience in marine mammal research useful. Common sense, a committed interest in whales and dolphins and willingness to work long hours as part of a small, highly motivated and focused field research team.

Work: Assist with humpback observations and with collection and collation of spatial and environmental data. General duties associated with daily operation aboard the vessel.

Lang.: English.

Accom.: Ship-style bunk. The present expedition vessel is a 12-metre catamaran. Information about what to bring, etc., will be provided to applicants.

Cost: Eco-Volunteers/Interns from 14–18 years of age pay AUS$950/week (approx. US$695). Graduate or post graduate students or teaching staff from an eligible educational institution are eligible to join as interns and pay AUS$1050/week (approx. US$842), otherwise AUS$1,350/week (approx. US$988). Cost includes living aboard the expedition vessel for 5 nights/6 days, all meals, participation in field research and on-board interpretation and education programmes. Transportation or accommodation to and from the departure point or personal insurance is not included.

Applic.: Application form is available online. See webiste for application and payment details.

Notes: The research programme is conducted and supervised by the expedition leaders, Trish and Wally Franklin. They are PhD Candidates at the Southern Cross University Whale Research Centre, see: http://www.scu.edu.au/research/whales/aboutus.html. Students or under-graduates may be able to receive credit towards marine science or environmental studies courses.

OKAVANGO DELTA LION MONITORING PROJECT, Botswana

Tau Consultants, Private Bag 83, Maun Botswana
E-mail: tau@dynabyte.bw
    2tau@bushmail.net (text only, no attachments or pictures)
www.taucon.com

Desc.: Tau Consultants have been carrying out baseline survey data on the Okavango Delta lions since 1997. Much of the published data to date has come from the Serengeti Lion Population and the Okavango Delta lions are different in their behaviour and physiology. This is the fourth largest remaining lion population in Africa and is one of only 5 large populations left.

Spp.: Lion (*Panthera leo*).

Hab.: Seasonally flooded delta.

Loc.: South-West Okavango Delta south of Moremi Game Reserve.

Travel: Meeting in Maun for flight or drive into camp. Arrival in Maun must be synchronised with camp movements.

Dur.: 1 month to 3 months.

Per.: Year round except December.

L. term: Inquire with the organisation.

Age: Min. 20.

Qualif.: Graduates preferred. The camp is very remote and consists of a small team, volunteers must be responsible, hard working, and dependable. Field-work involves off-road driving.

Work: Radio tracking lions, lion identification, social and behavioural observations, herbivore, vegetation and flood monitoring. Some maintenance work on camp or vehicles may be required along with computer and administrative work.

Lang.: English.

Accom.: Dome tent, shared bathroom. Need own sleeping bag.

Cost: US$1,500 for 1 month, US$2,500 for 2 months, $1,000 per month if 3 months or longer.

Applic.: Send application to both email addresses to ensure reception.

Notes: Max 2 volunteers at a time. 100% of fees goes directly into project. Volunteers need to arrange insurance and visas.

OPERATION OSPREY, Scotland

RSPB – The Royal Society for the Protection of Birds
The Lodge, Sandy
Bedfordshire SG19 2DL UK
Tel.: ++44 (1767) 680 551
Fax: ++44 (1767) 692 365
www.rspb.org.uk

Desc.: Within its Residential Volunteering Scheme, RSPB (see Organisation list) offers special projects, such as Operation Osprey, an opportunity for bird protection and conservation work. Ospreys are an endangered species in Scotland.

Spp.: Osprey (*Pandion haliaetus*).

Hab.: Scots pine woodland, lochs, moors.

Loc.: Abernethy Forest Reserve, Loch Garten, Scotland.

Travel: Travel details are given to selected applicants.

Dur.: Min. 1 week (Saturday to Saturday); max. 2 weeks.

Per.: Late March to early September.

Age: Min. 18.

Qualif.: Good spoken English and willingness to be part of a team.

Work: Osprey nest site protection and surveillance, information to visiting public.

Lang.: English.

Cost: Accommodation is provided free. Food and travel expenses are not included.

L. term: N/A.

Accom.: In chalets.

Applic.: Information and application form is available on www.rspb.org.uk/volunteering or write to the Volunteer Unit at the above address for further details and for an application form. Enclose a self-addressed label with 2 first class and one first class stamp (in the UK) or 2 International Postage Coupons.

ORANGUTAN FOUNDATION, Indonesia

7 Kent Terrace, London, NW1 4RP   UK
Tel.: ++44 (20) 7724 2912
Fax: ++44 (20) 7706 2613
E-mail: info@orangutan.org.uk
www.orangutan.org.uk

Desc.: The Orangutan Foundation is a charity that actively conserves the orangutan and its rainforest habitat in Indonesia and Malaysia. The Foundation conducts long-term research on the ecology of orangutans and operates a rehabilitation programme that returns orangutans to a life in the wild. The Foundation operates a volunteer programme in the Tanjung Puting National Park, Kalimantan.

Spp.: BorneanOrangutan (*Pongo pygmaeus*).

Hab.: Tropical rainforest.

Loc.: Tanjung Puting National Park, Kalimantan, Indonesian Borneo.

Travel: By airplane to Jakarta, train or flights to Semerang. From Semerang flight or boat to Pangkalan Bun.

Dur: Min. 6 weeks.

Per.: 3 teams of 12 people, from May to September.

L. term: Max. 6 weeks.

Age: Min. 18.

Qualif.: Previous experience in the field is desirable but not necessary. Good health, team spirit and a willingness to do manual work.

Work: The main area of the programme is Camp Leakey, the historical research site of Dr. Biruté Galdikas. Help is needed to continue the ongoing renovation and expansion project. Proposed activities include repairing existing structures, increasing boundaries of the study area, trail cutting, installing walkways and signs and developing facilities for conservation education.

Lang.: English or Indonesian.

Accom.: Very basic. In huts on the floor or hammocks in the forest.

Cost: GB£500 (approx. EUR 725) for food and accommodation, volunteers are responsible for their own travel arrangements.

Applic.: Contact the UK office for an application form.

ORANGUTAN HEALTH, Indonesia

Dr Ivona Foitova – Principal Investigator
c/o Leuser International Foundation
Jl. Bioteknologi, Kampus USU, Medan 20155 Indonesia
E-mail: orangutanhealth@nusa.net.id
www.orangutan-health.org

Desc.: This unique & fascinating project is investigating the special behaviours and ecological conditions necessary for the maintenance of health in wild orangutans. As part of a 17-day volunteer team, volunteers perform various research tasks necessary for the project's work. At the same time they have the chance to visit and experience a living, breathing rainforest in one of the most beautiful areas of the world.

Spp.: Orangutan (*Pongo pygmaeus*).

Hab: Tropical rainforest.

Loc.: Bukit Lawang, Sumatra, Indonesia.

Travel: By airplane to Medan via Jakarta, Kuala Lumpur, Singapore or Penang. Volunteers are met at the airport.

Dur.: Min. 17 days.

Per.: Year round.

L.term: Possible, inquire with the organisation.

Age: Min. 18.

Qualif.: A good level of fitness – able to hike 10km during 1 day in difficult terrain, without health problems, allergies or phobias. Volunteers are required to be patient and attentive.

Work: Work will be split between 3–4 day treks in the jungle, and computer/lab work at base camp. This will be rotated and will depend on people's strength in certain areas.

Lang: English.

Accom.: Accommodation is very basic: a bed, a mosquito net and a basic Asian toilet. No shower, but a supply of water to wash.

Cost: US$1,169 (approx. GB£650) excluding travel.

Applic.: Request an application form via e-mail.

Notes: There is no physical contact whatsoever with orangutans. A medical certificate of good health is mandatory.

ORKNEY SEAL RESCUE CENTRE, Scotland

Dyke End, South Ronaldsay
Orkney, KW17 2TJ, Scotland   UK
Tel./Fax: ++44 (1856) 831 463
E-mail: selkiesave@aol.com

Desc.: The care of 50 seal pups every year with a variety of problems. Most of the seals that come into the centre have been separated from their mothers. Others have been injured by discarded fishing nets or have been injured by gun shot.

Spp.: Marine mammals: grey seals (*Halichoerus grypus*); common and harbour seals (*Phoca vitulina*).

Hab.: Marine/coastal.

Loc.: Northern Islands of Scotland.

Travel: By airplane to London, Glasgow, Edinburgh, Inverness or Aberdeen; bus or train by sea from Thurso or from Aberdeen to Orkney.

Dur.: Min. 4 weeks.

Per.: Year round except April and May.

L. term: Possible after initial period and approval.

Age: Min. 18.

Qualif.: A strong motivation to work with animals.

Work: Cleaning, food preparation and feeding the seals at the centre; possible involvement in rescue and release of seals; participate in cooking (vegetarian) and house cleaning.

Lang.: English.

Accom.: Shared in a house with 2 attic bedrooms with bathroom.

Cost: GB£15–20/week (approx.EUR/US$22–30) for the cost of food.

Appilc.: Send an application form to Orkney Seal Rescue (the Green Volunteers application form is accepted).

Notes: The work at Orkney Seal Rescue can at times be wet and cold with long hours. Once volunteer positions for the year are full, applications are no longer considered; please do not send reminders. Positions are filled very rapidly. As an alternative see Irish Seal Sanctuary (www.irishsealsanctuary.ie).

PANDRILLUS FOUNDATION, Nigeria

Drill Rehabilitation & Breeding Center
H.E.P.O. Box 826 Calabar   Nigeria
Tel.: ++234 (87) 234 310
E-mail: drill@hyperia.com - stephanie@pandrillus.org
(many websites describe the project: type"Pandrillus" in a search engine;
see http://limbewildlife.org for Limbe Wildlife Centre, see Notes)

Desc.: The centre (from 1991) recovers captive drill orphans and rehabs them into breeding groups: 160 drills born to date. The project is closely involved in conservation of Afi Mountain Wildlife Sanctuary where wild drills, gorillas and chimps survive and where drills will be released. The project also maintains 25 non-breeding chimpanzees. Animals are kept in enclosures of natural habitat of up to 9 ha. Pandrillus also runs the Limbe Wildlife Center (Cameroon) where volunteers may apply..

Spp.: Drill (*Mandrillus leucophaeus*), chimpanzee (*Pan troglodytes*).

Hab.: Tropical rainforest.

Loc.: Southeast Nigeria.

Travel: Flight to Lagos then to Calabar.

Dur.: Min. 1 year.

Per.: Year round.

L. term: Highly encouraged.

Age: Min. 25.

Qualif.: Mature persons with 1) animal, veterinary or medical experience/skills or practical skills (carpentry, electrical, etc.); 2) appropriate educational background; 3) developing country experience; 4) sincere interest in conservation; 5) good human relations ability ; 6) administrative or management experience.

Work: Staff management and training, animal management and record-keeping, administration, public relations, education, construction and maintenance. Versatility is a must.

Lang.: English.

Accom.: House at urban site, open-walled cabins at field site.

Cost: Room and board provided. Travel to project not provided.

Applic.: Send CV with references, a photograph and a letter of intentions. Interview with an appointed person will follow.

PIONEER MADAGASCAR

Azafady UK
Studio 7, 1a Beethoven Street, London W10 4LG UK
Tel.: ++44 (20) 8960 6629
Fax: ++44 (20) 8962 0126
E-mail: mark@azafady.org – info@azafady.org
www.madagascar.co.uk

Desc: Azafady is a registered UK and Madagascar-based NGO. Through Pioneer Madagascar, volunteers can experience working with a grass-roots organisation fighting the problems of extensive deforestation and extreme poverty on this unique island. The programme focuses on integrated conservation and development working closely with the Malagasy people.

Spp.: Primates, reptiles and birds, eg. brown collared lemur (*Eulemur fulvus collaris*), various botanical Spp.

Hab.: Littoral forest (tropical coastal forest), coastal zone.

Loc.: Southeast Madagascar.

Travel: Airplane to Antananarivo, then to Fort Dauphin.

Dur.: Project placements are 10 weeks.

Per.: Year round; schemes start in January, April, July and October.

L. term: Long-term stay as a coordinator or specialist can be arranged.

Age: Min. 18, no max.

Qualif.: No special skills needed; enthusiasm and sensitivity are a must; practical and research experience welcome.

Work: Work varies depending on the time of year, project programme and schedules of co-ordinators. Projects include counts of lemurs and birds in fragmented forest areas, conservation of loggerhead turtles, building facilities, pharmacies and schools.

Lang.: English or French; intensive course in Malagasy is given.

Accom.: Very basic under canvas, located near the rural village of Saint Luce; occasional use of other Azafady residences.

Cost: Successful applicants must cover live costs (flight, insurance, medical expenses, visa and equipment) and raise a minimum donation to the charity of GB £2,000 for UK applicants and GB£2500 (approx: EUR/US$ 3,800) for overseas applicants.

Applic.: Fill in forms available from the website.

PROJECTO JUBARTE DO CABO VERDE

Swiss Whale Society
Via Nolgio 3, CH–6900 Massagno Switzerland
Tel.: ++41 (91) 966 09 53
Fax: ++41 (91) 966 09 53
E-mail: jann@dial.eunet.ch
www.whales.ch

Desc.: The project's objective is to study the distribution and behaviour of Humpback whales around the Cabo Verde islands, and to identify the threats faced by the whales during their stay in the waters of the archipelago (fisheries, traffic, pollution, etc.).

Spp.: Humpback whale (*Megaptera novaeangliae*).

Hab.: Coastal waters and open ocean.

Loc.: Cabo Verde Islands, Atlantic Ocean.

Travel: Flight to island of Sal (international airport) and meet the ship or continue with domestic flight to another island where the ship may be located. Meeting point to be confirmed in advance.

Dur.: Min. 2 weeks.

Per.: March to May.

L. term: Max. length of stay is 2 months.

Age: Min.18.

Qualif.: No particular skills needed; photography welcome; relatively good physical condition to be able to live and work on a boat.

Work: Help in observation work; recording data on behaviour under supervision of scientists; photography.

Lang.: English, German, Italian (Portuguese is also spoken).

Accom.: On board a research ship.

Cost: About EUR1,600 (approx. GB£ 1,100) for 2 weeks on board the ship. Flight from Europe costs about EUR 700.

Agents: Travelchannel Ag., Haeldelstrasse 19, CH-8712 Staefa. Fax: ++41 1928 2031, e-mail: info@olimar.ch.

Applic.: Contact Beatrice Jann of the Swiss Whale Society at the address above or the agent.

PROVCA – PROGRAMA DE VOLUNTARIOS PARA LA CONSERVACION DEL AMBIENTE, Costa Rica-Panama

San José Avs. 10, calle 19 transversal, casa # 1020
P.O. Box 085–3007, Heredia   Costa Rica
Tel.: ++(506) 848 9428
Tel./Fax: ++(506) 221 8590
E-mail: provca@racsa.co.cr - mam271@racsa.co.cr

Desc.:	Provca works with Costa Rican National Parks developing environmental projects, and with Panama National Parks; it also carries on social projects in native Americans reserves.
Spp.:	Various species of flora and fauna of Costa Rica and Panama.
Hab.:	Tropical rainforest or cloudforest; tropical coast.
Loc.:	National parks of Costa Rica, National Parks of Panama and Indian reserves of Panama.
Travel:	Airplane to San José, then by bus to the National Parks.
Dur:	Min. 2 weeks.
Per.:	Year round.
L. term:	1–3 or more months depending on the project.
Age:	Min.18 for individual participants; min. 16 for groups accompanied by a group leader.
Qualif.:	Ability to work in occasional difficult conditions, understanding of rural environmental problems and preservation of natural resources and capacity to deal with the public.
Work:	Depends on the project; some activities are, for example, general maintenance of facilities, cleaning of beach, providing information to tourists or language classes to park personnel, assisting on different duties at turtles nesting sites, support on administrative duties, etc.
Lang.:	English, some Spanish knowledge helpful.
Accom.:	At the park facilities (volunteers often have to share rooms).
Cost:	US$14 per day to cover room and board in Costa Rica. Depending on project in Panama.
Applic.:	By e-mail or fax.
Notes:	Panama address: Ciudad de Panama, San Francisco, tel.: ++(507) 5973 656. E-mail: provca@cwpanama.net It is possible to take Spanish classes while volunteering.

PROYECTO CAMPANARIO, Costa Rica

Campanario Biological Reserve
Apdo. 263-1260 Escazu Costa Rica
Tel.: ++506 258 5778
Fax: ++506 256 0374
E-mail: campanario@racsa.co.cr
www.campanario.org

Desc.: Founded in 1990, Proyecto Campanario maintains a tropical rainforest biological reserve in southwest Costa Rica. Through tropical ecology courses and eco-tourism, funds are generated to keep the reserve in its natural state. In addition, the programme offers opportunities for eco-tourists, student groups (of all ages) and researchers to learn more about the biodiversity and ecology of the Osa Peninsula to then promote the cause of rainforest protection in their own communities.

Spp.: Rainforest and tropical coastal flora and fauna.

Hab.: Tropical rainforest; mangrove forest, coastal zone.

Loc.: Osa Peninsula, southwest Costa Rica (near Corcovado NP).

Travel: Flight to San Jose, bus to Palmar, then boat to Campanario.

Dur.: Min. 3 weeks.

Per.: Year round.

L.term: Possible with project leader's approval.

Qualif.: No particular skills are needed, only enthusiasm and a positive attitude. Every effort is made to utilize skills of volunteers. They should be able to swim, be able to work without supervision and be in good physical and emotional health.

Work: Variable; includes manual labour restoring trails, taking species inventories, building observation points, sometimes under hot or wet conditions.

Lang.: English, Spanish helpful but not essential.

Accom.: In a rustic field station (no hot water) or in a tent cabin close to the beach. Shared room or tent with at least 1 other volunteer.

Cost: Volunteers give a non-refundable US$25/day contribution for food, prior to arrival.

Applic.: Request application form via e-mail or fax.

Notes: A medical, accident and evacuation insurance is compulsory.

PROYECTO KARUMBÉ — TORTUGAS MARINAS DEL URUGUAY

Calle Juan Paullie 1198, Apto 101. Montevideo Uruguay.
Tel.: ++598 (2) 401 0101
Fax: ++598 (2) 401 0101
E-mail: maririos34@adinet.com.uy
www.karumbe.8k.com

Desc.: Proyecto Karumbé is part of an NGO devoted to the conservation of the sea turtles of Uruguay. The organization combines conservation and research activities in different areas such as environmental education, monitoring sea turtles feeding areas and bycatch in artisanal and industrial fishing fleets.

Spp.: Green (*Chelonia mydas*), Leatherback(*Dermochelys coriacea*) and Loggerhead (*Caretta caretta*) turtles.

Hab.: Coastline and shallow rocky oceanic areas close to the shore.

Loc.: Barra de Valizas/Cabo Polonio, South Eastern Uruguay.

Travel: Airplane to Montevideo or Ferry from Buenos Aires (Argentina) to Montevideo, where volunteers are met.

Dur.: Min. 15 days, max. 1 month.

Per.: Mid January to mid February.

Age: Min. 18.

Qualif.: No specific qualifications are required. Veterinary or biology studies, and good physical condition helpful but not necessary.

Work: 1.Sighting and capturing, with nets, juveniles of green turtle. 2.12 km walk, searching for stranded sea turtles. 3.Help researchers with necropsies of dead turtles. 4.Collecting data of the artisanal fishery carried out locally, from onboard or at port. 5.Involvement in talks and workshops for the community and tourists.6.Rehabilitation of sick and weak sea turtles. 7.Help in the field station duties such us cleaning and cooking

Lang.: Spanish, but staff also understands English.

Accom.: Shared room in a house or tent accommodation with indoor bathroom and shower as well as electricity and drinkable water.

Cost: Room, accommodation and simple meals are provided.

Applic.: Via e-mail with subject 'Volunteer Barra de Valizas'. In the text, include CV, photograph, letter of intentions and dates.

189

PRZEWALSKI HORSE REINTRODUCTION PROJECT, Mongolia

The Ecovolunteer Network
Meyersweg 29, 7553 AX Hengelo The Netherlands
Tel.: ++31 (74) 250 8250
Fax: ++31 (74) 250 6572
E-mail: info@ecovolunteer.org   www.ecovolunteer.org

Desc.: Fieldwork at the steppe in Mongolia, participating in the research on the released, reintroduced Przewalski horses. The goal is to establish a self sustaining viable population of this species that became extinct in the wild during the 20th century.

Spp.: Przewalski horse (Equus ferus).

Hab.: Mountain steppe.

Loc.: Hustai National Park, Mongolia.

Travel: Travel by plane or train to the Mongolian capital Ulaanbatar; meeting at the airport or train station.

Dur.: Min. 3 weeks.

Per.: March to November.

L. term: Inquire with the organisation.

Age.: Min. 18.

Qualif.: Good health.

Work: Monitoring and making behavioural observations of mares before, during and after birth; 2-year-olds before and during separation from the harem and new born foal observation of the behaviour of horses, their locations and their home-range; wildlife and vegetation research along with bird observation. Activities will mainly consist of taking long walks to reach the harems whenever necessary.

Lang.: English.

Accom.: In shared Mongolian tents in the steppe.

Cost: US$1,090 for 3 weeks; US$52 for every extra day.

Agents: The Ecovolunteer Network at www.ecovolunteer.org.

Applic.: The Ecovolunteer Network (see Organisation list).

RE-AFORESTATION PROJECT, Ghana

Save the Earth Network
P. O. Box CT 3635, Cantonments, Accra Ghana
Tel.: ++233 (28) 203 006
E-mail: ebensten@yahoo.com – eben_sten@hotmail.com

Desc.: The purpose of the project is to plant trees on 50 acres of land, to restore a tropical rainforest destroyed by excessive lumbering for timber, firewood and charcoal production. An additional objective of the project is to protect the watershed and to restore the habitat for wildlife and birds through nursing and planting of Leucaena trees, 'the miracle tree'.

Spp.: Leucaena and Mahogany trees.

Hab.: Tropical rainforest, villages and farms.

Loc.: Eastern region of Ghana, West Africa.

Travel: Plane to Accra, bus to Adawso.

Dur.: 1 week to 4 months.

Per.: Year round.

L. term: Volunteers can join for up to 4 months, with project leader's approval, after the regular volunteer period.

Age: Min. 18, max. 60 or older if in good physical condition.

Qualif.: No particular skills needed.

Work: Volunteers work 4 days a week, 2 hours per day.

Lang.: English.

Accom.: In a house with water and electricity.

Cost: US$595/month. Room and board are included. Volunteers provide transportation to the project site.

Applic.: A standard form must be requested from the project to be completed and returned. There are no deadlines or membership requirements.

Notes: There are many small villages near the project area where volunteers can visit on their free time for cultural exchange.

REEF CHECK GLOBAL CORAL REEF MONITORING

P.O. Box 1057
17575 Pacific Coast Highway
Pacific Palisades, California 90272–1057 USA
Tel.: ++1 (310) 230 2371 – Fax: ++1 (310) 230 2376
E-mail: rcinfo@reefcheck.org
www.ReefCheck.org

Desc.: Reef Check is an international programme working with communities, governments and businesses to scientifically monitor, restore and maintain coral reef health. Reef Check objectives are to: educate the public about the coral reef crisis; to create a global network of volunteer teams trained in Reef Check's scientific methods who regularly monitor and report on reef health; to facilitate collaboration that produces ecologically sound and economically sustainable solutions; and to stimulate local community action to protect remaining pristine reefs and rehabilitate damaged reefs worldwide.

Spp.: Coral reef organisms, include fish, invertebrates and coral.

Hab.: Tropical and subtropical coral reefs.

Loc.: Volunteers are needed in all coral reef countries.

Travel: Travel arrangements are the responsibility of the participant.

Dur.: Min.1 week.

Per.: Year round.

L. term: To be arranged with Headquarters.

Age: Min. 18

Qualif.: Participants must be confident swimmers and comfortable with snorkeling for long periods of time. SCUBA may be used at some locations. Non-divers help organizing Reef Check activities, sponsorship, training sessions, etc.

Work: Volunteers will be trained in RC methods and carry out coral reef surveys in water no deeper than 10m.

Lang.: Language used in country of choice.

Accom.: Accommodations vary with location.

Cost: Cost vary with location.

Applic.: See website or contact e-mail address above for information.

RE-HYDRATION OF THE EARTH, Kenya

Westerveld Conservation Trust
Flevolaan 34, 1399 HG Muiderberg The Netherlands
Tel.: ++31 (294) 261 457
Fax: ++31 (294) 262 080
E-mail: mg.vanwesterop@ncd.nl
www.westerveld.nu

Desc.: Re-hydration and water conservation project. Recreation of water catchments and rehabilitation of sunken water table.

Spp.: Various East African Savannah species.

Hab.: Semi-arid area in sub-saharan Africa; bush country.

Loc.: Bufferzones of national parks, among others Tsavo and Amboseli National Park, Kenya and Manyara N.P., Tanzania.

Travel: By air to Nairobi, Kenya or other airport near project location. Meeting point will be discussed before travel.

Dur.: Min. 2 weeks.

Per.: Year round.

L. term: Possible. Students and initiatives from engineers, biologists, etc. welcome. Volunteers must cover their stay.

Age: Min. 18.

Qualif.: Good health and physical condition. Willing to work in the field for long hours with hot temperatures.

Work: Assist staff of Westerveld Safari and rangers of Kenya Wildlife Service with the construction of water catchments in the Tsavo and Amboseli Region.

Lang.: English.

Accom.: Simple camps or lodges nearby project location.

Cost: Volunteers pay for their own accomodation and meals. Estimated cost EUR 800 (approx. GB£550) for 2 weeks and EUR 315 (approx. GB£210) for every extra week. Transport to and from project and during fieldwork are included. Entry and camping fees for the National Parks included if the project is located within the national park boundaries. WCT membership, EUR 15/person, is required.

Applic: Westerveld Conservation Trust for information and booking.

Notes: Fieldwork dates at request. Individual insurance required.

RESERVA PACUARE, Costa Rica
Avenida 10 (entre calle 27 y29) N.2550
San José, Costa Rica
Tel.: ++ (506) 224 85 68
E-mail: fdezlaw@racsa.co.cr – reservapacuare@yahoo.com
www.reservapacuare.org

Desc.: Reserva Pacuare is a 800ha tropical rainforest area in Costa Rica owned by the NGO Endangered Wildlife Trust where conservation, education and research projects are carried out.

Spp.: Leatherback, green and hawksbill sea turtles, howler, whitefaced and spider monkeys, 211spp of birds, 17spp of amphibians, 70spp of butterflies, occasionally peccary, anteater, paca, jaguarundy. Crocodiles and caiman are often seen in the canals, iguanas and basiliscs near the cabins.

Hab.: Lowland rainforest, coastal and freshwater lagoons and canals

Loc.: Province of Limón, on the Caribbean Coast, South of the mouth of the Pacuare River, Costa Rica.

Travel: Airplane to San José, bus to Matina, taxi to the canal dock, where boat transportation will be provided to the Reserve.

Dur.: Min. 1 week.

Per.: Mid February to October.

L. term: There is no limit of time for long-term stays.

Age: Min. 18.

Qualif.: No qualifications needed, just good physical condition to be able to walk the soft sandy beach everyday.

Work: Assistance on all conservation and research projects carried out at the reserve. Walking the beach at night to monitor the turtles and nests, and during the day for nest excavations.

Lang.: Spanish and English are spoken by everyone.

Accom.: Cabins with shared bathrooms and showers.

Cost: US$120/115/110/100 for 1st, 2nd, 3rd and 4th week respectively; includes boat transportation, room and board.

Applic.: Via e-mail, preferred dates must be indicated.

Notes: Positions for long term Research Assistants are available. Independent research can be carried out.

RHINO RESCUE PROJECT, Swaziland

The Ecovolunteer Network
Meyersweg 29,   7553 AX Hengelo The Netherlands
Tel.: ++31 (74) 250 8250
Fax: ++31 (74) 250 6572
E-mail: info@ecovolunteer.org
www.ecovolunteer.org

Desc.: Hands-on participation in various activities such as the daily monitoring of endangered species, a regular check of the fence enclosing the Reserve, maintenance work and assist with anti-poaching activities.

Spp.: White rhinoceros (*Ceratotherium simum*), black rhinoceros (*Diceros bicornis*); many other species such as elephants, buffaloes, antelopes, crocodiles, hyppopotamus, zebra, giraffes, monkeys, leopards, etc, can be observed.

Hab.: African savannah.

Loc.: Swaziland, Africa.

Travel: Airplane to Mbabane; a visa and a passport valid for at least 6 months after leaving Swaziland are necessary.

Dur.: Min. 2, max. 5 weeks.

Per.: Year round.

L. term: Max. 5 weeks.

Age: Min. 18.

Qualif.: Volunteers must be able to walk long distances and tolerate heat. Some knowledge of wildlife and birds is helpful.

Work: Participation in daily monitoring of endangered species, nightly detecting of poaching activities from watchtowers, animal surveys, maintenance work. Most working days start before sunrise. Cooking and cleaning tasks are rotated.

Lang.: English.

Cost: 2 weeks US$1200; 3rd week US$257; 4th week US$157, 5th week free. Flights, visa, local taxes and insurance not included.

Accom.: Simple huts or tents close to the working area. Overnight camping is very primitive with cold-water shower and pit latrine.

Applic.: The Ecovolunteer Network (see Organisation list).

Notes: Volunteers can visit nearby parks. Malaria treatment required.

RIVER OTTER PROJECT, Brazil

The Ecovolunteer Network
Meyersweg 29   7553 AX Hengelo The Netherlands
Tel.: ++31 (74) 250 8250 – Fax: ++31 (74) 250 6572
E-mail: info@ecovolunteer.org
www.ecovolunteer.org

Desc.: Hands-on participation in biological field research on South American otters on an attractive island in southern Brazil. Most of the work consists in fieldwork, but also some laboratory analysis is involved.

Spp.: American river otter (*Lutra longicaudis*).

Hab.: Streams and lakes, estuaries, coastal lagoons, mangroves.

Loc.: Piri Lake, Island of Santa Catarina, Atlantic Ocean, about 1,000 km south of Rio, Brazil.

Travel: Flight to Florianopolis, Santa Catarina State.

Dur.: Min. 1 week.

Per.: Year round.

L.term: Long-term encouraged; price decreases for longer stays.

Age: Min. 18.

Qualif.: Good health and physical condition. Willing to work in the field for long periods under varying weather conditions. Able to walk for long periods and spend evenings in the forest at wildlife observation posts.

Work: Activities vary and include analysis of the otter's frequency at the shelters, monitoring of nests, ethological studies and food habits. Most of volunteers' work is in the field, but also some laboratory analysis is involved. Work involves treks through the Atlantic forest, dunes, use of canoes and kayaks and nocturnal observations. Approx. 10 hours/day.

Lang.: English, Portuguese, Spanish.

Accom.: Research bases have toilets and hot water; 2 meals per day.

Cost: US$364, 318, 273, 227, for first, second, third and every extra week respectively or US$27,50 per day for long-term participation.

Applic.: The Ecovolunteer Network (see Organisation list).

THE SAN WILD WILDLIFE TRUST, South Africa

PO Box 418
Letsitele, 0885 South Africa
Tel.:: ++27 (15) 318 7900 Fax: ++27 (15) 318 7900
Mob.: ++27 (83) 459 4913
E-mail: sanwild@pixie.co.za
www.sanwild.org – www.afritrust.com

Desc.:	SanWild is an NGO devoted to the rehabilitation of animals and release into it's own reserve. Often animals have been rescued from malpractices like the canned hunting industry.
Spp.:	African wild dog, lion, white rhino, cheetah, impala, kudu, blue wildebeest, Burchell's zebra, eland, brown hyena, waterbuck, red hartebeest, giraffe, common reedbuck, mountain reedbuck, common duiker, steenbok, nyala, bushbuck, klipspringer, baboons, vervet monkey, warthog, bush pig, pangolin, aardvark, caracal, serval, genet, mongoose, civet, aardwolf, and various birds of prey.
Hab.:	Mixed broadleaf woodland/thornveld type bush, riverine forest and open grasslands, alternating flat plains, hills and ridges.
Loc.:	16km south of Gravelotte, between Tzaneen and Phalaborwa.
Travel:	Flight to Johannesburg, then flight to Phalaborwa or by bus to Tzaneen. Transportation from Airport or Bus-station provided.
Dur.:	Min. 1 week.
Per.:	Year round.
L. term:	There is no limit of time for long-term stays.
Age:	Min. 20
Qualif.:	Good physical condition.
Work:	Feeding the animals, cleaning enclosures, maintenance.
Lang.:	English.
Accom.:	Shared dome-tents in a bush-camp with all daily living facilities.
Cost:	US$500/week. Occasionally there are special offers on the website. Includes accommodation, meals and soft-drinks, 3 lectures /week, e-mail access, 2 trips to Tzaneen or Phalaborwa, daily game drive or bush-walks, airport pick-up.
Applic.:	Via e-mail with the subject heading: 'Volunteer program'.
Notes:	Health insurance and anti-malarial tablets mandatory.

SANTA MARTHA RESCUE CENTERS, Ecuador

Santa Martha, Tambillo, near Quito, Ecuador
Tel.: ++ 593 (2) 317 188
E-mail: santamartha@mail.com
www.santamartharescue.org

Desc.: Santa Martha is a volunteer supported NGO devoted to the rescuing of animals from unhealthy and illegal situations, rehabilitating and restoring them to their natural habitat.

Spp.: The rescue centers take every animal possible that the authorities confiscate, monkeys, jaguars, pumas, lions, ocelots, parrots, macaws, and a variety of other South American species .

Hab.: Hilly dairy farmland, rainforest.

Loc.: In the hills above Tambillo; in rainforest near Mera.

Travel: Airplane to Quito, then bus to Tambillo then taxi to the center.

Dur.: Min. 1 month.

Per.: Year round.

L. term: There is no limit of time for long-term stays.

Age: Min. 18.

Qualif.: No special qualifications. Enthusiastic, hard-working people with a strong motivation to help and care for animals

Work: Feeding, cleaning and repairing enclosures, helping to build new enclosures and improving existing facilities to provide more natural environment for the animals.

Lang.: English or Spanish, with opportunities to learn Spanish

Accom.: Volunteers share a house with hot showers, laundry, stereo, TV and fully equipped kitchen.

Cost: An average volunteer spends about 310$ per month.

Applic.: Via e-mail with the subject heading: 'Volunteer programme". In the text, include CV, letter of intentions and possible dates.

Notes: Further detailed information can be found on the website.

SCOTTISH WHALE & DOLPHIN PROJECT, Scotland

The Hebridean Whale and Dolphin Trust, HWDT
28 Main Street, Tobermory
Isle of Mull, Argyll PA75 6NU Scotland UK
Tel. ++44 (1688) 302 620 – Fax: ++44 (1688) 302 728
E-mail: volunteerco-ordinator@hwdt.org – admin@hwdt.org
www.hwdt.org

Desc.: The Trust conducts educational and research projects on whales, dolphins and porpoises inhabiting the waters of western Scotland. Including boat-based projects.

Spp.: Cetaceans (whales, dolphins), seals, otters, basking sharks.

Hab.: Temperate sea and coast.

Loc.: Western Scotland.

Travel: Train or bus to Oban; ferry from Oban to Isle of Mull.

Dur.: Min. 1 month in the centre or 6 days for boat-based projects.

Per.: April to November.

L. term: Long-term positions possible for outstanding volunteers.

Age: Min. 18.

Qualif.: Tailored to projects e.g. Education experience for education projects; administration/marketing/fund-raising skills for centre projects; student/graduate in a biological science for research.

Work: Boat based projects involve visual and acoustic monitoring of marine mammals. Other projects involve research and education of marine mammals coupled with working in the discovery centre.

Lang.: English.

Accom.: Hostel or caravans, depending on volunteer budget. Trust staff will help with booking and arrangement.

Cost.: No cost for projects in the discovery centre. Volunteers pay for accommodation and food approx. GB£75-100/week (approx. EUR110-150). Boat-based research costs GB£585 (approx. EUR850) for 10 days.

Applic.: E-mail or phone for application form to be sent in with CV and cover letter. Phone interviews for short-listed applicants.

Notes: Volunteers must be enthusiastic, efficient, friendly, willing to work as part of a team and able to converse with the public.

SCOTTISH WILDLIFE RESCUE, Scotland

Hessilhead Wildlife Rescue Trust
Hessilhead, Gateside, Beith Ayrshire KA15 1HT Scotland UK
Tel.: ++44 (1505) 502 415
E-mail: info@hessilhead.org.uk
www.hessilhead.org.uk

Desc.: Rescue, repair, rehabilitate and release all native species of wild birds and mammals. Hand rearing, cleaning and feeding animals; maintenance and construction work and monitoring the casualties after release. Some groups of birds will be ringed, and hopefully some species will be radio-tracked.

Spp.: All Scottish wild birds and mammals.

Hab.: Urban, woodland, farmland, coast, moorland.

Loc.: West central Scotland.

Travel: The Centre is within easy travelling distance from Glasgow.

Dur.: Min. 2–3 weeks.

Per.: March to October.

L. term: Suitable volunteers may be able to stay for 6 months or more.

Age: Min. 18.

Qualif.: Ability to work as part of a team. Training will be given. Experience of radio tracking could be useful. Veterinary experience useful.

Work: Volunteers may help with all aspects of the Trust's work. This includes rescue, treatment, feeding, cleaning, preparing of birds and animals for release and post-release monitoring. Educational work with the public may be possible.

Lang.: English.

Accom.: Log cabins.

Cost: GB£10 per week for cabins. Food must be provided by the volunteer. Volunteers must arrange their own transport, though can be collected from Glasgow.

Applic.: Apply directly to HWRT with relevant details and a contact number or address. More information will be supplied.

SEA TURTLE CONSERVATION PROGRAM, Costa Rica

Asociación ANAI Apdo. 170–2070,
Sabanilla de Montes de Oca, San José   Costa Rica
Tel.: ++ (506) 224 3570/224 6090
Fax: ++ (506) 253 7524
E-mail: volunteers@racsa.co.cr – anaicr@racsa.co.cr
www.anaicr.org

Desc.: Asociación ANAI has over 15 years of experience working in the Caribbean coastline of Costa Rica, mainly in the region of Talamanca; one of the biologically richest areas of the planet with over 2% of the entire world's biodiversity. The Sea Turtle project was started in 1986 in Gandoca Beach and the success of that project has led to its expansion in year 2000 to cover Playa Negra. Before an unknown beach for sea turtles nesting, now the most important beach for the Hawksbill sea turtle, which is critically endangered worldwide.

Spp.: Seaturtles: Leatherback (*Dermochelys coriacea*), Hawksbill (*Eretmochelys imbricata*), and Green (*Chelonia Mydas*).

Hab.: Caribbean, tropical coast.

Loc.: Gandoca and Playa Negra Beaches, region of Talamanca, Caribbean coastline of Costa Rica.

Travel: Airplane to San Jose, then bus to Talamanca.

Dur.: Min. 1 week, max. 6 months.

Per.: Gandoca: March to July; Playa Negra: March to November.

L.Term.: Generic volunteers can stay for the entire nesting season. Professional volunteers typically come for 8–12 months.

Age: Min. 18.

Qualif.: ANAI has 2 kinds of volunteers: generic and professional. For generic volunteers no specific skills are required, but a strong motivation is a must. Ability to walk long hours at night and to withstand hot tropical temperatures. Professional volunteers have skills in fields such as economy, business administration, accounting, agriculture, and forest management work and in the process developing new skills and experiences.

Work: Generic volunteers help patrol the beach to protect the turtles, assist with the scientific monitoring of the species, guard nests and work with the hatchlings on their journey to the ocean. Professional volunteers will put their skills at the disposal of the organisation while helping in the tasks of generic volunteers.

Lang.: English, Spanish useful.

Accom.: In Gandoca with local families; in Playa Negra in the project accomodations.

Cost: There is a registration fee of US$30. Full room and board at Gandoca for volunteers range from US$7/day with own tent in camping area (food can be bought in the community) to US$30/day in private cabins. Family homestays for volunteers are US$15/day. Playa Negra volunteers pay US$12/day. Professional volunteers stay with staff at the ANAI facilities for US$10/day. Optional services include US$7/night lodging in ANAI office in San José upon arrival and US$30 airport pick-up.

Agents: Contact Asociación ANAI directly.

Applic.: Use on-line application form.

Notes: Gandoca Beach is in the Gandoca-Manzanillo Wildlife Refuge, a protected area that also includes mangrove, coral reefs and tropical rainforest. Playa Negra is within the Cahuita National Park. Volunteers at both projects sites will be able to explore the amazing marine and land wildlife of the region during their stay.

SEA TURTLE CONSERVATION PROJECTS, Costa Rica

PRETOMA - Sea Turtle Restoration Program of Costa Rica
Apdo. 1203-1100 Tibás
San José Costa Rica
Tel.: ++ (506) 241-5227   – Fax: ++ (506) 236-6017
E-mail: info@tortugamarina.org   – alexandergaos@tortugamarina.org
www.tortugamarina.org

Desc.: Each year olive ridley sea turtles nest on the beaches of Punta Banco and San Miguel, Costa Rica. Participants tag and collect data on nesting sea turtles and manage hatchery.

Spp.: Olive ridley sea turtle (*Lepidochelys olivacea*).

Hab.: Subtropical coast, rainforest jungle.

Loc.: Punta Banco and San Miguel small beach towns on Pacific coast of Costa Rica.

Travel: Flight to San José, then small plane orbus to site.

Dur.: From 2 weeks to 5 months.

Per.: July to December.

L. term: Long-term stays encouraged for getting to know project and local community.

Age: Min. 18 unless with parent permission.

Qualif.: No qualifications required. Volunteers should be in good health.

Work: Beach patrols for nesting turtles, transfer eggs to hatchery and optional participation in environmental education programmes in small local schools. Tag and measure adult and juvenile turtles, record data on hatching success and work with community and local biologists.

Lang.: Spanish helpful but not necessary.

Accom.: Station house and cabins operated by local community members, homestays.

Cost: US$500/2wks, US$800/4weeks,US$1,400/8 weeks. Longer stays available, prices include meals and lodging; transportation not included, travel assistance available.

Applic.: Contact Alexander Gaos, Ingrid Yanez at Pretoma.

Notes: Leasure activities include: jungle hikes, swimming, surfing, viewing abundant wildlife, Spanish practice, interaction with local community.

SEA TURTLE RESCUE CENTRE, Greece

Archelon – Sea Turtle Protection Society of Greece
Solomou 57, GR–104 32 Athens Greece
Tel./Fax: ++30 (210) 523 1342
E-mail: stps@archelon.gr
www.archelon.gr

Desc.:	Archelon is a non-profit organisation that conducts sea turtle conservation projects in Greece with the support of international volunteers. This project focuses on treatment and rehabilitation of injured, sick or weak turtles. Raising of public awareness is part of the activities, as well as expanding and improving the Sea Turtle Rescue Network in Greece.
Spp.:	Sea turtles.
Hab.:	Mediterranean coast.
Loc.:	Glyfada, about 20 km from Athens, Greece.
Travel:	Airplane to Athens. Inquire with the organisation for further instruction.
Dur.:	Min. 4 weeks.
Per.:	Year round.
L. term:	After the initial stay of 4 weeks.
Age:	Min. 18.
Qualif.:	A strong motivation.
Work:	Treatment of turtles, construction and maintenance work, painting, building, cleaning.
Lang.:	English. German and Greek are useful.
Accom:	At the Centre.
Cost:	Participation fee is approximately EUR100 (approx.GB£70). Volunteers must also pay for their own travel expenses and pay a min. of EUR9/day to cover food costs.
Applic.:	Prospective volunteers must fill out an application form.
Notes:	Participation fee includes a 1-year subscription to the newsletter *Turtle Tracks* as a Archelon supporter. Volunteers must carry international health insurance.

SEA TURTLE SUMMER FIELD WORK, Greece

Archelon – Sea Turtle Protection Society of Greece
Solomou 57, GR–104 32 Athens Greece
Tel./Fax: ++30 (210) 523 1342
E-mail: stps@archelon.gr
www.archelon.gr

Desc.: Archelon is a non-profit organisation that conducts sea turtle conservation projects in Greece with the support of international volunteers. Summer field work includes monitoring turtle nesting activities on the beaches, tagging nesting female turtles, protecting nests and raising public (visitor and local) awareness.

Spp.: Loggerhead sea turtle *(Caretta caretta)*.

Hab.: Mediterranean coast.

Loc.: Peloponnesus and the islands of Zakynthos and Crete, Greece.

Travel: Airplane to Athens, then bus or ferry boat.

Dur.: Min. 4 weeks.

Per.: May to October.

L. term: Volunteers applying for long-term are particularly welcome.

Age: Min. 18.

Qualif.: On site training provided. Tolerance for hot weather necessary.

Work: Based upon project requirements; include beach surveys, nest relocations, on-site nest protection as well as tagging nesting female turtles at night and raising public awareness through information stations, slide shows and beach patrolling.

Lang.: English. German, Italian, Dutch, Swedish and Greek useful.

Accom: Designated free campsites in tents. Basic sanitary and cooking facilities with limited water supply.

Cost: Participation fee is approximately EUR100 (approx.GB£70) plus a min. EUR9/day to cover food costs. Travel expenses paid by volunteer.

Applic.: Prospective volunteers must fill out an application form.

Notes: Participants receive a 1-year subscription to *Turtle Tracks* newsletter. International health insurance required. Groups (over 2 persons) not accepted for the same area.

SIBERIAN/EAST RUSSIAN VOLUNTEER PROGRAM

Building the Great Baikal Trail
Earth Island Institute
300 Broadway, Suite 28, San Francisco, California 94133 USA
Tel.: ++1 (415) 788 3666 – Fax: ++1 (415) 788 7324
E-mail: baikalwatch@earthisland.org
www.earthisland.org

Desc.: Earth Island and the Buryat Federation for Ecotourism and Mountain-climbing are building the Great Baikal Trail (GBT). The GBT will be the first system of hiking trails in Russia. It will lead some 1,600 km around Lake Baikal, through 3 national parks and 3 nature reserves. Again in 2005, multiple teams of volunteers will be organised to help build the trail. Teams will be international, with many local Siberians mixing with foreign participants. At least 5 project sites are planned. Examples would be: 1) in Zabaikalski National Park, where a 40-mile trail extension needs to be constructed from the foot of the Barguzin Mountains, along the shores of Baikal, to the wooden Siberian village of Ust-Barguzin; 2) in Baikalski Nature Reserve, where a 3-mile trail needs improving from the Reserve's visitor centre up into an old-growth forest and right up to the edge of a secluded waterfall; 3) along the southern shores of Baikal, where the Round Baikal Railroad is now being partially converted to a hiking and biking trail, leading through tunnels, gables, and many cliff-front passages that face Baikal. For more information on all the work sites for volunteers in the summer, please www.baikal.eastsib.ru/gbt/index_en.html

Spp.: Varies greatly: along the trail one might see Baikal seal, bears, eagles, sable or red deer. Divers may see many exotic species of fish and even coral.

Hab.: Lakeshore habitat, temperate mountain forests, wetlands and meadowlands.

Loc.: Lake Baikal region of south central Russia, near the Mongolian border.

Travel: Airplane to Irkutsk (via Moscow or the Far east) or the Trans-Siberian train, which takes 3 days of travel from Moscow.

Dur.:   2–4 weeks.

Per.:   Summer, from May to September.

L. term.: Opportunities for volunteering for several projects around Baikal are available for those who wish to stay on longer.

Age: Min.18.

Qualif.:   Helpful (but not required) trail-building experience. Good health and ability to do hard work are a must, since some heavy tools will be used, with training provided.

Work: Mostly physical, all outdoors, with opportunities to assist design and strategy teams as they choose the best sites and methods for building each trail.

Lang.:   Some knowledge of Russian would be helpful but not required. At least 1 English-language interpreter will be working on every team.

Accom.: Field work involves sleeping on boats or in tents; sleeping bag required.

Cost: Earth Island charges no fees for referring to the trail-building crews. However, the Federation is a non-profit group and will depend on international volunteers to pay for their own travel and food costs at Baikal. Training will be provided for volunteers at the site. Volunteers should also bear the cost of insurance and accommodations in Russia before and after the work period.

Agents: Prospective volunteers can communicate directly with Earth Island's staff (at baikalwatch@earthisland.org) or with the Russian partners at the national parks and nature reserves, through their colleagues at the Federation (ariadna_gbt@mail.ru) who are fluent in English.

Applic.:   No application form to fill out, simple inquiries will be sufficient.

Notes: There are many other volunteer and internship opportunities with Siberian environmental groups available, where knowledge of Russian is a requirement. For more information on these programmes, contact Earth Island Institute.

SKAFTAFELL NATIONAL PARK, Iceland

BTCV Conservation Centre
Balby Road, Doncaster DN4 0RH   UK
Tel.: ++44 (0) 1302 572 244
Fax: ++44 (0) 1302 310 167
E-mail: information@btcv.org.uk
www.btcv.org.uk

Desc.:	A dramatic landscape of green oasis surrounded by black sand, dark rivers and white glaciers. The park was opened to the public 20 years ago and erosion from tourists has become a serious problem. Constructing footpaths directs visitors to certain areas and helps conserve this unique landscape.
Spp.:	Subarctic species of flora and fauna (ptarmigan, arctic fox).
Hab.:	Glacier area, subarctic tundra.
Loc.:	Skaftafell National Park, southeast Iceland.
Travel:	Meet at Heathrow Airport or at Reykjavik BSI.
Dur.:	1 to 2 weeks.
Per.:	Summer.
L. term:	Contact organisation for details.
Age:	Min. 18.
Qualif.:	Strenuous work: a reasonable level of fitness required.
Work:	Constructing the construction of the footpath network.
Lang.:	English.
Cost:	GB£300-500. Flights approx. GB£600.
Agents:	Contact BTCV directly.
Applic.:	Deposit of GB£100 required.
Notes:	Conservation Holiday brochure available on request.

SOUTHWESTERN RESEARCH STATION, Arizona

American Museum of Natural History
P.O. Box 16553 Portal, Arizona 85632 USA
Tel./Fax:++1 (520) 558 2396
E-mail:swrs@amnh.org
http://research.amnh.org/swrs/

Desc.: The volunteer programme offers students in biological sciences outstanding opportunities to observe and become involved with scientists doing field research. Food and lodging are provided to volunteers in exchange for 24 hours per week of routine chores, with the remaining time available for research activities. The program is open to both undergraduate and graduate students; the latter may pursue their own research projects. The program is open to non-students as well, particularly in the spring and fall.

Spp.: Birds, reptiles, amphibians, mammals, insects, plants.

Hab: Five life-zones are encountered, from desert to alpine.

Loc.: Portal, southeastern Arizona.

Travel: Airplane to Tucson, then shuttle to Douglas (meeting place).

Dur.: Generally 6-week commitment, although shorter commitments are allowed in spring and fall.

Per.: Mid-March through the end of October.

L. term: Possible with the Station director's approval, after initial period.

Age: Min. 18, no max.

Qualif.: Some biological background is helpful, but not necessary.

Work: Volunteers work 24 hours on routine Station chores, e.g., housekeeping, grounds keeping, assisting in the kitchen/dining room, in exchange for room and board. Remaining time is available for research activities.

Lang.: English.

Accom.: Shared rooms are provided. All linens are provided. Meals are in a common dining room.

Cost: There is no cost to volunteers, other than transportation.

Applic.: Contact the Director, Dawn S. Wilson, Ph.D. An application must be submitted with letter(s) of reference.

SPANISH DOLPHINS, Spain

Earthwatch Institute (Europe)
267 Banbury Road
Oxford OX2 7HT   UK
Tel.: ++44 (1865) 318 831 – Fax: ++44 (1865) 311 383
E-mail: projects@earthwatch.org.uk
www.earthwatch.org/europe

Desc.: Monitoring the distribution and dynamics of cetaceans, in particular the declining common dolphin populations in the region, using photo-ID and bio-acoustic surveys. Research is carried out onboard the *Toftevaag*, an old 1910 Norwegian fishing boat converted into a research vessel.

Spp.: Common dolphin (*Delphinus delphis*), striped and bottlenose dolphins, long-finned pilot whales, Risso's dolphins.

Hab.: Temperate sea (Mediterranean Sea).

Loc.: Southeast Spain.

Travel: Airplane to Almería; bus or taxi to the ship (Almerimar).

Dur.: 10 days.

Per.: Throughout the year.

L. term: Volunteers can join the project for more than 1 period.

Age: Min. 16.

Qualif.: No particular skills needed.

Work: Volunteers share all duties with the research crew, including navigation, helping with the feeding of computer data, lookout watch, water sampling and analyses and bio-acoustic watch. Volunteers, depending on their experience, can participate in other activities such as inflatable-boat driving, photo-ID and underwater filming. During days of bad weather researchers will show slides, videos and publications.

Lang.: English.

Accom.: In bunks aboard research vessel.

Cost: About US$ 2,395 (GB£1,250) including food.

Agents: Contact the Earthwatch Institute (Europe) (see Organisation list).

Applic.: Apply on-line at www.earthwatch.org/europe/.

SUSTAINABLE LIVELIHOOD DEVELOPMENT ASSOCIATION, Sri Lanka

Aang Serian Peace Village
No 258, Moragoda Road, Mudungoda,
Gampaha Sri Lanka
Tel.: ++94 (33) 222 9003
E-mail: damilda@sltnet.lk

Desc.: An NGO involved in conserving and propagating lesser known traditional food plants beneficial to rural communities. The organisation is active in running native plant nursery and arboretum for the purpose of conservation and distribution of plants such as medicinal, wild fruits, yam and herbal drinks. Volunteers are able to involve in the nursery in the arboretum and at community level. Volunteers' posts are mainly community based and provide a unique opportunity to understand the local culture and values.

Spp.: Low impact sustainable crops.

Hab: Hilly tropical farmland.

Loc.: Western province of Sri Lanka.

Travel: Airplane to Colombo then bus to project area.

Dur.: Depending on the time availability of the volunteers.

Per.: Year round, but rainy season (Apr. -Jul./Oct. - Dec.) preferable.

L. term: Volunteers can stay as long as they want.

Age: Above 25 years. Elderly people are welcome.

Qualif.: No particular skills required; initiative, adaptability, compassion for nature and traditional knowledge are important requisites.

Work: Regeneration of traditional environmental values by practically implementing the programmes with hands on experience at family level in rural areas. Volunteers will learn from a mentor who will look after them during their stay.

Lang.: English.

Accom.: With local families: basic, but clean and comfortable.

Costs: Volunteers pay fro their living expenses US$ 10/day. They receive food and lodging and are free to make a contribution.

Applic.: Send a detailed CV to the above e-mail address.

Notes: Expect a genuine hospitality by a local Sri Lanka family.

SUSTAINABLE MANAGEMENT OF THE NATURAL RESOURCES OF SOUTHERN ECUADOR

Fundación Ecológica Mazán
Casilla Postal 01–01–844
República 1-62 y Huayna Cápac, Cuenca Ecuador
Tel.:/Fax.: ++593 (7) 868 989/ 869 718
E-mail: mazan@etapaonline.net.ec – marmosqs@yahoo.es

Desc.: Fundación Ecológica Mazán is working with communities to protect natural resources in the South of Ecuador. The Fundación's main activities include environmental education, reforestation, alternative agriculture, and diffusion and communication.

Spp.: The most common plant species are: *Chinchona spp., Podocarpus spp., Weinmannia descendens, Guarea spp, Cedrela rosei, Dendropanax spp., Clusia spp., Eugenia spp.*

Hab.: Andean forest (2,800–3,200m of altitude).

Loc.: Southern Ecuadorian Andes.

Travel: Airplane to Quito or Guayaquil, then bus to Cuenca and surrounding communities.

Dur.: No limits, depending on the experience and adaptability to the projects goals and personnel.

Per.: Year round.

L. term: Volunteers staying over 1 year are preferred. Short-term (1–3 months) work is mainly manual labour.

Age: Min. 21.

Qualif.: Various qualifications relevant to the activites listed below.

Work: Agroforestry, community training, environmental education, small business management, computer graphic design, maintenaince of web pages, and various other positions.

Lang.: All volunteers must have an intermediate Spanish level.

Accom: Apartment (or rented room). Room and board in Cuenca starts at US$300/mcnth.

Cost: No charge, however no services (room and board, transportation, etc.) are provided. The Foundation will help volunteers with logistic details and cultural assimilation.

Applic.: Interested volunteers may send a CV and cover letter.

TAITA DISCOVERY CENTRE, Kenya

The Savannah Group
P.O. Box 48019-00100, Nairobi Kenya
Tel.: ++254 (20) 312 137 – 222 075
Fax: ++254 (20) 311 361 – 216 528
E-mail: discoverycentre@originsafaris.info
www.originsafaris.info/community-volunteer.htm

Desc.: Tsavo is Kenya's largest wildreness area. It forms a vital migratory corridor across the Taru Desert for elephants and lions, between the Galana River in Tsavo East and south to the foothills of Mt. Kilimanjaro and Lake Jipe in Tsavo West. A purpose-built African Village of 16 traditional rondavels is dedicated to environmental education. Scientists, educators, local communities, students, volunteers and conservationists have access to work, study and explore.

Spp.: Large mammals.

Hab.: Savannah and acacia woodlands.

Loc.: Kenya. 30 km southeast of Voi at Bachuma, adjacent to southeast boundary of Tsavo East National Park.

Travel: 375 km, 7–8 hour drive via Voi from Nairobi on the Nairobi/Mombasa Trans African Highway. 100 km, 2 1/2 hour drive via Bachuma from Mombasa. Voi Railway Station has daily service between Nairobi and Mombasa. Flights available to Mombasa.

Dur.: Education programmes: 10 days. Volunteer work: 1–3 months.

Per.: Year round.

L. term: Possible. Inquire with the organisation.

Age: Min. 12; under 18 must be accompanied by an adult.

Qualif.: No particular skills required. However, the TDC has often opportunities for skilled volunteers, such as computer trainers, who can apply for a reduced fee. See website for details.

Work: Monitoring wild game movement; land management and community service projects.

Lang.: English.

Accom.: Dormitory and Chaperone rooms; full board..

Cost: Cost start at US$244/week. Park fees are payable directly.

Applic.: Download form from website.

TAMBOPATA RESIDENT NATURALIST PROGRAM, Peru

TReeS
P.O. Box 33153
London NW3 4DR UK
E-mail: safaris@amauta. rcp.net.pe
www.geocities.com/resident_naturalist/

Desc.: The Explorer's Inn, a tourist lodge and research station along the Tambopata River, offers a Resident Naturalist (RN) programme. RNs are volunteers at the lodge and help undertake numerous simple scientific-based tasks associated with an ongoing environmental monitoring programme. RNs also help train resident Peruvian guides in European languages and tropical natural history interpretation.

Spp.: Tropical rainforest species.

Hab.: Sub-tropical moist forest.

Loc.: Tambopata region, Peru southeast province of Madre de Dios.

Travel: Airplane to Lima, then to Puerto Maldonado, then river boat.

Dur.: Min. 4 months; 6 months preferred.

Per.: Year round. Applicants should arrive 1 week earlier for training.

L. term: RNs who wish to stay at least 6 months are preferred.

Age: Min. 22.

Qualif.: Graduates in natural sciences, biology or related disciplines.

Work: RN duties include: training to Peruvian staff in languages and natural history; recordings of weather data; maintaining wildlife sightings logs; monitoring giant otters, macaws and parrots; helping maintain the trail system; giving natural history lectures to arriving guests; writing monthly reports to RN Co-ordinator.

Lang.: English, priority to people with working knowledge of Spanish.

Accom.: Shared room in one of the lodge bungalows.

Cost:: Free room and board in return for undertaking RN activities. RNs pay for their travel to Puerto Maldonado.

Applic.: Contact TRees or Peruvian Safaris (via e-mail). UK applicants must send an A4 SAE. Applications can also be made online.

Notes: RNs may also undertake their own research during their stay with approval of RN Co-ordinator and Lodge Administrator.

TILOS PARK ASSOCIATION, Greece

Eristos
GR-85002 Tilos   Greece
Tel.: ++30 (22460) 44235
E-mail: tilos-park@otenet.gr
www.tilos-park.org

Desc.:   Tilos Park is an NGO devoted to the conservation of wildlife on the island of Tilos, Dodecanese, Greece. Tilos and its fourteen islets are classified as a Special Protection Area for the birds (SPA) and a Natura 2000 site under EU laws.

Spp.:   102 bird species have been recorded on Tilos with 27 of them classified in Annex 1 of the Bird Directive of the European Union as being under threat of extinction. 377 flora species and many reptile species have also been recorded..

Habitat: Coastal Mediterranean with 16 different types of biotopes. .

Loc.:   The Greek island of Tilos is located in the Dodecanese Archipelago of the Aegean Sea in the Eastern Mediterranean.

Travel: By airplane to Rhodes, bus to the Rhodes port, ferry or high speed hovercraft to the Livadia port of Tilos.

Dur.:   Minimum 1 month, subject to renewal every 3 months.

Per.:   Year round.

L.Term: There is no limit of time for long-term stays.

Age: Min. 18 with no upper age limit.

Qualif.:   Ability to work in a team, experience in mountain trekking can be useful, ornithological or veterinary experience and/or construction experience also helpful.

Work: Assistance with the ecological programmes, wildlife record keeping and observation, assistance on wildlife rehabilitation, facility and nature trail maintenance.

Lang.:   English and/or Greek.

Acccom.: Room in a house with indoor bathroom and shower.

Cost: EUR50 non-refundable, payable at registration.

Applic.:   Via e-mail with subject : 'Volunteer program'; applicants must send CV, letter of intentions and possible dates.

TOLGA BAT HOSPITAL, Australia

Tolga Bat Rescue & Research, Inc.
P.O. Box 685 Atherton 4883 Australia
Tel.: ++61 (7) 4091 2683
Fax: ++61 (7) 4091 2683
E-mail: jenny.maclean@iig.com.au
www.athertontablelands.com/bats

Desc.: Tolga Bat Hospital works with spectacled flying foxes and their habitat. It involves rescuing bats with tick paralysis or with problems from barbed wire, electrocution, shotguns, car accidents, etc. It also deals with education and research.

Spp.: Spectacled flying foxes, little red flying foxes (*Pteropus spp.*), several species of microbats.

Hab.: Tropical rainforest.

Loc.: Atherton, near Cairns, Australia.

Travel: Airplane to Cairns, then bus to Atherton.

Dur.: Minimum 4 weeks in busy season; 1 week for rest of year.

Per.: Year round but especially from October to January.

L. term: A stay of 2-3 months in the busy season is welcome.

Age: Min. 21 years, no max.

Qualif.: Ability to work well in teams and for long hours. Experience with bats not necessary, though experience with wildlife, veterinary or zoo work is a plus. Cooks and Vets are welcome.

Work: Extremely varied in busy season: it involves searching the colony daily for tick paralysis bat; hospital treatments; feeding babies; preparing food for adults and babies; cleaning; washing; cooking; weighing and measuring bats; computer work. In low season work in the vegetable and bush gardens.

Lang.: English necessary.

Accom.: Excellent tourist accommodation (Pteropus House). Single, twin or triple room available. Some form of 'soft volunteering' is possible where people can pay more and work less.

Cost: AUS$30-50 per day for food and accommodation.

Applic.: Application form online.

Notes: Vaccination for rabies is mandatory from October to January, although Bat Lyssavirus is rare in Spectacled flying foxes.

TREE PLANTERS FARM, Australia

Willing Workers on Organic Farms
2 Deserio Rd., Cedar Pocket, Gympie
Queensland   4570 Australia
Tel.: ++61 (7) 5486 6147
E-mail: forest@spiderweb.com.au
www.spiderweb.com.au/~forest

Desc.:	This privately owned organic working farm aims to establish rainforest tree species through rainforest regeneration and tree planting on former rainforest sites. Special interest on the farm is in rare rainforest tree species. Adjoining the state forest, the farm has large rainforest trees, walking trails, swimming holes, a creek, a camping cave, an isolated visitors hut and an small orchard of tropical fruit trees.
Spp.:	Rainforest trees.
Hab:	Rainforest.
Loc.:	Southeast Queensland.
Travel:	Train or bus to Gympie, about 160 km north of Brisbane,the meeting point.
Dur.:	2 nights to make sure that both parties are happy and after that by negotiation.
Per.:	Any time of the year.
L. term:	Longer terms can perhaps be arranged.
Age:	Min. 18.
Qualif.:	No specific qualifications required, just enthusiasm.
Work:	To assist with the establishment of the forests and perhaps some other farm jobs.
Lang:	Only English is spoken but the project manager will assist those that wish to improve their English.
Accom.:	Either in a spare bedroom in the house or a self-contained old converted dairy behind the house. Sleeping bags required.
Cost:	No cost. Work is done in return for keep.
Applic.:	Contact Bob Whitworth, owner, directly either by telephone or writing to the above address.

TREES FOR LIFE, Scotland

The Park, Findhorn Bay, Forres, IV36 3TZ, Scotland UK
Tel.: +44 (1309) 691 292
Fax: +44 (1309) 691 155
E-mail: trees@findhorn.org
www.treesforlife.org.uk

Desc.: Trees for Life is an ecological restoration charity, working with volunteers to restore the Caledonian Forest to the Highlands of Scotland.

Spp.: Tree planting weeks may include Scots pine, silver and downy birch, hazel, willow, alder and juniper. Fauna inlcudes red or roe deer, red squirrel, black grouse, many small birds and, occasionally, capercaille or pine marten.

Hab.: Caledonian Forest.

Loc.: Highlands of Scotland, west of Inverness.

Travel: Transport is provided from Inverness station.

Dur.: Min. 1 week, Saturday to Saturday.

Per.: March – June and September – October.

L. term: Long-term opportunites are possible.

Age: Minimum 18 years.

Qualif.: None required, although volunteers would need to be reasonably fit to take part.

Work: Tree planting, removing redundant fences, small scale stock fencing and tree tubing, wetland restoration, felling non-native trees and seed collection.

Lang.: English.

Accom.: Simple but comfortable, ranging from a renovated croft house to well appointed bunkhouse with all facilities.

Cost: GB£90 (GB£55 unwaged: ie students, unemployed, pensioners), includes accommodation, vegetarian food and transport from Inverness.

Applic.: Via e-mail or online.

Notes: The website has testimonials and experiecens form volunteers.

TURTLE CONSERVATION PROJECT (TCP), Sri Lanka

389, Godagama, Kosgoda Sri Lanka
Tel.: ++94 (777) 810 509/++94 (91) 226 4765
Fax: ++94 (38) 31 919
E-mail: turtle@sltnet.lk or tcpsl@sltnet.lk
Website: www.tcpsrilanka.org

Desc.: TCP is an NGO devoted to the conservation of marine & Coastal resources in Sri Lanka through Community participation.

Spp.: Green (*Chelonia mydas*), hawksbill (*Eretmochelys imbricata*), loggerhead (*Caretta caretta*), olive ridley (*Lepidochelys olivacea*) and leatherback turtles (*Dermochelys coriacea*).

Hab.: Tropical – marine and coastal.

Loc.: Marine and coastal areas of Sri Lanka.

Travel: Airplane to Colombo. Transportation to project site provided.

Dur.: Minimum 2 weeks, a minimum of 3 months is preferred.

Per.: Year round.

L. term: There is no limit of time for long-term stays.

Age: Min. 18.

Qualif.: No special skills required. A degree of stamina is required for the long shifts and occasional variations in climate. Volunteers must be enthusiastic, efficient, willing to work as part of a team and have a strong adaptability.

Work: Measuring turtles, beach patrols and mapping, conduct education programmes, environmental hotel presentations, English teaching in monasteries and schools, office administration, fundraising, IT development work, promotion of responsible nature tourism.

Lang.: English.

Accom.: The type of accommodation will vary and may include basic standards of living compared to Western standards.

Cost: US$750/1,200/2,250/3,300, for 2 weeks,1, 3 or 6 months respectively; includes accommodation, food, visa depending on the duration and any transport incurred through TCP work. A local family will provide all required meals.

Applic.: Contact the organization by e-mail for Application Form.

TURTLES OF TORTUGUERO, Costa Rica

Caribbean Conservation Corporation
4424 NW 13th Street, Suite A-1
Gainesville, Florida 32609 USA
Tel.: ++1 (352) 373 6441 – Fax: ++1 (352) 375 2449
E-mail: resprog@cccturtle.org – ccc@cccturtle.org
www.cccturtle.org

Desc.: Caribbean Conservation Corporation (CCC) has been tagging and monitoring the green turtles of Tortuguero for over 40 years. CCC is now in its third year gathering information also on leatherback turtles, which nest at Tortuguero Beach in impressive numbers.

Spp.: Green turtles (*Chelonia mydas*).

Hab.: Tropical coast.

Loc.: Tortuguero, Costa Rica.

Travel: Airplane to San José, Costa Rica.

Dur.: 1–2 weeks.

Per.: June to September.

L. term: Volunteers can stay longer than 2 weeks with prior approval.

Age: Min. 18.

Qualif.: Volunteers must be in good physical condition, be able to live in rustic setting and tolerate harsh weather.

Work: Volunteers assist researchers with tagging turtles and collecting data on size, tag numbers, nest location, etc.

Lang.: English. Spanish may be useful.

Accom.: Volunteers stay in local lodges at Tortuguero.

Cost: US$1,554 for 1 week; US$1,999 for 2 weeks. Cost includes 2 nights in San José, transfers to Tortuguero, all room, meals and training while at Tortuguero. A deposit is required. Flight to San José not included.

Agents: Holbrook Travel, tel. 1 (800) 451 7111 in North America.

Applic.: Contact Daniel Evans at CCC or agent to confirm dates.

VOLUNTEER PETEN, Guatemala

Parque Nueva Juventud
San Andres, Peten, Guatemala
Tel.: ++ (502) 5711 0040/5496 2276
E-mail: volunteerpeten@hotmail.com
www.volunteerpeten.com

Desc.: Volunteer Peten is a small independent non-profit organization dedicated to: 1) protect and manage a 150-acre ecological reserve in San Andres, Peten; 2) provide environmental education programs to all the schools in the San Andres area; 3) assist and develop small sustainable community projects; 4) provide quality volunteer opportunities for international travellers and students.

Spp.: Volunteer Peten has identified in the area over 160 bird species, 120 medicinal plant species, 95 tree species, and countless insect and reptile species in the park.

Hab.: Semi-humid, deciduous tropical rain forest.

Loc.: Northern Guatemala. San Andres, Peten.

Travel: San Andres is 30 min. by bus from Santa Elena\Flores.

Dur.: Volunteers can stay for one month to one year.

Per.: Year round.

L. term: Volunteers can stay for as long as they want.

Age: Min. 18.

Qualif.: No specific skills required.

Work: Volunteers work Monday though Friday from 8-12. Most work is outside and includes trail management, reforestation, gardening, minor construction, environmental education, and making arts and crafts.

Lang.: English, basic Spanish is highly desirable.

Accom.: With local families, which provide food and accommodations.

Cost: US$ 350/650/950 for 4, 8 or 12 weeks respectively; includes all food, housing (with local family), training, activities, and resources for projects. Spanish lessons available at US$3/hour.

Appl.: Via e-mail by confirming date of arrival at least one week in advance.

WAKULUZU: FRIENDS OF THE COLOBUS TRUST, Kenya
Colobus Trust
P.O. Box 5380, Diani Beach 80401 Kenya
Tel./fax: ++ (254) 40 320 3519
E-mail: info@colobustrust.org
www.colobustrust.org

Desc.: The Colobus Trust is committed to saving the rare Angolan colobus monkey and preserving the coastal forest habitat.

Spp.: Primates: Angolan colobus (*Colobus angolensis*), yellow baboons, sykes, vervets, bush babies.

Hab.: Tropical coral rag forest.

Loc.: Diani Beach, South Mombasa Coast, Kenya.

Travel: Airplane to Mombasa via Nairobi or direct.

Dur.: 3 months.

Per.: Year round.

L. term: Subject to prior approval.

Age: Min. 22.

Qualif.: Preferably undergraduates or graduates with experience in conservation, education, zoology, journalism, ecology or veterinary medicine.

Work: Ecological and primate surveys, primate rescue and rehabilitation, desnaring, public awareness, and various other conservation actions.

Lang.: English. German, Dutch, French, useful but not essential.

Accom.: Shared rooms and facilities in house overlooking Indian Ocean. Mosquito net required. Bed linen provided.

Cost: Accommodation costs EUR$400/month. Food costs approx. EUR$15/week.

Applic.: There is a standard form to be completed from the website www.colobustrust.org.

WHALE AND DOLPHIN PROJECT, La Gomera, Spain

M.E.E.R. e. V.
Bundesallee 123
12161 Berlin Germany
Tel./Fax: ++49 (30) 8507 8755
E-mail: praktika@m-e-e-r.de
www.m-e-e-r.de

Desc.: Observation of cetaceans. Scientific study aboard a small whale-watching vessel. Documentation of the behaviour of cetaceans and the kind of interaction between the vessel and the whales.

Spp.: Dolphins, whales, turtles, sharks.

Hab.: Coastal and offshore subtropical waters of the Atlantic Ocean.

Loc.: Southwest of La Gomera (Canary Islands, Spain).

Travel: Airplane to Tenerife, then ferry to La Gomera.

Dur.: 2 weeks.

Per.: Springtime, autumn.

L. term: Not possible.

Age: Min. 18.

Qualif.: No particular skills needed. Previous experience in marine mammal research, photography or ethology are welcome.

Work: Volunteers participate in the whale-watching trips, gather data and enter it in a database. A full training programme, written working materials, scientific supervision and a certificate of attendance are provided.

Lang.: English, German.

Accom.: Tourist apartments (2–4 persons).

Cost: EUR875 (approx. GB£ 600). The cost includes accommodation, a donation to MEER e.V., all whale-watching trips and all other expenses related to the project. Travel costs are not included.

Applic.: Apply directly through praktika@m-e-e-r.de.

Notes: During the 14 days stay there are 7 whale-watching trips (4-hours trips and one 8-hour day trip). A detailed brochure on the courses can be downloaded at www.m-e-e-r.de.

WHALE RESEARCH IN THE ST.LAWRENCE ESTUARY

Swiss Whale Society, Niederwielerstr. 12, CH-5524 Nesselnbach Switzerland

Centre Mériscope, 64 rue du Barrage, Longue-Rive, Québec Canada

Tel.:++1 (418) 231 2033 (summer)/++41 (76) 530 9192(winter)

Fax:++1 (418) 231 2033 (summer)/++41 (56) 426 0609(winter)

E-mail: info@whales.ch - dany@whales.ch www.whales.ch

Desc.: The 'Mériscope' is a small research base on the North shore of the St. Lawrence estuary. Research projects include bioacoustics of minke, finback and blue whales as well as habitat utilisation and social behaviour of baleen whales (by photo-identification). Work is conducted with 2 rigid-hulled inflatable boats; day trips typically last 5–6 hours. Slide talks and land excursions complete the courses in marine biology.

Spp.: Baleen whales: blue, finback, minke, and humpback whales. Toothed whales: belugas, sperm whale, harbour porpoises.

Hab.: Subarctic estuary (coastal waters).

Loc.: St. Lawrence estuary, about 350 km northeast of Québec City.

Travel: Flight to Montreal or Quebec, then bus to Portneuf-sur-Mer.

Dur.: Courses last 2 weeks, 7 courses per summer, 10 people max.

Per.: June to September.

L. term: Biologists may join for 2-4 months.

Age: Min.18 (younger participants only accompanied by parents).

Qualif.: No particular skills needed; reasonably good physical condition (living in prospector tents and working on board inflatable boats for several hours); photography and computer skills welcome.

Work: All work under supervision of staff biologists: data collection at sea; observation and identification of marine mammals; behavioural sampling; navigation (GPS); sound recording; photo-ID. Data entry and sound analysis in the lab.

Lang.: English, German or French.

Accom.: 3 ten places tents by the sea; cooking in a big kitchen tent.

Cost: US$1,160; students US$1,020. Includes food and accommodation, lectures and thermo suit.

Agents: Contact Dany Zbinden, project coordinator directly.

Applic.: A standard form is also available from the website.

WHALES AND DOLPHINS OFF CôTE D'AZUR, France

Swiss Cetacean Society (SCS)
Max-Olivier Bourcoud
PO Box 1430, CH–1001 Lausanne   Switzerland
Tel.: ++41 (21) 403 2114 – Fax: ++41 (21) 351 2751
E-mail: scs1@vtxnet.ch
www.swisscetaceansociety.org

Desc.: Study of the distribution, abundance and dynamics of cetaceans in the Mediterranean Sea, between Côte d'Azur and Corsica.

Spp.: Cetaceans.

Hab.: Mediterranean French coast.

Loc.: South of France (Provence-Côte d'Azur).

Travel: Airplane to Nice; bus or train to Hyères or Toulon (depending on the research ship).

Dur.: Min. 6 days.

Per.: June to September.

L. term: Negotiable (max. 4 months).

Age: Min. 18.

Qualif.: Strong interest in cetacean research and conservation, strong willingness to work and learn, navigation experience, photography, good hearing and sight, ability to swim and not prone to seasickness.

Work: Scanning the horizon for whales and dolphins; assisting the researchers with bioacoustic survey, photo-ID, skin and faces sampling, recording specific data, etc. cooking, dishwashing and ship upkeep.

Lang.: French (good knowledge required).

Accom.: On the ship. Volunteers must bring sheets or sleeping bags.

Cost: Approx. EUR780 (approx. GB£ 540/US$ 1,000) for 6 days and nights for accommodation and food.

Applic.: E-mail a short CV and a statement of purpose.

WHITE SHARK TRUST, South Africa

Field Research Assistantship

P.O. Box 1258, Gansbaai 7220, Western Cape South Africa

Tel.: ++27 (28) 384 03 31

E-mail: FRA@WhiteSharkTrust.org

www.WhiteSharkTrust.org www.WhiteSharkTrust.org/assistant.html

www.SharkResearch.org

Desc.: The White Shark Trust is a non-profit organisation for research, conservation and educational projects on the Great White Shark (*Carcharodon carcharias*). Michael Scholl, founder and head of the White Shark Trust, is leading one of the most extensive and long-term population study of Sharks worldwide. Since 1998, he has been collecting information on the White Sharks visiting the Dyer Island area for a population study using a technique developed specifically for the project: photographic identification. To date over a thousand different White Sharks have been identified, and the project is monitoring their residency, spacial- and temporal- patterns. The data collected is used for an extensive population structure and dynamics study.

Spp.: Great white shark (*Carcharodon carcharias*).

Hab.: Southeastern Atlantic-Pelagic, coastal and in shore waters.

Loc.: Dyer Island and Geyser Rock (5 nautical miles offshore of Kleinbaai, Gansbaai, Western Cape, South Africa) / Haibaai, Holbaai and Geelbekgat (3 nautical miles east of Kleinbaai).

Travel: Flight to Cape Town. Shuttle transport from Cape Town city center or airport to Gansbaai (190 km) is organised by the White Shark Trust.

Dur.: Minimal duration is one month. Preference is given to 2+ months applications.

Per.: Year round.

L.term: With project leader's approval after 3-month trial period.

Age: Minimum 21.

Qualif.: Priority is given to applicants with an academic background, with preference towards students having or aiming at a marine biology/biology/zoology degree. Applicants without any academic qualification can be considered based on their degree of passion/ interest and reason (a personal motivation letter is highly recommended along with the application). A minimum of three non-related references are requested with the application for every applicant.

Work: Assisting Michael Scholl in the field work: collecting information on the location and environmental conditions of the field work, presence times of sharks around the boat, identification features and markings on the sharks, take photographs for individual identification, handling of the bait line, prepare the chum/bait, boat/equipment maintenance and cleaning, etc.

Lang.: English.

Accom.: Field research assistants will be lodged in a comfortable independent flat above the house of the project leader: balcony overlooking Walker Bay, large lounge and open kitchen, one bathroom, one toilet room and two sharing rooms.

Cost.: The donation fee includes room and board, and return transport from Cape Town to Gansbaai.

Applic.: Online application form on the White Shark Trust website.

Notes: The assistantship was created to offer students with a unique opportunity to gain valuable and exciting field experience working with an endangered marine animal. The program is not a holiday, and there is a no-tolerance, no-refund and immediate expulsion policy for any assistant unwilling or neglecting to work or assist in any of the tasks at hand. That said however, the atmosphere is always relaxed on the boat and on shore. Important aspects of the working and living conditions absolutely require the ability to work in a team, be extroverted, open, talkative and friendly. Working conditions and hours require a certain passion and dedication for sharks, field research and nature. The photo gallery on the website is updated on a regular basis and illustrates the fieldwork and life at the White Shark Trust.

WILD BIRD REHABILITATION, Bulgaria

BTCV Conservation Centre
Balby Road, Doncaster DN4 ORH   UK
Tel.: ++44 (0) 1302 572 244
Fax: ++44 (0) 1302 310 167
E-mail: information@btcv.org.uk
www.btcv.org.uk

Desc.: The project is carried out in association with the local conservation group "Green Balkan". Its priorities are: treatment, rehabilitation, breeding and release of wild, rare and threatened species in the wild.

Spp.: Dalmatian pelican, red-breasted goose, imperial and golden eagle, Egyptian and griffon vulture.

Hab.: Eastern European Boreal Forest.

Loc.: Stara Zagora Wildlife Rehabilitation & Breeding Centre, Bulgaria.

Travel: Flight to Bourgas airport.

Dur.: 2 weeks.

Per.: August.

L. term: Contact organisation for details.

Age: Min. 18.

Qualif.: No specific skills required.

Work: Construction/repair of specialised cages to increase capacity; bird care, fencing, pond making. The experience allows volunteers to observe birds from close and to assist to activities related to their rehabilitation and release.

Lang.: English.

Accom.: Camping.

Cost: GB£495 (approx. EUR750) excluding flight.

Agents: BTCV.

Applic.: £100 deposit required. Go to: www.btcv.org.

Notes: Conservation Holidays brochure available on request.

THE WILD DOLPHIN PROJECT, Bahamas

The Wild Dolphin Project
P.O. Box 8436
Jupiter, Florida 33468   USA
Tel.: ++1 (561) 575 5660 – Fax: ++1 (561) 575 5681
E-mail: wdpcindy@earthlink.net
www.wilddolphinproject.org

Desc.: The Wild Dolphin Project (WDP) has been studying a specific pod of Atlantic spotted and bottlenose dolphins, in the Bahamas, since 1985. WDP is a non-profit organization dedicated to research, education and conservation. While continuing to collect long-term baseline data WDP researches many other aspects of dolphin society, including behavior, communication, vocalizations, social structure, genetics and habitat. Participants will assist the researchers in various tasks and get to snorkel with the dolphins and may also visit other snorkel spots, such as coral reefs and shipwrecks. .

Spp.: Spotted dolphins (*Stenella frontalis*) and Bottlenose dolphins (*Tursiops truncatus*).

Hab.: Shallow sandbanks 40 miles offshore (offshore anchorage).

Loc.: Northern Bahamas.

Travel: Airplane to Grand Bahama Island.

Dur.: 9 day and 6 day trips.

Per.: Field season: May-September (contact WDP for trip dates).

Age: Minimum 18 without parent.

Qualif.: Volunteers must be able to swim and snorkel safely.

Work: Help with routine data collection and dolphin watches. Observe (while snorkeling) the wild spotted and bottlenose dolphins underwater, in addition to surface observations.

Lang.: English.

Accom.: All food and sleeping accommodations are provided aboard a 62 feet (20m) power catamaran, 2 to 4 to a room.

Cost: US $2,495 for 9 days, US $1,745 for 6 days, airfare to and from Florida and/or Grand Bahama Island not included.

Applic.: Inquire about trip dates and request application form.

Notes: Portion of trip price is tax deductible for US citizens.

WILDLANDS CONSERVATION TRUST RESEARCH EXPEDITIONS, South Africa

PO Box 1138, Hilton, 3245 South Africa
Tel: ++27(33) 343 1917
Fax: ++27(33) 343 1976
E-mail: wildlandstrust@wol.co.za
www.wildlandsvolunteers.org.za

Desc.: Volunteers join a team of biodiversity researchers conducting red data and big mammal research in Northern KwaZulu-Natal. Participants spend most of their time in the bush.

Spp.: Elephant, lion, crocodile, and various endangered species.

Hab.: World Heritage Site Costal wetlands and various private and state-owned "Big 5" game reserves.

Loc.: St. Lucia Wetlands, Northern KwaZulu-Natal, South Africa.

Travel: Airplane to Durban or Johannesburg. Then flight or bus to Richards Bay.

Dur.: Min. 2-4 weeks up to 6 months.

Per.: January to December.

L. term: Possible to stay up to 12 months.

Age: Min. 17.

Qualif.: Interest in nature and outdoors. Prepared to work and stay in remote, isolated, hot and humid wilderness. Physically fit.

Work: Help collect field data by vehicle or on foot: telemetry tracking, transect walks, rapid field surveys, behavioural observation, identification of individual animals, vegetation work. Administrative duties and data capture. Activities dependent on seasonal requirements. Assist with organizing daily logistics.

Health: Malaria precautions and rabies innoculation required.

Lang.: Basic English.

Accom.: Vary from rustic hutted camps, tented camps, research staff accommodation and traditional beehives huts.

Cost: Approximately GB£700/US$1,100 per 4 weeks; including local transportation and accommodation, excluding flights and food.

Agents: BTCV (see listing) & GNF (Global Nature Fund) volunteers.

Applic.: Request the application forms. Medical and insurance for working in areas with dangerous game is compulsory.

WOLF AND BEAR CONSERVATION, Slovakia

BTCV, Conservation Centre, Balby Road, Doncaster DN4 0RH UK
Tel: ++44 (0)1302 572244
Fax: ++44 (0)1302 310167
Email: information@btcv.org.uk
www.btcv.org.uk

Desc.: Project works in association with the local conservation group Slovak Wildlife Society, (www.slovakwildlife.org.uk), and deals with the research and conservation of the Tatra chamois. This is indeed an ambitious project aimed at resolving the conflicts between large carnivores, people and livestock.

Spp.: Wolf, bear, lynx and chamois.

Hab.: Mountains and forests.

Loc.: Tatra Mountains, Slovakia.

Travel: Flight to Vienna Schwechat International Airport.

Dur.: 2 weeks.

Per.: May or September.

Age: Min 18.

Qualif.: No specific skills required.

Work: Observing and recording behaviour of livestock guarding dogs and monitoring forest predator populations.

Lang.: English.

Cost: GB£680 (approx. EUR1000) excl flight.

Agents: BTCV.

Applic.: GB£100 Deposit required. Go to www.btcv.org.

Notes: Conservation Holidays Brochure available on request.

WOLF PROJECT, Bulgaria

The Ecovolunteer Network
Meyersweg 29   7553 AX Hengelo The Netherlands
Tel.: ++31 (74) 250 8250 — Fax: ++31 (74) 250 6572
E-mail: info@ecovolunteer.org
www.ecovolunteer.org

Desc.: Hands-on participation in biological field research on European wolves in Bulgaria, and assist in reintroduction of the Karakachan shepherd dogs as livestock guarding dogs to safeguard livestock against attacks by wolves, that is seen as a key factor for wolf conservation in Bulgaria.

Spp.: European wolf, *Canis lupus* and Karakachan livestock guarding dogs.

Hab.: Mixed mountain forests of deciduous trees and pine trees.

Loc.: Kraishte area in central-western Bulgaria.

Travel: Flight to the Bulgarian capital Sofia, pick-up from the airport upon arrival.

Dur.: Min. 2 weeks.

Per.: Year round.

L.term: Not possible.

Age: Min. 18.

Qualif.: Good health and physical condition and to be able to walk long distances in rough terrain.

Work: 1) participate in wolf research: fieldwork recording all the signs of presence of wolves and other species are one of the main activities. 2) Karakachan livestock guarding dogs care: assisting in dog raising will be a big help to the staff: walking the dogs and participate in visits to shepherds.

Lang.: English.

Accom.: Volunteers will stay in a house where running water and facilities for cooking are available; or tents in summer time during the field work. All meals included.

Cost: EUR831,- for the first two weeks; EUR376 for extra weeks.

Agents: The Ecovolunteer Network at www.ecovolunteer.org.

Applic.: The Ecovolunteer Network (see Organisation list).

INDICES

TABLE OF ORGANISATIONS AND PROJECTS BY GEOGRAPHIC LOCATION AND COST

(cost is intended approximately per week, with or w/o food, travel to project site is always not included)

Organisation	Africa	Asia	Europe	Mediterranean	Centr. America	South America	North America	Oceania	US$ 0-100	US$100-500	US$ 500-1500	Over US$ 1500
A' Pas de Loup	X		X	X	X				X			
African Conservation Experience	X											X
African Experience	X									X		
American Bear Association							X		X			
Appalachian Trail Conference							X		X			
ARCAS - Asociación de Rescate y Conservación de Vida Silvestre			X		X				X			
Arcturos									X			
ASVO - Asociacion de Voluntarios para el Servicio en las Area Protegidas					X				X			
Biosphere Expeditions	X	X	X	X	X	X	X	X			X	
Les Blongios			X						X			
Blue Ventures	X										X	
Brathay Exploration Group	X	X	X							X	X	
BTCV	X	X	X							X	X	X
Carapax - European Center for Conservation of Chelonians			X	X			X	X	X			
Centre for Alternative Technology			X	X					X			
Chantiers de Jeunes Provence Cote d'Azur			X	X						X		
Conservation Volunteers New Zealand								X	X			
Coordinating Committee for International Volunteers			X	X					X			
Coral Cay Conservation (CCC)			X	X	X			X	X	X	X	
Cotravaux				X					X			
CTS - Centro Turistico Studentesco e Giovanile			X	X						X		
CVA - Conservation Volunteers Australia								X		X		
CVG - Conservation Volunteers Greece			X	X					X			
Earthwatch Institute	X	X	X	X	X	X	X	X			X	X
Ecovolunteer Network	X	X	X	X	X	X	X	X		X		
EUROPARC Deutschland			X						X			
Expedition Advisory Centre (RGS)	X	X	X	X	X	X	X	X	X	X	X	X
Frontier	X	X		X	X			X	X		X	

234

TABLE OF ORGANISATIONS AND PROJECTS BY GEOGRAPHIC LOCATION AND COST

(cost is intended approximately per week, with or w/o food, travel to project site is always not included)

	Africa	Asia	Europe	Mediterranean	Centr. America	South America	North America	Oceania	US$ 0-100	US$100-500	US$ 500-1500	Over US$ 1500
Global Service Corps	X	X									X	
Global Vision International	X				X	X					X	
Greenforce – Careers in Conservation	X	X			X						X	
Hellenic Ornithological Society		X	X						X			
i to i	X	X				X			X			
International Otter Survival Fund	X		X	X	X	X	X	X			X	
Involvement Volunteers Association	X	X	X	X	X	X	X	X		X		
IUCN – The World Conservation Union	X	X	X	X	X	X	X	X	X			
Legambiente			X	X						X		
LIPU – Lega Italiana Protezione Uccelli, Birdlife Italy			X	X						X		
Mingan Island Cetacean Research Expeditions			X		X		X				X	
The National Trust									X			
The Nature Corps							X		X			
NZTCV - The New Zealand Trust for Conservation Volunteers								X	X			
Oceanic Society Expeditions	X				X	X	X	X				X
Operation Crossroads Africa	X										X	
Operation Wallacea	X	X			X						X	
Peru Verde	X	X				X			X			
Raleigh International	X	X	X		X	X	X	X			X	
RSPB – The Royal Society for the Protection of Birds	X								X			
SANCCOB – South African Foundation for the Conservation of Coastal Birds							X		X			
San Gorgonio Wilderness Association (SGWA)							X		X			
SCA – Student Conservation Association, Inc.							X		X			
SCI – Service Civil International			X				X	X	X			
Tethys Research Institute			X	X						X		
Trekforce Expeditions					X						X	
United Nations Volunteers (UNV)	X	X			X	X	X		X			
University Research Expeditions Program (UREP)	X	X	X		X	X	X				X	
U.S. Department of Agriculture - Forest Service	X	X	X		X	X	X		X			

235

TABLE OF ORGANISATIONS AND PROJECTS BY GEOGRAPHIC LOCATION AND COST

(cost is intended approximately per week, with or w/o food, travel to project site is always not included)

	Africa	Asia	Europe	Mediterranean	Centr. America	South America	North America	Oceania	US$ 0–100	US$100–500	US$ 500–1500	Over US$ 1500
U.S. Fish and Wildlife Service							X		X			
U.S. National Park Service							X		X			
Volunteer for Nature							X		X			
Volunteers for Outdoor Colorado (VOC)							X		X	X		
Volunteers Sri Lanka		X							X	X		
The Wilderness Foundation	X						X			X		
WWF Italy			X	X	X	X						
YCI – Youth Challenge International	X				X	X		X			X	
PROJECTS												
American Conservation Experience (ACE)							X		X			
Acorus Restoration Native Plant Nursery, Canada							X		X			
Adriatic Dolphin Project, Croatia				X						X		
African Conservation Trust, South Africa	X								X			
Amigos de las Aves, Costa Rica					X					X		
Animal Rescue Project, Florida							X		X			
ARFA – Asociación de Rescate de Fauna, Venezuela						X			X			
Ayutthaya Elephant Camp, Thailand		X								X		
Bimini Lemon Shark Project, Bahamas					X						X	
Birds of Tortuguero, Costa Rica					X				X			
Black Howler Monkey Project, Argentina						X			X			
Black Rhino, Kenya	X										X	
Black Sheep Inn, Ecuador						X			X			
Blue-fronted Parrot Project, Argentina						X			X			
Bohorok Environmental Centre, Indonesia		X								X		
Bottlenose Dolphin Project, Belize					X				X			
Bottlenose Dolphin Project, Italy				X							X	
Brown Bear Project, Russia			X								X	
Cano Palma Biological Station, Costa Rica					X				X			

236

TABLE OF ORGANISATIONS AND PROJECTS BY GEOGRAPHIC LOCATION AND COST

(cost is intended approximately per week, with or w/o food, travel to project site is always not included)

Organisation / Project	Africa	Asia	Europe	Mediterranean	Centr. America	South America	North America	Oceania	US$ 0–100	US$100–500	US$ 500–1500	Over US$ 1500
Cape Tribulation Tropical Research Station, Australia								X	X			
Caretta Research Project, USA							X				X	
Cats of Rome, Italy			X						X			
Centre for Rehabilitation of Wildlife (CROW), South Africa	X									X		
CERCOPAN, Nigeria	X								X	X		
Cetacean Research & Rescue Unit (CRRU), Scotland			X								X	
Cetacean Sanctuary Research, Italy-France				X							X	
Charles Darwin Foundation, Galapagos						X			X			
Cheetah Conservation Fund, Namibia	X									X		
Cheetah Conservation, Botswana	X											X
Cochrane Ecological Institute (CEI), Canada							X		X			
Comunidad Inti Wara Yassi, Bolivia						X			X			
Conservation Project Utila Iguana (CPUI), Honduras					X				X			
Dolphin Research Center, Florida							X			X		
Dolphins and Sea Life around the Maltese Islands, Malta				X						X		
Donkey Sanctuary, the Netherlands Antilles					X				X	X		
Ecolodge San Luis and Research Station, Costa Rica					X				X	X		
Ecology and Conservation of Deer in Patagonia, Argentina						X			X			
Elephant Nature Park, Thailand		X								X		
Elephant Project, Thailand		X								X		
Environmental Volunteer Programme, Murcia Spain			X	X					X			
Fauna Forever Manu Programme, Peru						X			X			
Forest Restoration, USA							X			X		
Genesis II Cloudforest Preserve and Wildlife Refuge, Costa Rica					X				X			
Gibbon Rehabilitation Project, Thailand		X								X		
Golden Boomerang Landcare, Australia								X			X	
Great Whales in their Natural Environment, Canada							X		X			
Grey Whales Research Expeditions, Canada-Mexico					X		X				X	
Grey Wolf Project, USA							X		X		X	

TABLE OF ORGANISATIONS AND PROJECTS BY GEOGRAPHIC LOCATION AND COST

(cost is intended approximately per week, with or w/o food, travel to project site is always not included)

	Africa	Asia	Europe	Mediterranean	Centr. America	South America	North America	Oceania	US$ 0-100	US$100-500	US$ 500-1500	Over US$ 1500
Griffon Vulture Conservation Project, Croatia				X						X		
Grupo Lobo, Portugal			X							X		
Hawaiian Forest Restoration Project, USA							X		X			
Hellenic Wildlife Hospital, Greece				X					X			
Humpback Research Project, Brazil						X					X	
Intag Andean Bear Research Project, Ecuador						X			X			
International Conservation Volunteer Exchange, Nevada							X		X			
Ionian Dolphin Project, Greece				X						X		
Iracambi Atlantic Rainforest Research and Conservation Center, Brazil						X			X	X		
Ischia Dolphin Project, Italy				X							X	
Jatun Sacha, Ecuador						X			X			
Leatherback Seaturtle Tagging Programme, Grenada					X					X		
Leatherback Turtle Project, Costa Rica					X					X		
Leopards of Phinda, South Africa	X										X	
Libanona Ecology Centre, Madagascar	X								X			
Lifeline Cat Research and Rehabilitation Centre, Belize					X					X		
Loggerhead Sea Turtles in Linosa, Italy				X						X		
Management Plan for Pylos Lagoon, Greece				X					X			
Manatee Research Project, Belize					X						X	
Manga del Mar Menor Restoration and Research Project, Spain				X					X			
The Marine Mammal Center (TMMC), California							X		X			
Marine Turtle Adriatic ARCHE' Project, Italy				X						X		
Marine Turtle & Youth Environmental Education, Mexico					X				X			
Monk Seal Project, Turkey				X						X		
The Monkey Sanctuary, England			X						X			
Monte Adone Wildlife Protection Centre, Italy			X						X			
Moray Firth Wildlife Centre, Scotland			X						X			
Munda Wanga Wildlife Park and Sanctuary, Zambia	X								X	X		
Naucrates Conservation Project, Thailand		X							X	X		

TABLE OF ORGANISATIONS AND PROJECTS BY GEOGRAPHIC LOCATION AND COST

(cost is intended approximately per week, with or w/o food, travel to project site is always not included)

	Africa	Asia	Europe	Mediterranean	Centr. America	South America	North America	Oceania	US$ 0-100	US$100-500	US$ 500-1500	Over US$ 1500
Noah's Arc, Greece				X					X			
The Oceania Research Project, Australia								X			X	
Okavango Delta Lion Monitoring Project, Botswana	X									X	X	
Operation Osprey, Scotland			X						X			
Orangutan Foundation, Indonesia		X								X		
Orangutan Health, Indonesia		X								X		
Orkney Seal Rescue Centre, Scotland			X						X			
Pandrillus Foundation, Nigeria	X								X			
Pioneer Madagascar	X										X	
Projecto Jubarte do Cabo Verde	X										X	
PROVCA – Prog.de Voluntarios para la Cons. del Ambiente, Costa Rica-Panama					X				X			
Proyecto Campanario, Costa Rica					X					X		
Proyecto Karumbe – Tortugas Marinas del Uruguay						X			X			
Przewalski Horse Reintroduction Project, Mongolia		X								X		
Re-Aforestation Project, Ghana	X									X		
Reef Check Global Coral Reef Monitoring, USA		X			X	X	X	X	X	X		
Re-Hydration of Earth, Kenya	X								X	X		
Reserva Pacuare, Costa Rica					X				X			
Rhino Rescue Project, Swaziland	X									X		
River Otter Project, Brazil						X				X		
The San Wild Wildlife Trust, South Africa	X										X	
Santa Martha Rescue Centers, Ecuador						X			X	X		
Scottish Whale and Dolphin Project, Scotland			X						X	X		
Scottish Wildlife Rescue, Scotland			X						X	X		
Sea Turtle Conservation Program, Costa Rica					X				X	X		
Sea Turtle Conservation Projects, Costa Rica					X				X			
Sea Turtle Rescue Center, Greece				X					X			
Sea Turtle Summer Field Work, Greece				X					X			
Siberian-East Russian Volunteer Program		X							X	X		

TABLE OF ORGANISATIONS AND PROJECTS BY GEOGRAPHIC LOCATION AND COST

(cost is intended approximately per week, with or w/o food, travel to project site is always not included)

	Africa	Asia	Europe	Mediterranean	Centr. America	South America	North America	Oceania	US$ 0-100	US$100-500	US$ 500-1500	Over US$ 1500
Skaftafell National Park, Iceland			X							X		
Southwestern Research Station, Arizona							X		X			
Spanish Dolphins, Spain				X								X
Sustainable Livelihood Development Association, Sri Lanka		X							X			
Sustainable Management of the Natural Resources of Southern Ecuador						X			X			
Taita Discovery Centre, Kenya	X									X		
Tambopata Resident Naturalist Program, Peru						X			X			
Tilos Park Association, Greece				X					X			
Tolga Bat Hospital, Australia								X	X			
Tree Planters Farm, Australia								X	X			
Trees For Life, Scotland			X						X	X		
Turtle Conservation Project (TCP), Sri Lanka		X							X	X		
Turtles of Tortuguero, Costa Rica					X				X			
Volunteer Peten, Guatemala					X				X			
Wakuluzu: Friends of the Colobus Trust, Kenya	X								X			
Whale and Dolphin Project La Gomera, Spain	X								X		X	
Whale Research in the Saint Lawrence Estuary, Canada							X				X	
Whales and Dolphins of Cote D'Azur, France				X							X	
White Shark Trust, South Africa	X									X	X	
Wild Bird Rehabilitation in Bulgaria			X							X		
Wild Dolphin Project, Bahamas							X					X
Wildlands Conservation Trust Research Expeditions, South Africa	X									X		X
Wolf and Bear Conservation, Slovakia			X							X		
Wolf Project, Bulgaria			X							X		

TABLE OF ORGANISATIONS AND PROJECTS BY SPECIES OR GROUP OF SPECIES

(species or group of species are indicated with common names)

Organisation	Various Spp.	Trees/Vegetat.	Birds	Sea Turtles	Amph./Reptile	Corals	Sharks	Seals/Manatee	Whales/dolph.	Oth. Mammals	Wolves	Felines	Primates	Bears	Bats	Africa Herbiv.
A' Pas de Loup				X				X			X					X
African Conservation Experience		X	X		X											X
African Experience												X				X
American Bear association														X		
Appalachian Trail Conference	X															
ARCAS - Asociación de Rescate y Conservación de Vida Silvestre	X		X	X	X					X	X	X	X	X		
Arcturos											X			X		
ASVO - Asociacion de Voluntarios para el Servicio en las Area Protegidas	X	X	X	X	X					X	X	X	X	X		X
Biosphere Expeditions	X		X							X	X	X	X			
Les Blongios	X	X														
Blue Ventures						X										
Brathay Exploration Group	X	X	X													
BTCV	X				X					X	X					
Carapax - European Center for Conservation of Chelonians	X			X												
Centre for Alternative Technology	X															
Chantiers de Jeunes Provence Cote d'Azur	X															
Conservation Volunteers New Zealand	X	X														
Coordinating Committee for International Volunteers	X					X										
Coral Cay Conservation (CCC)						X										
Cotravaux	X															
CTS - Centro Turistico Studentesco e Giovanile			X						X	X				X		
CVA - Conservation Volunteers Australia				X	X				X	X	X	X				
CVG - Conservation Volunteers Greece		X	X	X												
Earthwatch Institute	X	X	X	X	X				X	X	X	X				X
Ecovolunteer Network	X	X	X	X					X	X	X	X	X	X		X
EUROPARC Deutschland	X	X														
Expedition Advisory Centre (RGS)	X					X										
Frontier	X	X														

TABLE OF ORGANISATIONS AND PROJECTS BY SPECIES OR GROUP OF SPECIES

(species or group of species are indicated with common names)

Organisation / Project	Africa Herbiv.	Bats	Bears	Primates	Felines	Wolves	Oth. Mammals	Whales/dolph.	Seals/Manatee	Sharks	Corals	Amph./Reptile	Sea Turtles	Birds	Trees/Vegetat.	Various Spp.
Global Service Corps	X															X
Global Vision International							X				X				X	X
Greenforce – Careers in Conservation				X			X				X			X		X
Hellenic Ornithological Society														X		
i to i														X	X	X
International Otter Survival Fund							X									
Involvement Volunteers Association																X
IUCN – The World Conservation Union																X
Legambiente																X
LIPU – Lega Italiana Protezione Uccelli, Birdlife Italy														X		
Mingan Island Cetacean Research Expeditions								X								
The National Trust															X	
The Nature Corps															X	X
NZTCV – The New Zealand Trust for Conservation Volunteers															X	X
Oceanic Society Expeditions							X	X			X					
Operation Crossroads Africa													X			
Operation Wallacea		X		X	X		X				X	X	X	X	X	X
Peru Verde				X	X		X					X		X	X	X
Raleigh International																
RSPB – The Royal Society for the Protection of Birds														X		
SANCCOB – South African Foundation for the Conservation of Coastal Birds														X		
San Gorgonio Wilderness Association (SGWA)																
SCA – Student Conservation Association, Inc.															X	X
SCI – Service Civil International															X	X
Tethys Research Institute								X								
Trekforce Expeditions															X	X
United Nations Volunteers (UNV)															X	X
University Research Expeditions Program (UREP)															X	X
U.S. Department of Agriculture - Forest Service															X	

TABLE OF ORGANISATIONS AND PROJECTS BY SPECIES OR GROUP OF SPECIES

(species or group of species are indicated with common names)

Name	Various Spp.	Trees/Vegetat.	Birds	Sea Turtles	Amph./Reptile	Corals	Sharks	Seals/Manatee	Whales/dolph.	Oth. Mammals	Wolves	Felines	Primates	Bears	Bats	Africa Herbiv.
U.S. Fish and Wildlife Service	X															
U.S. National Park Service	X	X														
Volunteer for Nature		X														
Volunteers for Outdoor Colorado (VOC)		X														
Volunteers Sri Lanka	X	X	X	X		X				X						
The Wilderness Foundation	X	X		X												
WWF Italy	X	X	X						X		X			X		
YCI - Youth Challenge International	X	X														
PROJECTS																
American Conservation Experience (ACE)	X	X														
Acorus Restoration Native Plant Nursery, Canada		X														
Adriatic Dolphin Project, Croatia									X							
African Conservation Trust, South Africa	X											X				X
Amigos de las Aves, Costa Rica			X													
Animal Rescue Project, Florida	X															
ARFA – Asociación de Rescate de Fauna, Venezuela					X					X		X	X			
Ayutthaya Elephant Camp, Thailand										X						
Bimini Lemon Shark Project, Bahamas							X									
Birds of Tortuguero, Costa Rica			X													
Black Howler Monkey Project, Argentina													X			
Black Rhino, Kenya																X
Black Sheep Inn, Ecuador		X	X											X		
Blue-fronted Parrot Project, Argentina			X													
Bohorok Environmental Centre, Indonesia		X											X			
Bottlenose Dolphin Project, Belize									X							
Bottlenose Dolphin Project, Italy									X							
Brown Bear Project, Russia														X		
Cano Palma Biological Station, Costa Rica	X		X		X					X						

TABLE OF ORGANISATIONS AND PROJECTS BY SPECIES OR GROUP OF SPECIES

(species or group of species are indicated with common names)

Organisation / Project	Africa Herbiv.	Bats	Bears	Primates	Felines	Wolves	Oth. Mammals	Whales/dolph.	Seals/Manatee	Sharks	Corals	Amph./Reptile	Sea Turtles	Birds	Trees/Vegetat.	Various Spp.
Cape Tribulation Tropical Research Station, Australia		X													X	
Caretta Research Project, USA													X			
Cats of Rome, Italy					X											
Centre for Rehabilitation of Wildlife (CROW), South Africa	X			X	X		X					X		X	X	X
CERCOPAN, Nigeria				X												
Cetacean Research & Rescue Unit (CRRU), Scotland								X								
Cetacean Sanctuary Research, Italy-France								X								
Charles Darwin Foundation, Galapagos									X			X		X	X	X
Cheetah Conservation Fund, Namibia					X											
Cheetah Conservation, Botswana					X											
Cochrane Ecological Institute (CEI), Canada							X									
Comunidad Inti Wara Yassi, Bolivia				X			X					X		X	X	X
Conservation Project Utila Iguana (CPUI), Honduras												X				
Dolphin Research Center								X					X	X		
Dolphins and Sea Life around the Maltese Islands								X					X	X		
Donkey Sanctuary, the Netherlands Antilles							X									
Ecolodge San Luis and Research Station, Costa Rica				X	X		X					X		X	X	X
Ecology and Conservation of Deer in Patagonia, Argentina							X									
Elephant Nature Park, Thailand							X									
Elephant Project, Thailand							X									
Environmental Volunteer Programme, Murcia Spain														X	X	X
Fauna Forever Manu Programme, Peru				X	X		X							X	X	X
Forest Restoration, USA															X	
Genesis II Cloudforest Preserve and Wildlife Refuge, Costa Rica				X										X	X	X
Gibbon Rehabilitation Project, Thailand				X												
Golden Boomerang Landcare, Australia															X	
Great Whales in their Natural Environment, Canada								X								
Grey Whales Research Expeditions, Canada-Mexico								X								
Grey Wolf Project, USA						X										

244

TABLE OF ORGANISATIONS AND PROJECTS BY SPECIES OR GROUP OF SPECIES

(species or group of species are indicated with common names)

Organisation / Project	Africa Herbiv.	Bats	Bears	Primates	Felines	Wolves	Oth. Mammals	Whales/dolph.	Seals/Manatee	Sharks	Corals	Amph./Reptile	Sea Turtles	Birds	Trees/Vegetat.	Various Spp.
Griffon Vulture Conservation Project, Island of Cres, Croatia														X		X
Grupo Lobo, Portugal						X										
Hawaiian Forest Restoration Project, USA															X	
Hellenic Wildlife Hospital, Greece							X									
Humpback Research Project, Brazil								X								
Intag Andean Bear Research Project, Ecuador			X													
International Conservation Volunteer Exchange, Nevada															X	
Ionian Dolphin Project, Greece								X								
Iracambi Atlantic Rainforest Research and Conservation Center, Brazil							X					X		X	X	X
Ischia Dolphin Project, Italy								X								X
Jatun Sacha, Ecuador							X							X	X	X
Leatherback Seaturtle Tagging Programme, Grenada													X			
Leatherback Turtle Project, Costa Rica													X			
Leopards of Phinda, South Africa	X				X											X
Libanona Ecology Centre, Madagascar				X											X	X
Lifeline Cat Reserach and Rehabilitation Centre, Belize					X											
Loggerhead Sea Turtles in Linosa, Italy													X			
Management Plan for Pylos Lagoon, Greece												X		X	X	
Manatee Research Project, Belize									X							
Manga del Mar Menor Restoration and Research Project, Spain												X		X	X	
Marine Mammal Center (TMMC), California									X				X			
Marine Turtles Adriatic ARCHE' Project, Italy													X			
Marine Turtle & Youth Environmental Education, Mexico													X			
Monk Seal Project, Turkey									X							
The Monkey Sanctuary, England				X												
Monte Adone Wildlife Protection Centre, Italy				X	X		X					X		X		X
Moray Firth Wildlife Centre, Scotland								X								
Munda Wanga Wildlife Park and Sanctuary, Zambia	X		X	X	X		X					X		X		X
Naucrates Conservation Project, Thailand											X		X		X	

245

TABLE OF ORGANISATIONS AND PROJECTS BY SPECIES OR GROUP OF SPECIES

(species or group of species are indicated with common names)

Organisation / Project	Various Spp.	Trees/Vegetat.	Birds	Sea Turtles	Amph./Reptile	Corals	Sharks	Seals/Manatee	Whales/dolph.	Oth. Mammals	Wolves	Felines	Primates	Bears	Bats	Africa Herbiv.
Noah's Arc, Greece	X									X						
The Oceania Research Project, Australia									X							
Okavango Delta Lion Monitoring Project, Botswana			X									X				
Operation Osprey, Scotland			X													
Orangutan Foundation, Indonesia													X			
Orangutan Health, Indonesia													X			
Orkney Seal Rescue Centre, Scotland								X								
Pandrillus Foundation, Nigeria													X			
Pioneer Madagascar			X		X								X			
Proyecto Jubarte do Cabo Verde									X							
PROVCA – Prog.de Voluntarios para la Cons. del Ambiente, Costa Rica-Panama	X	X	X	X	X					X		X	X			
Proyecto Campanario, Costa Rica	X	X	X		X					X		X	X			
Proyecto Karumbe – Tortugas Marinas del Uruguay				X												
Przewalski Horse Reintroduction Project, Mongolia										X						
Re-Aforestation Project, Ghana		X														
Reef Check Global Coral Reef Monitoring, USA						X										
Re-Hydration of Earth, Kenya																X
Reserva Pacuare, Costa Rica	X	X	X	X	X					X		X	X			
Rhino Rescue Project, Swaziland															X	X
River Otter Project, Brazil										X						
The San Wild Wildlife Trust, South Africa	X	X	X		X					X		X	X	X		X
Santa Martha Rescue Centers, Ecuador	X		X		X		X	X		X		X	X	X		
Scottish Whale and Dolphin Project, Scotland								X	X	X						
Scottish Wildlife Rescue, Scotland			X							X						
Sea Turtle Conservation Program, Costa Rica				X												
Sea Turtle Conservation Projects, Costa Rica				X												
Sea Turtle Rescue Center, Greece				X												
Sea Turtle Summer Field Work, Greece				X												
Siberian-East Russian Volunteer Program	X	X														

246

TABLE OF ORGANISATIONS AND PROJECTS BY SPECIES OR GROUP OF SPECIES

(species or group of species are indicated with common names)

Organisation / Project	Africa Herbiv.	Bats	Bears	Primates	Felines	Wolves	Oth. Mammals	Whales/dolph.	Seals/Manatee	Sharks	Corals	Amph./Reptile	Sea Turtles	Birds	Trees/Vegetat.	Various Spp.
Skaftafell National park, Iceland							X							X	X	X
Southwestern Research Station, Arizona							X					X		X	X	X
Spanish Dolphins, Spain								X								
Sustainable Livelihood Development Association, Sri Lanka															X	
Sustainable Management of the Natural Resources of Southern Ecuador															X	
Taita Discovery Centre, Kenya	X															
Tambopata Resident Naturalist Program, Peru				X	X		X					X		X	X	X
Tilos Park Association, Greece														X	X	
Tolga Bat Hospital, Australia		X														
Tree Planters Farm, Australia															X	
Trees For Life, Scotland															X	
Turtle Conservation Project (TCP), Sri Lanka													X			
Turtles of Tortuguero, Costa Rica													X			
Volunteer Peten, Guatemala				X	X		X					X		X	X	X
Wakuluzu: Friends of the Colobus Trust, Kenya				X												
Whale and Dolphin Project La Gomera, Spain								X								
Whale Research in the Saint Lawrence Estuary, Canada								X								
Whales and Dolphins of Cote D'Azur, France								X								
White Shark Trust, South Africa										X						
Wild Bird Rehabilitation in Bulgaria														X		
Wild Dolphin Project, Bahamas								X								
Wildlands Conservation Trust Research Expeditions, South Africa												X		X	X	X
Wolf and Bear Conservation, Slovakia			X		X	X	X									
Wolf Project Bulgaria						X										

ORGANISATION ALPHABETICAL INDEX

PROJECT ALPHABETICAL INDEX

THE *GREEN VOLUNTEERS* PHOTO CONTEST

Good photographs of wildlife and people together are extremely rare, especially those that give the idea of involvement and participation, which is what *Green Volunteers* is all about. *Green Volunteers* is therefore launching a contest among all its readers and active volunteers. We are looking for good pictures of wildlife together with people (possibly volunteers) to be published in our website and to be chosen as the cover picture (such as the picture on the current cover) for future issues of the Guide. If your pictures get published, you will not be paid by Green Volunteers but you will have the opportunity of helping your favourite project by allowing it to receive more volunteers, and you will have the satisfaction to see your picture published in our website. *Green Volunteers* will award EUR100 (US$ 130) to the pictures that will be chosen for covers of next issues of the Guide. Please send your pictures exclusively via e-mail (possibly in low density) to: network@greenvol.com No picture will be used for publication without prior permission of the photographer. If the picture is selected, you will be contacted, and asked if your picture can be added to our website. **Make sure, however, that for taking your pictures of volunteers in action you don't interfere with the work of the project. We look forward to seeing your great pictures. Good luck with your Green Volunteering!**

STANDARD APPLICATION FORM
Green Volunteers © 2005

(To be photocopied enlarged, retyped or downloaded from the *Green Volunteers* **Network Pages** at www.greenvol.com. This is not an official application form; many organisations have their own, others may accept this.)   (Please print)

Last name: .... First name: ....

Nationality: .... Date of birth: .... Passport n°:..............................

Occupation: ....

Address for correspondence: ....

Tel.: .... Fax: .... E-mail: ....

Next of kin (name, address and tel. number): ....
....

If you are a student, write the name and address of the school, College or University:
....

Mother tongue:... Other languages spoken:
excellent:.............................. very good:............................ good:............................ basic:..........................

Education:...

Indicate your experience in volunteering (also in other fields) or in participating in environmental projects, wildlife rescue centres, fieldwork, camping, backpacking or other outdoor activities:
....
....
....

Skills which may be useful to the project:
....
....
....

Are you a member of any environmental organization? If yes, specify:
....

Do you have any health problems? If yes, specify:
....

Indicate your preferences for project's dates and location:
....

Any additional relevant information (feel free to add additional pages):
....
....
....

Date: ..... / ..... /...... Signature: ....

From the same publisher

Green Volunteers The World Guide
to Voluntary Work in Nature Conservation
Over 200 projects worldwide for those who want to experience active conservation work as a volunteer. Projects are worldwide, year round, in a variety of habitats, from one week to one year or more. From dolphins to rhinos, from whales to primates, this guide is ideal for a meaningful vacation or for finding thesis or research opportunites.

Price £ 10.99 € 16.00 $ 14.95   Pages: 256

World Volunteers The World Guide
to Humanitarian and Development Volunteering
Nearly 200 projects and organisations worldwide for people who want to work in international humanitarian projects but don't know how to begin. Opportunities are from 2 weeks to 2 years or longer. An ideal resource for a working holiday or a leave of absence. A guide for students, retirees, doctors or accountants, nurses or agronomists, surveyors and teachers, plumbers or builders, electricians or computer operators... For everyone who wants to get involved in helping those who suffer worldwide.

Price: £ 10.99 € 16.00 $ 14.95   Pages: 256

Archaeo-Volunteers The World Guide
to Archaeological and Heritage Volunteering
Listing 200 projects and organisations in the 5 continents for those who want to spend a different working vacation helping Archaeologists. Placements are from 2 weeks to a few months. For enthusiastic amateurs, students and those wanting hands-on experience. Cultural and historical heritage maintenance and restoration and museum volunteering opportunities are also listed. The guide also tells how to find hundreds more excavations and workcamps on the Internet.

Price: £ 10.99 € 16.00 $ 14.95   Pages: 256